Palgrave Studies in Literary Anthropology

Series Editors
Deborah Reed-Danahay
Department of Anthropology
The State University of New York at Buffalo
Buffalo, New York, USA

Helena Wulff
Department of Social Anthropology
Stockholm University
Stockholm, Sweden

This book series aims to publish explorations of new ethnographic objects and emerging genres of writing at the intersection of literary and anthropological studies. Books in this series will be grounded in ethnographic perspectives and the broader cross-cultural lens that anthropology brings to the study of reading and writing. The series will explore the ethnography of fiction, ethnographic fiction, narrative ethnography, creative nonfiction, memoir, auto ethnography, and the connections between travel literature and ethnographic writing.

More information about this series at
http://www.springer.com/series/15120

Peter Wogan

Corner-Store Dreams and the 2008 Financial Crisis

A True Story about Risk, Entrepreneurship, Immigration, and Latino-Anglo Friendship

Peter Wogan
Willamette University
Salem, Oregon, USA

Palgrave Studies in Literary Anthropology
ISBN 978-3-319-84862-4   ISBN 978-3-319-52264-7 (eBook)
DOI 10.1007/978-3-319-52264-7

© The Editor(s) (if applicable) and The Author(s) 2017
Softcover reprint of the hardcover 1st edition 2017
This work is subject to copyright. All rights are solely and exclusively licensed by the Publisher, whether the whole or part of the material is concerned, specifically the rights of translation, reprinting, reuse of illustrations, recitation, broadcasting, reproduction on microfilms or in any other physical way, and transmission or information storage and retrieval, electronic adaptation, computer software, or by similar or dissimilar methodology now known or hereafter developed.
The use of general descriptive names, registered names, trademarks, service marks, etc. in this publication does not imply, even in the absence of a specific statement, that such names are exempt from the relevant protective laws and regulations and therefore free for general use.
The publisher, the authors and the editors are safe to assume that the advice and information in this book are believed to be true and accurate at the date of publication. Neither the publisher nor the authors or the editors give a warranty, express or implied, with respect to the material contained herein or for any errors or omissions that may have been made. The publisher remains neutral with regard to jurisdictional claims in published maps and institutional affiliations.

Cover illustration: © Peter Wogan

Printed on acid-free paper

This Palgrave Macmillan imprint is published by Springer Nature
The registered company is Springer International Publishing AG
The registered company address is: Gewerbestrasse 11, 6330 Cham, Switzerland

For Our Parents, Who Taught Us to Dream

Peter Wogan and Ranulfo Juárez

Editors' Preface

Palgrave Studies in Literary Anthropology publishes explorations of new ethnographic objects and emerging genres of writing at the intersection of literary and anthropological studies. Books in this series are grounded in ethnographic perspectives and the broader cross-cultural lens that anthropology brings to the study of reading and writing. By introducing work that applies an anthropological approach to literature, whether drawing on ethnography or other materials in relation to anthropological and literary theory, this series moves the conversation forward not only in literary anthropology, but in general anthropology, literary studies, cultural studies, sociology, ethnographic writing and creative writing. The "literary turn" in anthropology and critical research on world literatures share a comparable sensibility regarding global perspectives.

Fiction and autobiography have connections to ethnography that underscore the idea of the author as ethnographer and the ethnographer as author. Literary works are frequently included in anthropological research and writing, as well as in studies that do not focus specifically on literature. Anthropologists take an interest in fiction and memoir set in their field locations, and produced by "native" writers, in order to further their insights into the cultures and contexts they research. Experimental genres in anthropology have benefitted from the style and structure of fiction and autoethnography, as well as by other expressive forms ranging from film and performance art to technology, especially the internet and social media. There are renowned fiction writers who trained as anthropologists, but moved on to a literary career. Their anthropologically inspired work is a common sounding board in literary anthropology. In the endeavour to foster writing skills in different genres, there are now courses on ethnographic writing, anthropological writing genres, experimental writing, and even creative writing taught by anthropologists. And increasingly, literary and reading communities are attracting anthropological attention, including an engagement with issues of how to reach a wider audience.

Palgrave Studies in Literary Anthropology publishes scholarship on the ethnography of fiction and other writing genres, the connections between travel literature and ethnographic writing, and internet writing. It also publishes creative work such as ethnographic fiction, narrative ethnography, creative non-fiction, memoir, and autoethnography. Books in the series include monographs and edited collections, as well as shorter works that appear as Palgrave Pivots. This series aims to reach a broad audience among scholars, students and a general readership.

Deborah Reed-Danahay and Helena Wulff
Co-Editors, Palgrave Studies in Literary Anthropology

Advisory Board

Ruth Behar, University of Michigan
Don Brenneis, University of California, Santa Cruz
Regina Bendix, University of Göttingen
Mary Gallagher, University College Dublin
Kirin Narayan, Australian National University
Nigel Rapport, University of St Andrews
Ato Quayson, University of Toronto
Julia Watson, Ohio State University

A True Story

All this really happened.

Contents

1	Cutting the Cloth	1
2	Invitation	5
3	Teaming Up	9
4	Saints of the Casino	15
5	Car Crash	25
6	Trip to Mexico	31
7	Don Quixote Rides Again	39
8	Searching for The Key	49
9	A Moon Shot	65
10	Visit to Campus	75

11	Confronting the Enemy	87
12	Mysteries of Money	99
13	Garbage Dream	109
14	Crash Warning	125
15	Stopping Time	137
16	Into the Mystic	145
17	Plan B	157
18	Mr. Success or Mr. Worthless?	165
19	Financial Crisis	171
20	Wrecking Ball	179
21	Respect for the Turtle	197

Acknowledgments	207
Appendix A: Ranulfo's Reactions to This Book	211
Appendix B: Names in This Book	215
Bibliography	217
Index	225

CHAPTER 1

Cutting the Cloth

If the senior citizens at the Dairy Queen in Salem, Oregon, had walked across the street, they would have found a small corner store with a hand-painted sign in Spanish that read *El Palmar*. The door below that sign offered a portal into another world.

I didn't want to presume that anyone at the corner store would speak Spanish with me, a middle-aged Anglo, so when I walked through the door one morning in September, 2005, I spoke in a combination of English and Spanish, explaining that I was returning a film I'd rented the day before. It was a comedy about a poor guy who sells tacos on the streets in Mexico and gets snubbed by a high-class woman—apparently a classic, but, like a ten-year-old who just watched his first Shakespeare play, I didn't get most of the jokes or why everyone kept breaking out in song.

The man behind the cash register, wearing a baseball cap, long-sleeved shirt, and jeans, immediately responded in Spanish. "Ah, so did you like the movie? It was great, wasn't it?" Unlike other Latinos I'd met in town, he spoke with informal Spanish, the *tú* form used among equals.

We discussed the movie for so long that I had to step aside to make room for other customers, women buying soap for the laundromat next door and candy for their little kids. While the man rang up his customers, I walked up and down the aisles and marveled at my surroundings. The store was about the size of a large living room, and every inch was crammed with merchandise: tortillas, guava and mango juice, candles

© The Author(s) 2017
P. Wogan, *Corner-Store Dreams and the 2008 Financial Crisis*,
Palgrave Studies in Literary Anthropology,
DOI 10.1007/978-3-319-52264-7_1

with pictures of saints, leather boots, Budweiser and Tecate beer, sewing kits, rain jackets, Mexican cowboy movies, even a stone mortar and pestle tucked in the corner. I had entered a Mexican sanctuary in suburban America.

Back at the counter, the cashier introduced himself as Ranulfo, and, after I told him my name was Peter, he said, "OK, I'll call you Pete."

"You're one of the only *Americanos* who has ever rented a movie in here," he noted with a smile. I liked his directness. Other Latinos in town had just tiptoed around my obvious outsider status.

Continuing in Spanish, I asked, "So are you the owner?"

"Yes, along with the man you met yesterday, my younger brother, Pablo.[1] Before this, we used to work in the fields, growing plants. Getting this store was a giant step, the step of a dinosaur, you know what I mean?"

I chuckled in agreement, and Ranulfo continued, "This is a beautiful country. This is a place where you can climb to the top of the mountain and nobody tells you, 'Hey, get down off that mountain.'"

I agreed again, resisting the urge to point out how many Americans end up groveling in the dirt at the bottom of the mountain. It had been so long since I'd heard someone express such pure love for the United States that I wasn't sure what to say, but luckily Ranulfo followed up with a little joke.

Pointing to his belly, pressing against his untucked shirt, he said, "But this is the worst thing that's happened to me since I came to this country."

Ranulfo laughed at himself, so I joined in, though hesitantly, afraid to seem critical. He wasn't exactly overweight, but he was one of the most spherical people I'd ever met. An artist would have sketched his underlying geometric form with a series of circles. Chubby cheeks, round face, that little belly—all circles.

Turning the conversation back to me, he asked, "No work today?"

"Believe it or not," I said, "this is my work."

Pointing in the direction of downtown, about two miles away, I said, "I'm a professor at the university, and I'm studying Mexican-American culture."

I couldn't think of a simple way to explain that I used to do research with a small indigenous group in Ecuador, but once my young sons discovered baseball, I couldn't bear to keep leaving them every summer for the Andes.[2] Baseball tapped us into something transcendental, and I didn't want to miss any of it. I was starting all over with a culture I hardly knew anything about.

My truncated explanation still made perfect sense to Ranulfo, who quickly assumed the role of cultural interpreter. He taught me the main Mexican film genres and invited me to come back the next day, to check out his movie database.

He also left me with a tantalizing proverb: *Hay mucha tela de donde cortar*. "There are many places to cut the cloth."

I took that proverb to mean Ranulfo had more stories to tell, but I didn't realize the best one was about to unfold over the next few years. He was about to embark on a quest to add a small bakery to the back of his store, using his recently paid-off house as collateral, risking his toehold in America after gaining citizenship and scratching his way out of poverty. He wanted to bake bread and pastries. He wanted to create something with his hands and heart, and he wanted his wife to join him, so she wouldn't have to keep working at the cannery, pushing vegetables down the production line all day. But Ranulfo didn't simply want the bakery to provide for his family, just as Captain Ahab didn't want to kill Moby Dick for mere lamp oil. Like Captain Ahab, Ranulfo wanted to "strike through the mask," to find out what lay on the other side of observable reality, to know whether the universe loved him.[3] He was going to study his dreams every morning for clues to the future, the inner workings of the universe, and his place in it.

I would eventually need Ranulfo at a deep, subterranean level, but during our first meeting I didn't know any of this. I had no inkling Ranulfo might end up an innocent victim of a housing bubble about to burst and drown the whole country. I didn't even know if we could overcome our differences.[4]

Introductory Note

To prevent this endnotes section from ballooning out of control, I only include essential sources directly related to the main text. Also, sometimes I break with narrative chronology, citing sources that I had not read at the time of the events described in the main text.

Notes

1. Pablo is legally the owner of the store.
2. Wogan (2004a).
3. Melville (1851), Chapter 36, "The Quarter-Deck." To encourage more reading of *Moby-Dick*, all my citations of it come from the annotated first American edition, available in its entirety at http://www.powermobydick.com/, a website with excellent margin annotations by Margaret Guroff. To make it easier for readers who want to use other editions, I cite by chapter number and title, rather than page number. As noted in Chap. 4, "Saints of the Casino," and Appendix A, "Ranulfo's Reactions to this Book," Ranulfo agreed with my comparison between him and Captain Ahab. In fact, he read, commented on, and approved multiple drafts of every chapter in this book. Throughout the text, I try to make it clear where his voice leaves off and mine begins, and Appendix A adds further clarification about the writing process and his reactions to this book.
4. If by this point you're craving the type of introductory chapter found in most non-narrative, social-science books, please know that the theoretical justifications for this book emerge in the endnotes for later chapters. My hope, though, is that eventually the analysis, theoretical framework, ethnography, and narrative will become so thoroughly intertwined in the text that it will be hard to separate them.

CHAPTER 2

Invitation

September, 2005

The next morning back at the store, Ranulfo told me to come behind the counter, so I could look at his movie database in the computer sitting a few feet away from the main register. With those simple steps, my perspective changed completely. Suddenly I wasn't just a passing customer or gringo interloper. I was standing in the Inner Sanctum. Everything felt better behind the counter, standing side by side with the owner and taking in the entire store, from the tamarind snacks in front of the register to the juice and beer coolers at the far end of the packed aisles.

Ranulfo's spirits were also riding high. When I asked how business was, he stretched out his arms and said, "Ah, it's so good I feel like the Incredible Hulk. Yesterday I said to my wife, 'Look at me, I'm busting the buttons right off my shirt.'"

"Really?" I asked, playing along. "And what did your wife say?"

"Oh," he said with a sheepish smile, "she just said, '*Sí, sí*. You're a monster. A little monster.'"

We both laughed at the rapid rise and fall of his fantasy, but as the day wore on and I observed Ranulfo more closely, I realized that the comparison made sense. Ranulfo had both the mild-mannered reserve of Dr. Banner and the burning intensity of his alter ego, the Incredible Hulk. Outwardly, Ranulfo was perfectly calm. He rested his hands lightly on the counter, reserving gesticulations and funny faces for punchlines, keeping his mouth half closed when he laughed, never raising his voice. I caught glimpses of the Incredible Hulk, though, when Ranulfo talked about his dreams for his business, and when he hit me with a big request out of nowhere: Would I be willing to teach an English class?

Before I could answer, Ranulfo launched into his vision for the class. The students would come from the neighborhood: mostly first-generation immigrants from small Mexican ranches who worked in the fields outside Salem's city limits, picking blueberries, strawberries, grapes, and hops, but also the people who worked in the canneries, sorting and packing fruits and vegetables, and maybe some of the Latinos who worked in restaurants, nurseries, and landscaping.[1] In other words, they would be his friends, relatives, and customers. And I would be the teacher, but not the kind you usually find in Mexico, the ones that scold the students whenever they get something wrong, like the teacher in elementary school who made him walk around the school wearing toy donkey ears one time when he hadn't done his homework. Recalling how the other kids called him "dumb donkey" that day, Ranulfo laughed and said those jokes just make you stronger. Still, he didn't want to recreate that atmosphere here in the U.S. No, the students would call me by my first name and we'd be *compañeros*.

I was used to this kind of congenial atmosphere at my college, where we never used donkey ears for teaching aids, but I wasn't excited about taking on the ESL class, knowing how much time it would burn up. Ranulfo didn't give up easily, though. "These students have to understand that it's hard work," Ranulfo said. "It's not magic. It's like there's this giant wall of ice in front of us, and we're blasting through it with a jackhammer." As he said this, he grabbed an imaginary jackhammer, pushed out his already puffy cheeks, and made the "brrrrrr" sound of a motor.

When he quoted a Discovery Channel show about space travel and slipped into full, grammatically correct sentences in English, I discovered Ranulfo himself could speak English quite well, though with an accent, like most second-language learners, including me. I complimented him and started to speak in English, but he quickly switched back into Spanish.

Not content with a jackhammer, he kept looking for another image that might convey his hopes for the class. "They have to be like a boxer and give English a knockout punch," he said. A minute later he switched to swamp imagery. "They can't just fall in a swamp and expect to be rescued. You're there to throw them a rope, but they have to pull, too."

Adding that we would give prizes to the students with the best attendance records (students we didn't have yet, for a class I hadn't yet agreed to teach), Ranulfo proclaimed, "I'm going to be *El Animador*, The Class Motivator."

I wanted to beg off, but I couldn't resist Ranulfo's energy, so I took a leap of faith and agreed to teach the class, provided the students would spend the last 20 minutes talking to me in Spanish about Mexican films and culture. Also, the class would have to end in December because in January I was moving with my family to Mexico, to oversee a study-abroad program in Oaxaca.

Ranulfo agreed, joking that pretty soon all the Americans were going to live in Mexico and the Mexicans were going to live in America.

Note

1. *Hispano* was the Spanish term Ranulfo most often used to refer to U.S. immigrants from Latin America. However, when referring to someone like himself, a first-generation immigrant from Mexico, he almost always used the term *mexicano*, Mexican.

CHAPTER 3

Teaming Up

October–December, 2005

Over the next few weeks, Ranulfo and I posted a flyer for our ESL class in the store and we secured a classroom at an elementary school a few blocks down the street, surrounded by small ranch houses, tidy squares of grass, and trimmed bushes. We quickly had about 15 students, mostly men who worked in agriculture and landscaping, and women who worked minimum-wage jobs in restaurants or stayed home to take care of their families. Some had been in the United States for just a couple months, while others had been here for years without any regular chance to interact with English speakers. They were all trying their hearts out.

The only student I felt a bit concerned about was Manuel, who sat with his arms folded across his chest on the first night and tersely stated that his favorite actor was Jean-Claude Van Damme, the action hero. Unsure if I'd heard him right, I held up my finger like a gun and asked if that's what he meant, and he nodded in agreement.

Yet on the paper I handed out asking the students to tell me more about themselves, this was the single sentence that Manuel neatly printed in English:

"I want be with my beutiful son."

I liked this tough guy.

And Manuel made sure his wish came true. Starting the next week, he brought his bright-eyed, 11-year-old son to class with him every night, and they always sat together in the front row, with his son quietly drawing and doing homework while half listening to our class. Sometimes, when Manuel couldn't follow my English instructions, his son would whisper the Spanish translation in his ear.

There were other kids, too. One time, Ranulfo's son Mauricio, a fourth-grader with soulful brown eyes, instinctively raised his hand when I asked the class, "Where is the flag?" He had momentarily forgotten where he was, an understandable mistake, given that his own classroom was down the hall and similarly adorned with an American flag, maps, and giant posters of puppies and wild animals. When he looked up and saw all the adults smiling at him, he said, "Oops, sorry."

As adorable as the kids were, their presence reminded the adults they'd never speak with the effortless bilingualism and perfect accents of their children. Even Ranulfo's three-year-old daughter—who begged to be included in the class, until Ranulfo told her she was too noisy—was already soaking up English at home, mostly by watching Disney cartoons. Once, after the adults got stumped by an English word in class and a child quickly explained it, I heard a mother sigh.

Ranulfo's English was also far beyond the level of the class, yet he showed up faithfully every night, throwing in jokes to lighten the mood, reminding the adults not to call me *usted*, sir, and making coffee for *el convivio*, a wonderful Spanish word that denotes "the snack break," but literally means "the co-living."

And I was always glad to have Ranulfo there. After the students had gone home, he and I would stand around in the faculty lounge dissecting the class, analyzing who was excelling and who was struggling, and planning what we should do next. Often, unable to pull away, we'd continue our conversations in the parking lot, or I'd drive him the two blocks to his house and we'd talk for another hour or two in my car, parked in the driveway a few feet from his front door. And we didn't just talk about teaching, we talked about everything—Mexican and American culture, NASA missions to Saturn and Mars, immigration, where to get a good deal on tires for our cars. Stories, opinions, and reflections came pouring out of Ranulfo in a torrent, as if he'd been waiting for someone to finally ask what he thought about this strange, beautiful world.

He especially liked telling me about the poverty he grew up with in Mexico. He got his first full-time job at age 12 in Mexico, working at a sawmill to help provide food for his family, walking to work in the cold mornings in open-toe sandals, going to bed every night fantasizing about owning a bicycle. When he arrived in Oregon at age 19 and started working at a plant nursery, the first thing he bought was a bicycle. He was so happy that he rode that bike for ten straight hours, only stopping for food and bathroom breaks. The funny part, Ranulfo said, was that he had to call in sick for work the next morning because he was too sore to walk, the first time in his life he ever missed work. That was his reward for getting a bicycle.

Ranulfo's childhood poverty remained deep inside him, creating not only a sense of humor about the way the universe sometimes gave him a smack in the head right after something went his way, but also a constant sense of wonder and disbelief at his good fortune in the U.S. To that day, he picked pennies off the ground, paid his bills on time, and never bought anything special for himself. He had never owned a credit card—I used mine to make online purchases for him and he paid me back in cash—and the whole concept of borrowing was alien to his family. When I asked how his father bought their house in Mexico, Ranulfo said, "He didn't buy it, he built it little by little, with us living inside the whole time. He got wood from the forest outside the village, and whenever he could afford it he'd buy some cement, and add a little more." Ranulfo was the first member of his family to purchase a dwelling, a small, one-story house within walking distance of both the store and our ESL class. It wasn't much, but Ranulfo loved it, deeply grateful to have running water, linoleum floors, and a patch of grass in the backyard, a piece of America he could call his own.

Now that he had recently paid off his mortgage, Ranulfo dared to want a little more—a small bakery, to be added to the back of the store. Ranulfo confided in me that he and his younger brother Pablo had just recently started discussing this bold new plan. They wanted to bake bread and pastries, the kind that taste like Mexico. They wanted to work with their hands, as they had done most of their lives, first working on their parents' farm in Mexico, then at plant nurseries in Oregon.

The bakery had even more personal meaning to Ranulfo. It would give him a chance to work side by side with his wife, Lupe. She was working at that time in the fruit and vegetable canneries a couple months a year, pushing heavy pumpkins and other produce down the conveyer belt, so white people could eat pies on Thanksgiving. She needed something better, something more permanent and less physically demanding. Once their daughter went to preschool in another couple years, Lupe would be ready to work full time, but she wouldn't have many job options, given her lack of English and education beyond elementary school. Picking crops in the fields outside Salem would be back-breaking work, worse than the canneries, so that wasn't a viable option, nor was there any need for her behind the register at El Palmar. The ideal plan was for her to bake bread in the store. The bakery wasn't just a business plan, it was sustenance.

Lupe was truly the girl from next door: her family lived two houses over from Ranulfo's parents in their hometown, a tiny village in the Mexican countryside. She quit school when she was eight to work in the fields, and at age 17 she married Ranulfo and came to live with him in Salem. Lupe, now in her 40s, had long black hair, and she usually wore slacks and loose-fitting, colorful shirts. When she came in the store, she spoke so quietly—always in Spanish—that I had to strain to understand her. Sometimes, in response to my questions, a mischievous smile started to appear at the edges of her mouth and I thought she was about to let a wisecrack fly, but she never did, even when we all got together at their house or their son's soccer practices. Ranulfo assured me, though, that she had a great sense of humor, especially when it came to putting him in his place. She was good for him, and they wanted to work together in the store. The bakery was the answer.

On the other hand, the chances of crashing and burning were high. Adding a bakery was going to require major new construction and equipment, paid for with hundreds of thousands of dollars in bank loans, a massive financial risk. Of the more than one million new small businesses started every year in the United States, 66% fail within the first ten years.[1] If the store went under, Ranulfo would likely lose his life savings and house—everything he'd worked for his whole life. And the unknowns were as overwhelming as the stakes. Would his customers keep their jobs picking berries, washing dishes, and mowing lawns? Would they like his pastries? How long would that take? Despite his sharp accounting for every dollar in the store, Ranulfo couldn't answer these questions.

Ranulfo's risk-taking fascinated me. It's one thing when someone in their 20s takes a financial risk, but when a father in his 40s with two young kids and a wife puts his family savings on the line—I wouldn't have had the guts to do that. If I paid more than $10 for a shirt, I usually got overwhelmed with regrets and returned it by the end of the week. I had a steady income and never considered putting my house or savings on the line, so I was hugely impressed that Ranulfo had given up his secure job at the plant nursery to open the corner store with Pablo. Now that the store was finally looking like it would survive, I would have stopped there.

I couldn't understand how Ranulfo had the courage to risk everything to get to the next level.

And there seemed to be a spiritual dimension at work. By taking an all-or-nothing gamble on the bakery, I got the feeling that Ranulfo wanted to test the outer limits of his good fortune, to see how far the universe was willing to go before it struck him down. Against all the odds, all those internal demons and external constraints on how far a Mexican immigrant with a fifth-grade education and GED can go, he was fighting to reach higher ground.

NOTE

1. Small Business Administration, Office of Advocacy, "Frequently Asked Questions," updated January, 2011. www.sba.gov/sites/default/files/sbfaq.pdf. Accessed June 10, 2013. These figures about survival rates for small businesses come from 2000 U.S. census data.

CHAPTER 4

Saints of the Casino

December, 2005

Since I had a research sabbatical that fall and no other classes to teach, I spent four or five days a week at the store, standing behind the counter with Ranulfo, listening, laughing, taking it all in. I was employing anthropology's basic methodology of "participant-observation," or what one anthropologist rightly called "deep hanging out."[1] The method works like this: hang around for a long time, ask naïve questions, go back to your room at night, think about what you did wrong, type up your notes, and think of more dumb questions to ask the next day. Ranulfo had never heard of anthropology before, but my methods still made sense to him. I was a scientist, and scientists ask questions, take notes, and study everything.

What he didn't realize was that I was breaking away from anthropology's traditional focus on exotica. Instead of studying mystical shamanism or inexplicable Aztec secrets, like a typical anthropologist of days gone by, I spent my time talking with Ranulfo about everyday things like cowboy movies. It tickled me to imagine our dialogues sounding like this:

"Don Ranulfo, please tell me, why do some customers buy Budweiser instead of Corona?"

"Ah, my son, that is because Budweiser is cheaper."

This little parody reminded me that I was moving away from classic anthropology...toward beer. I was immersed in everyday commerce and loving it.

Ranulfo had even less interest in the occult. He'd never once in his life visited a *curandero*, a traditional healer, and on the few occasions when I tried to talk about them and Mexican spirit mediums, he dismissed them all as baseless *supersticiones* and *mitos*. He didn't even show much interest in Catholic saints, though he regularly sold candles with pictures of saints that customers used to pray for miracles and good fortune. Whenever I asked about the candles, he quickly changed the topic. He was Catholic, but almost never went to church, except for baptisms and weddings. He put his faith in science, technology, and business, and got more excited talking about astronauts and Bill Gates than shamans or saints.

Ranulfo stood in sharp contrast to Guillermo, one of the regulars who liked to buy saint candles. When Guillermo approached the register one afternoon in early December, I could tell something was wrong. Slowly placing two candles on the counter without looking up, he seemed more somber than usual, and I quickly learned why: he had just lost $15,000 playing the slot machines at the casino. My jaw almost dropped when Guillermo reported this news, but luckily he didn't notice. He was too busy picking up one of the candles, rolling it in his hand, and saying he really had to stay away from the casino. Like most of the guys who came in the store, he wore a baseball cap, tee shirt, and faded jeans, with the thin waist and strong arms of someone who worked outdoors with his hands. He didn't seem like someone who could afford to lose $15,000.

Ranulfo picked up one of his free 2006 calendars, reserved for loyal customers, handed it to Guillermo, and said, "Here. Now that you're not going to the casino, you're going to win calendars."

Guillermo looked up, forced a smile, and said, "*Gracias*, this will be good luck for me."

Then in a half whisper he confessed, "What's happening is that right now I can't get my thoughts together…I'm just in a very difficult part of my life."

At that point Ranulfo left to stock the shelves, leaving me at the counter with Guillermo and his unorganized thoughts, loosely connected by one main theme: magic rituals that bring good luck. His eyes lit up when he described the miraculous powers of saints like San Ramón and San Martín Caballero, and how they would help you win money at the casino if you combined prayers to them with certain tricks, like folding up dollar bills and putting them under a tree, or applying a special perfume to your feet, which is where all energy comes from, Mother Earth. By the time Ranulfo got back to the counter, Guillermo had moved from casino rituals to instructions on how to make sure a pregnancy results in the gender you want. While Ranulfo rang up customers at the register, I kept listening to Guillermo, nodding and inserting a quick follow-up question every five or ten minutes to keep him going. Soon Guillermo was telling me stories about gold coins hidden beneath the ground near his family's farm in Mexico, and how someday he was going to find them, once he solved this problem with the casino.

When Guillermo finally left, I was flying high, my head spinning with stories of saints and their cosmological implications. As much as I liked talking about Budweiser, I still had a place in my heart for miracles, too. And it didn't surprise me that Guillermo was an "over-sharer" by most standards. Other Americans share confidences with a hairdresser, bartender, or passenger on the bus. Guillermo chose me, the gringo at the corner store. And why not? As sympathetic outsiders, anthropologists often become privy like this to secrets and confidences that people wouldn't normally share with their best friends.[2]

I was feeling great—until Ranulfo turned to me and said, "I think he's crazy."

Ranulfo's terse comment brought my spirits crashing down, but after picking myself up, I had to admit that Guillermo did seem a bit unhinged. I also felt relieved when Ranulfo added, "You can't just walk around telling everything you think to everyone you meet; you have to hold some things back." That comment confirmed what I'd noticed that fall: Ranulfo might cross the line sometimes, but he didn't pour his heart out with just anyone who walked in the store. With self-control and social awareness, he adjusted his tone and level of formality according to the situation, quickly discerning who wanted to joke or swap stories and who just wanted to buy a gallon of milk or phone card and leave quickly. He seemed to get along well with everyone—the men and women in our ESL class, the little kids who begged their mothers for popsicles, the teenagers who stopped in for a snack after school, the older women and single men who washed their clothes at the laundromat. He was no Guillermo.

And yet…Ranulfo had his own casino problems.

For the last couple years, he had been visiting the same place as Guillermo: Spirit Mountain, a casino run by the Grande Ronde Indian tribe and located about 30 miles west of Salem, on the way to the coast. That fall Ranulfo visited Spirit Mountain two or three times a week to play the slot machines, sometimes staying until 2 or 3am, then driving back in time to work the next morning.

Ranulfo said he just went there for fun and recreation. He never spent more than $100 in a single night, and he always went with a couple other people, usually his wife and brother-in-law. But I knew plenty of gambling addicts started out the same way. It was a slippery slope. Ranulfo himself had once confessed, "I don't want to lose control." If he shared even a tiny fraction of Guillermo's obsession with the casino, he'd be in serious danger.

Since Ranulfo insisted the casino was just a diversion, I had to piece together my own interpretations. This didn't come easily. Getting me to understand the casino was like getting a Latin American farmer to understand why Americans spend billions of dollars every year on lawn products.[3] It just didn't make sense. If I'd thought about casinos before, I'd dismissed them as a rip-off scheme built on poor people's desperation. Now I had to take casinos seriously.

I concluded that, for Ranulfo, the casino was a controlled experiment in risk-taking. Ranulfo was at a major crossroads with the bakery, and that's where the casino came in. It helped him steel his nerves in a simulated business environment. Ranulfo hated to lose money, but he got to test out that awful sensation in controlled doses at the casino, if not learning to accept financial loss, at least reducing the pain through repetition. Referring to the risk of losing his house and life savings on the bakery, he used the exact same phrase he'd once used to describe the casino: *Me gusta el peligro y las emociones fuertes.* "I like danger and strong emotions."

Naturally he liked winning even more, not so much for the money, which never came to more than a couple hundred dollars a night, as what the winnings told him: he was on the right path, this was the right time to get the bakery, the United States loved him. Ilan Stavans, a famous Mexican-American scholar, said something similar about his grandfather, a Ukrainian immigrant who won the Mexican national lottery: "The experience made him forever grateful. Fortune had smiled. Mexico had opened its arms to him."[4] Ranulfo was searching in the casino for his own embrace from the United States. Even if the casino hadn't yet validated him with a giant pay-out, he still felt good sitting there side by side with Anglos, Latinos, and Asian-Americans, men and women, young and old, white-collar and blue-collar workers, the closest he would ever get to sitting in the same room with this sprawling, confusing place called America.

The casino was his Church of Gratitude, a way to thank America for giving him what he called "the best period of my life." Half-jokingly he once turned to me and said, "I'm thinking about putting a sign on the roof of the store with giant letters that say, 'I'M HAPPY!' That way, Santa Claus can fly overhead and know how I'm feeling."

Since Santa Claus was too busy to respond, Ranulfo turned to the casino instead, in search of return messages of love.

But this is where it got crazy. Buoyed by his optimism and gratitude, Ranulfo had recently created a saint of himself…

"Wait, you're creating a saint in your own name?" I had to be sure my ears had heard right, that I hadn't taken one of Ranulfo's Spanish expressions too literally.

"That's right. It's a pilot project. On the way to the casino, I think to myself, 'Please help me, San Ranulfo. On you, everything depends. I want to win. Thank you, San Ranulfo.'" He voiced these entreaties in a whisper, as if he were saying the rosary.

I couldn't believe it. This was outrageous. This was playing with fire. You don't go and canonize yourself. Even crazy Guillermo wouldn't do that.

"But it's a joke, right?" I was thrown off balance, once again not sure where the thin line stood between Ranulfo's fantasies, jokes, and serious ambitions.

"Well, it started out as a joke, but the saint is doing some good works. I won last week, so it's serious, too. And if the saint works well, I'll tell other people about him, so they can win, too." He didn't laugh, so I wiped the smile off my face, hoping he didn't feel like I was judging him.

"Wow, and you call the saint 'San Ranulfo'?"

"Exactly. I'm trying to give him a personality, a good image." Then, to break up the tension, Ranulfo quipped, "I want to make sure the saint isn't fat, like me."

Later, after reading more about gambling, I decided that the San Ranulfo Pilot Project wasn't as crazy as it first sounded. Magical charms are common among all sorts of gamblers, and some, just like Ranulfo, adopt new names to reflect their altered identities and increase their chances of winning.[5] As for Catholic saints, Mexico generated new saints as fast as the United States generated new technology companies and financial scams. Just in the last couple decades, large followings had developed for a saint who specialized in helping Mexicans cross the border (San Toribio), another who defended drug traffickers (Jesús Malverde), and another in the image of death itself (La Santísima Muerte). A saint of the casino wasn't that far-fetched. It sounded like a figure in a magical realist story or Kerouac's rhapsodies about a "new American saint" and other "riotous angelic particulars"—yet it made sense.[6]

Still, even as lucky charms and saints went, Ranulfo was going to extremes. By calling himself a saint, he was sticking his finger in the eye of the Catholic Church and the egalitarian culture he'd grown up with in Mexico. Creating a saint in his own image even crossed the line in the United States, the land of greasy cheeseburgers and indulgent individualism. He was probing the outer limits of America's love. He was tempting fate, daring the world to either grant his wishes or strike him down.

Ranulfo was acting, in other words, like Captain Ahab. Both challenged God and the prevailing social order. Both wanted the universe to reveal what lay behind its stony silence. Explaining his ultimate motive for hunting Moby Dick, Captain Ahab famously thundered, "All visible objects, man, are but as pasteboard masks. But in each event—in the living act, the undoubted deed—there, some unknown but still reasoning thing puts forth the mouldings of its features from behind the unreasoning mask. If man will strike, strike through the mask! How can the prisoner reach outside except by thrusting through the wall?"[7] In his quieter way, Ranulfo, too, wanted the universe to give him a sign of recognition—a wink, a wave, a peek behind the curtain, a sign that he was on the right track. If he could get past the indifference of the casino's machines—their unreasoning mask, randomness itself—he would know whether the universe really loved him.

Of course, Ranulfo and Ahab were exact opposites in other ways. Ahab's quest was motivated by hate and vengeance, Ranulfo's by love and gratitude. Ahab didn't care about his family, Ranulfo did everything for them. Ahab doubted God's existence and disdained commerce, Ranulfo had faith in both. Ahab went out to sea, Ranulfo stayed on land. Yet opposites have a strange way of turning into the same thing. It wasn't a coincidence that Ahab gave his speech about striking through the mask right after nailing a gold coin, a doubloon, to the masthead, offering it as reward for the crewman who first spotted Moby Dick. Though Ahab forswore interest in money, the doubloon was a central symbol in the story, referred to by the sailors as no less than the "ship's navel" and "the White Whale's talisman."[8] Money was as important to Ahab's mission as Ranulfo's, flip sides of the same doubloon.

Years later, while discussing an early draft of this book, I started describing Captain Ahab's desire to "strike through the mask," and Ranulfo immediately interjected, "So the captain wants to go beyond the ordinary. He wants to erase the sun".

"Exactly!" I said, thrilled to see that Ranulfo intuitively understood Ahab, even though he'd never read *Moby-Dick*. "In fact, right after Ahab says he wants to strike through the mask, he says he'd punch the sun if it insulted him."[9]

"Ah, so we're the same," Ranulfo said matter of factly. "I'd punch time if I had to. Same thing."

I started noting differences between him and Ahab, but Ranulfo showed no interest in belaboring such surface matters.

"So you don't mind the comparison?" I asked.

"No, it's good," Ranulfo immediately replied. *Mucha filosofía*. "Lots of philosophy here."

Ranulfo and I had many conversations like this after he checked over drafts of every chapter in this book. I made every change he asked for, mostly minor corrections to names and dates, but he didn't want me to change a thing about my Ahab comparison.

At the time, though, I didn't want to tell Ranulfo that he reminded me of either Captain Ahab or Guillermo. I figured detailed Ahab comparisons wouldn't make sense, and Ranulfo wouldn't appreciate the comparison with Guillermo, a man clearly caught in the grips of the casino.

Comparisons with Guillermo would have been even less appreciated once we saw what happened to him during the next couple years. Guillermo took out an equity loan on his house to pay off his debts, but he ended up gambling everything away at the casino. He lost his house, and then his wife left him and took the kids with her, forcing Guillermo to move in with his nephew. When Guillermo didn't emerge from his room in the attic one day, his nephew went up to check on him—and found him dead. The nephew later told me that his uncle died of a heart attack, probably brought on by Rock Star, the energy drink he'd been consuming the night he died.

I had to ask, "Do you think Rock Star was really the main cause?"

"Actually," the nephew said, pausing, "I think he died of a broken heart. The pain was too much."

The tragic specters of Ahab and Guillermo scared me, and what happened next made me even more convinced that Ranulfo could end up like them.

Notes

1. For more details on what James Clifford and later Clifford Geertz called "deep hanging out," see Wogan (2004b).
2. As Georg Simmel said, a stranger "often receives the most surprising openness—confidences which sometimes have the character of a confessional and which would be carefully withheld from a more closely related person" (1912, 404). Simmel probably wrote so insightfully about strangers and secrets because of his own liminal social position. He was admired by notable scholars like Max Weber, but, as a Jewish man in nineteenth-century Germany, Simmel was also discriminated against and unable to get a paid academic post until the end of his life. Another factor was Simmel's virtuoso, impressionistic writing style, which didn't go over well at a time when academic fields, aptly called "disciplines," were anxiously consolidating their professional identities within universities. In this latter sense, Simmel was the sociological equivalent of Friedrich Nietzsche, a contemporary German philosopher whom Simmel admired. This is the way Lewis Coser sums up Simmel's career: "As in the case of 'The Stranger,' of whom he wrote so perceptively and so movingly, his relations to the academy were a compound of nearness and remoteness" (Coser 1971, 213–214).
3. On the cost of lawn care, see Steinberg (2006), and on historical American views of gambling, see Lears (2003), who shows that gambling has been similarly dismissed and condemned throughout American history, especially by Protestant reformers and business leaders who celebrated hard work and rational, scientific management. He also shows that gambling, or "chance," has just as persistently endured, right through the celebrations of change and spontaneity by late twentieth-century business leaders. Even someone like Roger Caillois, one of the most influential theorists of play, slips into dismissals of modern gambling as nothing but the desperate acts of poor people: "Chance is courted because hard work and personal qualifications are powerless to bring such success about" (1961, 114).
4. Stavans (2004, xi).
5. For examples of "magical" thinking in gambling, including the use of separate names for one's gambling self, see Reith (1999).
6. Kerouac (1951, 34, 197).

7. Melville (1851), Chapter 36, "The Quarter-Deck."
8. Melville (1851), Chapter 36, "The Quarter-Deck," on Pip referring to the doubloon as the "ship's navel," and Chapter 99, "The Doubloon," on all the sailors revering the doubloon as the "White Whale's talisman."
9. In the original text, Ahab says, "Talk not to me of blasphemy, man; I'd strike the sun if it insulted me" (Melville 1851, Chapter 36, "The Quarter-Deck").

CHAPTER 5

Car Crash

December, 2005

On a cold Wednesday morning in mid-December, I pulled up to the store and saw that the entire driver's side of Ranulfo's Ford Explorer had been smashed up.

"*¡¿Qué pasó?!*" I asked as I entered the store, not even waiting for Ranulfo to finish ringing up the customers at the counter.

Ranulfo just said, "*Hola*, Pete," and flashed me a smile with a hint of embarrassment that I'd never seen before. Sensing he didn't want to talk in front of the customers, I came behind the counter, set my backpack in its usual spot along the back wall, waited for the customers to leave, then pointed to the parking lot and asked again, "So what happened?"

"Well, the thing is," he said slowly and carefully, "I was coming back from the casino with Lupe last night, about two in the morning. And I wasn't going that fast, but I went out into the second lane to pass a car, and suddenly I hit some ice, and whoof—the car started spinning like crazy! I couldn't stop it."

"Whoa, that's terrible!" I said. I had never seen Ranulfo so vulnerable.

"It was," he agreed. "The car spun around about two or three times... and then we were sitting in the ditch on the *other* side of the highway. And then Lupe started crying, she was so scared."

Ranulfo looked right at me and his eyes widened, as if to say, "Can you believe this?"

I couldn't. I just stood there, trying to wrap my mind around the scene.

"So then I asked her if she was all right, and I got out of the car and went to her side, to see. We both started checking ourselves. We were all right, except that Lupe got hit in the arm with some juice cans from the back of the car. They got thrown around when the car started spinning."

Then he added the most haunting part. "You know what? If our car had started spinning just a few seconds later, we'd be dead now, because just after we hit the ditch, I saw a tractor trailer come flying down the road, in the lane that we had just crossed over."

"But we were saved." His eyes opened slightly again, to emphasize the magnitude of his good luck.

I agreed when Ranulfo said, *Fue como de película*. "It was like out of a movie."

I couldn't bear to state the obvious: the accident was an indictment of the casino's dangers. I also didn't want to ask whether he was afraid, since I knew he didn't like that word. Earlier that fall, when I had asked if he felt any fear about the bakery plan, Ranulfo had said that word didn't exist for him, joking that he'd ripped the word *miedo* right out of his dictionary.

Nonetheless, without any prompting from me, Ranulfo announced, "San Ranulfo didn't work last night."

Still trying not to be critical, I said, "I was going to ask you about that...."

He said, "This is what I don't understand, this is what's making me think," and then recounted San Ranulfo's role in the night.

"Last night I said, 'San Ranulfo, I'm here.' But then I decided not to gamble. But then Lupe said she wanted to play the slot machines for about 20 minutes, and I went to redeem these free raffle tickets, and that took about 20 to 30 minutes because there was a long line. Then Lupe came back, and I had a soda and said again, 'I'm not going to play.'"

Here's where the mystery began, a hidden undertow that seemed to pull him toward the slot machines. "All of a sudden, I looked at the ATM there, and just decided to take out $100. And I changed it into $10 and $5 bills."

"To play?"

"Yes, to play." Ranulfo found this strange because he was usually decisive, not given to saying one thing and doing another two minutes later.

He continued, "And I was doing pretty well, winning. And I said, 'San Ranulfo, now is the time, show me if you're ready to be canonized.'"

At this point I couldn't suppress a little laugh, out of sheer nervousness and surprise that Ranulfo was going all the way with his self-canonization.

Ranulfo smiled and broke off his sentence, "Because...usually...to be canonized...." Then turning serious and regaining his footing, he said, "But, no, he failed me." I nodded in agreement, and Ranulfo quickly moved on to the next part of the story.

"I was working well for about an hour. I was collecting a lot of winnings. But all of a sudden I changed machines and I started to lose, and I lost my whole $100."

"So what do you think about San Ranulfo in terms of the accident?" I was giving him a chance to make a more explicit critique of San Ranulfo, but he didn't want to go that far. Suddenly he switched to more practical matters. "Pete, I want you to call the car insurance company for me, OK?"

Of course, I said yes, then spent the next couple hours making phone calls and filling out insurance forms. After that we planned out the next night's ESL class, rather than talk any more about the car accident and take the chance that the word "fear" might slip back into Ranulfo's imaginary dictionary.

The next night in class, the last of the year, I administered the same ESL oral comprehension quiz I had given on the first night, then handed back the original quizzes. As the students could clearly see by setting the two quizzes side by side, they had all significantly improved over the fall. Smiling in half-disbelief and joy, they pored over their quizzes like hidden treasure maps.

I also gave them "diplomas," typed pieces of paper with congratulations for each student. Everyone laughed when Ranulfo shouted out, "We're going to need teacher–parent conferences to tell your parents how well you're doing!" They also laughed when he added, "I think NASA is going to call to get some new astronauts." None of them knew that he often seriously wondered out loud to me about what it would be like to be an astronaut or extraterrestrial, but the joke worked because they probably knew Latinos like him who constantly watched educational documentaries about NASA and space travel. I sometimes heard Ranulfo, Pablo, and their customers discussing topics like Pluto's demotion as a planet and whether the universe is expanding. They weren't alone, either. An anthropologist who worked with Central American manual laborers near San Francisco reported that the men would go home at night and surf the web for educational documentaries. While standing on the corner waiting for day jobs, the men discussed science and history for hours, and the anthropologist lost bets to them over scientific matters like the exact speed of light and the differences between Asian and African elephants.[1]

I, too, couldn't keep up with Ranulfo's space references, so I just proceeded with our ceremony. After the students presented me with a cake, a gift certificate to a Mexican restaurant, and heartfelt speeches, it was all I could do, seeing them clutching their diplomas and quizzes, crowded around me in the faculty lounge, to steady my voice and deliver a few final words. I reminded them that Ranulfo would help one of my college students take over the class after the holidays. I told them how much I believed in them and admired what they were doing. Some students were on the verge of tears, so I wrapped up by imploring everyone to keep doing their homework while I was in Mexico, at which point Ranulfo interjected, "Pete's going there to become *un brujo*, a witch!" The students laughed at his final risqué joke, which played off the irony that Oaxaca gets stereotyped among Mexicans as a backward, indigenous state, yet, for that very same reason, American and European tourists see it as the "real" Mexico and flock there.

I didn't have much chance to let the full sadness of that goodbye sink in. I got busy packing, and later that week stopped by the store to pick up the plane tickets that Ranulfo had ordered for me. Ranulfo worried about my family having to change planes in Mexico City. "It's not just you, Pete. It's your wife and kids. You can't take chances," he said. I told him we'd be fine, but he didn't agree. He was so concerned that he started talking about buying a ticket and flying down with us, until I convinced him not to by promising we wouldn't leave the airport in Mexico City, no matter what. He finally accepted my assurances, then gave me some international phone cards, so I could call him as soon as we arrived.

That's what friends do: they look out for each other. I wished I could do something to protect Ranulfo from the casino, but just had to hope that the car accident had scared him straight.

Note

1. This devotion to educational documentaries emerges in the course of a recent book (Ordóñez 2015) about immigrant, Latino day laborers in the San Francisco Bay area. The parallels with Ranulfo, Pablo, and other people I met at the store are so striking that it's worth quoting Ordóñez at length: "Before coming to the United States, Eduardo…had a computer with which he surfed the Internet, favoring museum webpages from around the world and various documentaries.… On the corner [for day laborers in the Bay area], we talked for hours about science, history, and when joined by Luis—whose family nicknamed him *el animalitos* because of his appetite for nature documentaries—tested out one another's knowledge about common and obscure endangered species. I was never a contender in these conversations—both Eduardo and Luis had encyclopedic knowledge about these subjects, and I lost bets over the exact speed of light and the differences between Asian and African elephants" (Ordóñez 2015, 60–61).

CHAPTER 6

Trip to Mexico

January–May, 2006

The market women in Oaxaca were delighted with our kids, Zach, Liam, and Petie, ages ten, eight, and six. At just about every outdoor market, friendly vendors in large aprons complimented our kids—"How precious!" "Look at the blue eyes!" "They're right out of Hollywood!"—and compared them to the blocks on a marimba, "small, medium, and large." But the reaction at the local elementary school was less enthusiastic. One day my oldest son, a fourth grader, came home and reported what classmates had screamed at him during recess: "Your president is an assassin!…You robbed our country!…It's shameful to be an American!" He could understand their Spanish because he and his brothers had gone to a bilingual elementary school in Salem, but he had no idea where this resentment was coming from. Nobody had ever informed him he'd robbed Mexico.

My wife, a Spanish teacher, put the kids to bed that night with a long history lesson about Mexico's concession of half its territory to the U.S. in the mid-nineteenth century, following the Mexican–American War.

It was still hard for our kids to comprehend. A few days later our first grader, Petie, asked me, "So are we Canadian?"

"No, we're Americans. Why?"

"Because Canadians speak English, too" He was confused because the only other kid who spoke English at school was Canadian.

A couple years later we told our kids that they had it much easier in Oaxaca than the millions of immigrant kids who arrive in the U.S. not speaking English and struggling as minorities. By contrast, they had all the privileges of a white middle-class family, and no matter what happened in Oaxaca, they knew they would be going back to the U.S. at the end of the six months.

But telling our kids all this wouldn't have helped at the time. They were just trying to figure out if they were Canadian, and what the correct Spanish words were for the candy they wanted to buy at the little store around the corner.

Never having lived before in a major city, our kids were also trying to understand what happened to all the grass and wide-open spaces they had grown up with in Oregon. My wife and I kept telling them how lucky they were to be surrounded by such beautiful markets, museums, and art, but that didn't matter to them. They were just mad that it was spring, and, for the first time since T-ball, they weren't playing on a baseball team. Instead, they spent the afternoons playing soccer on the tiny driveway in front of our apartment, fighting constantly over whose turn it was to kick the ball. Between their fighting and picky food habits, I suddenly didn't find my kids as cute as usual.

After about a month of hearing the kids fighting and screaming every day, my wife and I couldn't take it anymore, so we did something with our family we would normally never do in Oregon: we all got on a bus and headed to the beach for the weekend. The hotel we found was a modest, two-story structure, but it had hammocks, a small feature that changed everything. The hammocks hung on the balcony outside our second-floor room, looking right over the crystal-blue water. Gazing at the ocean waves while lying in the hammocks, my wife and I felt as if we were floating on magic carpets. Our boys, on the other hand, preferred whacking their magic carpets together. Every time their hammocks collided, they laughed, amazed and delighted that they could hit each other and not get hurt. The hammocks provided the illusion of safety, and the sun and salt water washed away their worries, so a bonk from a brother that would have set off a howling argument a day ago was now taken as good fun. Except for the time we spent body surfing and walking the beach, we stayed in those hammocks for the entire weekend—three days and nights of swaying, rocking, and whacking.

Lying in the hammocks after the sun went down, the closeness of our bodies and the absence of visual cues tapped us into another dimension, a relaxed world of reveries. In this altered state we invented a game: one person quoted a line from a movie, and then the others had to guess which movie it came from. It was a simple game, but we played it for hours, lying there quietly in our hammocks, trying to recall obscure movie images.

When our middle son, eight-year-old Liam, got stuck trying to find a good, tough line, I suggested, "How about something from *Rainbow Fish*?"

The kids immediately laughed at this outrageous suggestion. *Rainbow Fish* was one of those shows they watched when they were three or four years old, back in the days when they watched videos just to see the pretty colors flickering by. Recalling *Rainbow Fish* was like hitting reverse and going back light years in time to those far-away days before Woody or Simba, before the days of plot, character, or irony. The kids had changed so much since then that they looked at their earlier selves as some sort of stranger, and the sudden intrusion of that stranger cracked them up. For the next few minutes, they could barely concentrate on the game. They just kept laughing and saying, "*Rainbow Fish*?!" They were trying to comprehend—and reject—the connection between their past and present selves.

That weekend itself erected another comforting division between their past and present selves. Back at our apartment in Oaxaca, our boys stopped fighting, and their classmates soon forgot about American foreign policy and focused on more pressing matters, like playing marbles and soccer with these three newcomers. Our boys made friends and settled into their new life. The hammocks got the healing done.

I, on the other hand, still had my own adjustment issues. I was disappointed to find that the cowboy movies Ranulfo's customers loved couldn't be found anywhere in Oaxaca, even the street stalls. Just about everybody watched contemporary American movies, especially action thrillers and Disney movies. And I couldn't blame them. I, too, liked buying cheap Hollywood DVDs on the street and taking my kids to see the new *Pink Panther* movie in the big multiplex in town.[1] Surrounded by all these Hollywood movies, I couldn't help feeling like the old Mexican cowboy movies arose from a time and place that could no longer be recovered.

I had that same feeling of stepping out of time while spending a week in a tiny hamlet in the mountains outside Oaxaca, during a service trip with my students. There were no Hollywood movies there…and hardly any people, either. Finding the farming life too hard, especially after NAFTA led the U.S. to flood Mexico with cheap, subsidized corn, all the young people had moved to other parts of Mexico or the U.S. One of the elderly farmers said, "We're all that's left. When we die, this whole village might die, too."

These farmers didn't have a cinema, but they had something even better: stories about *naguales*, people who turn into coyotes, birds, and other animals at night. A few farmers even reported seeing these coyotes reduce humans to stuttering fools. Hearing these stories, I felt it again—the call of the wild.

These stories reminded me of Carlos Castaneda, the anthropologist who wrote best-selling books in the 1970s about a Mexican shaman named Don Juan Matus who doled out spiritual wisdom, including accounts of coyotes that convert into human form. Along with millions of other readers, I had devoured Castaneda's books in high school, finding in them an invitation to other worlds, other realities. Then in graduate school I found out that critics had denounced Castaneda for embellishing his accounts. That charge, together with the usual academic disdain for "popularizers," made Castaneda persona non grata in anthropology, so I hadn't thought about him again—until now, hearing these uncannily similar stories in the mountains of Oaxaca. The son of the local healer even told me he'd read all of Castaneda's books, and not only were they all true, he used them as guides to living right. That shocked me. Maybe I had gotten Castaneda wrong all these years?

I felt compelled to re-read Castaneda when I got back to the bookstores in Oaxaca city, but didn't get far. Even though Castaneda's stories of shape-shifters were uncannily close to the ones I'd just heard in the mountains, I still couldn't forgive him for failing to refute his critics with concrete evidence. Writers like him made it hard for those of us telling the truth.

Even when you have your facts straight, it's still difficult to translate them in a comprehensible way for people who weren't there. I was reminded of this translation problem when my wife and I went out to dinner with American acquaintances, a lovely, liberal-minded couple passing through Oaxaca on vacation. Hearing my descriptions of the human coyotes up in the mountains, the wife said, "I know. It's like a couple years ago we got this book from the library on Native American folktales, for bedtime stories for the kids, but the first one was all about a coyote who reaches in his butt and pulls out a huge turd! And then he throws the turd around and creates the mountains or something!"

We all laughed, especially when the normally quiet husband chimed in, "It wasn't exactly bedtime reading."

The wife added that the next story was about a coyote peeing backwards, so she told her kids, "Let's just find another book, OK?"

As the dinner conversation quickly moved on to other topics, I thought to myself, *Sure, that sounds like coyote. He's a profound trickster, a cross between Prometheus, bringer of fire and knowledge, and Bugs Bunny, bringer of carrots and humor.*

Eileen Kane, an anthropologist who wrote a beautiful memoir about fieldwork with the Paiute Indians of Nevada, described coyote this way:

"he creates things and smashes them; he's clever and a fool; he can invent things and then he's so immature.... He seems to do good by accident, while he's doing something completely selfish."[2]

I couldn't stop the dinner conversation, though, and go into a long anthropological discourse on coyote figures. It would take a whole book like Kane's to explain why coyote pees backwards, and to make any sense of the Mexican coyotes would require another book or two. Coyote would have to remain a bizarre mystery that night.

I liked shape-shifter stories so much, I was actually tempted to start researching Mexican coyotes and shamanism. But, no, I decided I couldn't jump ship at the first coyote sighting. I was already committed to studying Ranulfo's store. I had to resist the call of the coyotes.

The problem was, I couldn't manage to find anyone like Ranulfo in Oaxaca, no matter how hard I tried. I finally arranged the next best thing: a visit with his parents in central Mexico.

Preparing me for the visit with last-minute advice before our phone conversation got cut off, Ranulfo sounded as excited as I'd ever heard him. "Pete, it's really isolated and it's going to be cold at night, but at least my parents have a hot water heater now, not like when we were kids and we had to boil the water in pots to take a bath…And don't forget, I'm picking you and your family up at the airport when you get back from Mexico…. But you know what I miss the most about my village? The sound of the roosters in the morning!"

On the scheduled day, close to Easter time, I arrived by bus in Ranulfo's home state, Michoacán, located north of Oaxaca, about halfway between Mexico City and the coast, and completely unlike all three. Ranulfo was right about the isolation. It was farm country, the boondocks.

At the station Ranulfo's father, Don Pablo, gave me a big smile and hearty handshake. He had short gray hair and wore black jeans, boots, a collared shirt, and, like most other men there, a white cowboy hat. Though in his 70s, he seemed healthier than people half his age. Ranulfo's mother, Doña Carmen, had a wide, pleasant face and shoulder-length hair, and didn't get around quite as well, because of a slight limp from a car accident.

Don Pablo threw my bags in the back of their old Ford pick-up truck, then we piled in the front seat together and Don Pablo barreled out of town, quickly heading down small dirt roads. A couple times the pot holes bounced me so high that my head almost hit the roof, but Ranulfo's parents never moved off their seats, having long ago mastered the art of riding a pick-up truck like a horse.

Don Pablo talked and laughed and occasionally pulled his right hand off the steering wheel to gesticulate, repeating that Ranulfo and Pablo had both called to say I was a special friend and they should take good care of me. Apparently I was the first gringo ever to visit them.

All I could see were farms interspersed with donkeys, horses, evergreens, and tiny houses. When I asked Ranulfo's mother what sort of industry they had around there, she said matter of factly, "There is none."

"Nothing at all?"

No, ninguna. "No, not one."

Aside from a woman selling snacks through her house window, I certainly didn't see any commerce when we arrived in their village, La Palma, a tiny *rancho* of about 200 households. Despite the village's wishful name, "The Palm Grove"—the inspiration for Ranulfo and Pablo's store name, El Palmar—I didn't see a single palm tree, just more pines.

Ranulfo's wife, Lupe, and their kids, Mauricio and Laura, happened to be visiting as well, taking an extended spring break with Lupe's parents, who still lived two houses away from Ranulfo's. Over the next couple days we drove around together in Don Pablo's pick-up, visiting the markets in nearby towns and buying supplies. At first I rode up front with Ranulfo's parents, but after we stopped for tacos and popsicles one time, I switched to the back with Lupe and the kids. They were used to the farms and landscapes rushing past us, but I kept lapping up the sights like a dog with his tongue hanging out the car window. I was especially excited when we returned to the village and got to watch Lupe's relatives planting corn with plows pulled by a bull and horse. Best of all, the men let me follow along in the field, poking tiny openings in the soil for seed.[3] They seemed amused to find that anyone could get excited about something so prosaic.

My other favorite moments arose at the house. At night Ranulfo's parents and I talked at their metal kitchen table, surrounded by rows of matching cups and glasses on shelves along the bare, concrete wall by the sink, a functional artwork that displayed artistic order and readiness to host 30–40 people if necessary. With his cowboy hat resting on the table, Don Pablo recounted the way he got his start many years ago selling bottles of Coke, which he bought in town and carted back to the village on a *burro.* Eventually he got a truck and then an electric mill, for grinding corn into tortilla flour. Most recently, he grew avocados and sold them to a middleman, whom he imagined sold everything to supermarkets in America. The avocados—a vegetable native to Central Mexico—got harvested twice a year, paying their bills for food, electricity, and water. Don

Pablo and Doña Carmen could have lived in the U.S. with their kids, but they preferred it here in the countryside, with the avocados and fresh air.

At bedtime we retired to our separate rooms, directly across the hall from each other. Mine had no outdoor windows, just a small glass window facing the hallway, and the clock on the wall didn't work, making me imagine I was in a magical realist story where time had stopped. In reality, Ranulfo's parents had probably unplugged the clock to save electricity.

In those quiet moments, it sunk in—I was staying with Ranulfo's parents, sleeping in the same room where Ranulfo slept with his siblings as a child, blankets up over his face for security.

Every night I could hear his parents across the hall reciting their bedtime prayers, alternating lines together, one after the other in rapid succession. Lying in the dark hearing those prayers, I felt like a little kid.

The day before I left, Don Pablo and I pulled two kitchen chairs out in the hallway so we could listen to the *corrido* music that I had bought at a small store in town, a cassette tape filled with country ballads that Don Pablo had picked out for me. We sat there right in front of the speakers, listening to the songs, nodding, tapping our feet. While rays of afternoon sunlight came streaking through an open doorway and lit the hallway, almost nothing was said between us, except for Don Pablo's occasional shouts of ¡*Es buena*!

It was a perfect moment.

Early the next morning, about 7am, a half-dozen women wrapped in black shawls stood in the courtyard on the side of the house, conversing together. Ranulfo's parents were grinding the women's sacks of corn in a small machine the size and height of a barbeque grill, set up at the edge of the barn, with old truck parts and wood scraps lying a few feet away. They were maintaining a business they'd started more than 40 years ago, grinding corn for villagers who were happy to turn over a peso or two in return for corn flour to make tortillas, the core of the daily diet. As a child, young Pablo had learned the art of grinding corn from his mother, back when he had to crank up the diesel motor with a giant handle. In the last decade, the business had declined steeply, since villagers started buying pre-made tortillas in nearby towns, but for the families that still made tortillas by hand, Don Pablo and Doña Carmen's mill was indispensable. They were helping feed the village, just as their sons hoped to do with a bakery in Salem, Oregon.

On the drive back to the bus station, Don Pablo reflected, "It's good to have friendships with someone like you. Maybe this gives us…" He paused, searching for the right word, then his eyes lit up, and he shot his right index finger in the air and exclaimed, "an experience!"

Notes

1. *Pink Panther*, Director Shawn Levy, 2006.
2. Kane (2010, 123). Kane's book has some of the best writing I've ever found in anthropology—beautiful, novelistic, poignant, and insightful. The book is worth the read not only for Kane's subtle reflections on tricksters and her fieldwork as a budding anthropologist among the Paiute Indians in Nevada, but also her tender portraits of her family life in Youngstown, a working-class Ohio town.
3. For a good account of culture in rural Michoacán and urban Chicago, including individualism and language patterns, see Farr (2006).

CHAPTER 7

Don Quixote Rides Again

May–July, 2006

When I returned from Mexico in May, Ranulfo saw me in a new light. I had gone to the other side and come back. I had stayed in his childhood home. By travelling with an open heart along the emotional fault line that ran from Oregon to Michoacán, I had unwittingly shifted a tectonic plate in our relationship.

Ranulfo proudly told customers, *Este hombre visitó a mi tierra.* "This man visited my land." When a couple new customers asked what I was doing in the store, assuming I couldn't understand their rapid-fire Spanish, even though I was only standing a few feet away at the counter, Ranulfo put on a straight face and said, "Oh, this man is from Mexico. His parents were gringos, but they didn't want him, so they left him in Oaxaca when he was a baby. He's *El Gringo Oaxaqueño.*"

That cracked me up. My Anglo parents had never lived in Mexico, and I only learned to speak Spanish in my 30s. I was far from *El Gringo Oaxaqueño*, though that didn't stop me from playing along with Ranulfo's orphan jokes until the customers realized we were kidding.

Other times, while I carefully placed tortillas or coconut treats in small plastic bags for customers at the counter, Ranulfo would joke with them, "Can you believe it, an American working for a Mexican?" Most froze up, until they saw me laughing.

It felt great to be back in my favorite spot in the world, behind the counter, joking around again. I hung out more than ever at the store, about six hours a day, five days a week. And since I was there all the time, Ranulfo and Pablo put me to work: fixing the printer, typing up notices about their checking-cashing policies, filling out government forms, calling the help line at city offices and software companies, bagging the customers' groceries.

I loved my new role, a cross between sidekick, aide, buddy, and anthropologist. Sometimes I even welcomed customers to the counter with the same ritualistic phrases I'd heard Ranulfo and Pablo repeatedly use—*Buenas tardes, ¿Qué le damos? ¿Algo más?*—as if I were co-hosting this magnificent ritual encounter. Each interaction was like a compressed Japanese tea ceremony. The customer's entrance through the doorway and the greetings separated the outside world from the inner ritual sphere. The standard phrases and questions at the counter provided comforting familiarity and sometimes spurred jokes, stories, and extended conversations. The thanks and exit through the door completed the framing of the moment. Like a good ritual or narrative, these customer interactions had a clearly marked beginning, middle, and end, creating a break from the shapeless flow of everyday life.[1]

A cynic could say I was making too much out of people buying tortillas, but that would be like telling the Japanese to stop doing the tea ceremony and just gulp down their tea. The everydayness of tea and tortillas makes them even more meaningful as ritual objects, at least if they're handled properly, with gratitude and mindfulness. The same went for money, which, as anthropologist Mary Douglas said, is "only an extreme and specialised type of ritual."[2]

El Palmar was like a Mexican town plaza, a public space where people went out to stroll or buy a popsicle and talk with relatives and neighbors. When I had asked my ESL students what they missed about Mexico, plazas always showed up at the top of the list. Salem's malls and grocery stores just weren't the same. Neither was El Palmar, but it got closer. Customers at El Palmar even put out small cardboard boxes with handwritten notes in Spanish asking for donations for medical operations and funeral expenses. This wasn't just a convenience store, it was a community.

The vendors also belonged to this community, such as CD salesman José Luis, who called me *profe* and gave me a fist bump every time he stopped in.

I was thrilled to be part of this community, right down to the first time I got to check the Budweiser delivery. Two cases of Bud Lite in cans, two cases in bottles, four cases of Bud regular in cans: everything listed on the invoice was stacked on the delivery man's hand truck, so I signed the slip and told him to put the beer in the coolers along the back wall. Without even checking my count, Ranulfo dropped the invoice in the drawer next to the register. For a survivor of extreme poverty, that was an act of faith.

Ranulfo's trust in me also led him to share more details about his life. I couldn't help finding irony, in a clash-of-cultures way, in the stories he told about his brief marriage with Kate, a white Oregonian who worked at Kmart and didn't speak any Spanish or have much tolerance for traditional Mexican gender roles. Ranulfo recalled, "I was Mr. Vacuum Cleaner, Mr. Dishwasher, everything. She got home late from work, too tired to cook, so she ordered a lot of pizza, and on Saturday mornings I had to cook her breakfast or she'd get mad."

Ranulfo still didn't want to criticize Kate. He softly repeated that she was a good person and he learned a lot from her about respect, communication, give and take, all the things that go into a marriage. "We were both young" was how he explained their divorce.

That same willingness to cross language and cultural barriers explained Ranulfo's later success. At the plant nursery, Monrovia, he went from being a worker in the fields to a middle manager, supervising more than 50 Hispanic workers and serving as a trusted adviser to the white bosses, translating for both sides across the cultural divide. He liked seeing situations from multiple perspectives, and he was good at it.

At the store, Ranulfo continued to serve as a translator, on a more subtle level. He interacted smoothly with customers from diverse regions of Mexico and other parts of Central America, areas as tonally different from each other as Mississippi, New York, and Montana. If he hadn't been able to adjust his approach and make them all feel at home in his store, they would have found another one.

Having built up a base of loyal customers through such good service, Ranulfo and Pablo were now eager to expand. In early July they started looking into purchasing a Mexican restaurant on the verge of bankruptcy in Albany, about 25 miles south of Salem. They started exploring this option because Mr. Hanning, the owner of the store building, had recently said he wasn't ready to sell; he wanted to keep leasing the building, which meant they couldn't make major modifications to its physical structure.

Ranulfo still hoped Mr. Hanning would change his mind and let them add the bakery, but he couldn't wait for that to happen. He talked more and more excitedly about the Albany restaurant, going so far as to say, *Quiero comer billete.* "I want to eat dollar bills." He was joking that time, but he wasn't when he said, *Me urge ganar dinero.* "I'm in a hurry to make money." In all seriousness, he said he had to make his big move before he got past his 40s and lost this race against time.

I was happy to see the restaurant replacing the casino in his thoughts. He'd cut way back on the casino while I was in Mexico, though it took him a long time to admit that had anything to do with the car accident in December with Lupe. When I returned in May, Ranulfo simply said he wasn't visiting the casino often and was thinking of giving it up altogether. During a different conversation later in the month, he said the problem with the casino was that losing puts you in a bad mood. Still not mentioning the accident, he said, "You have to share with your family. When you go to the casino and lose, you come back feeling down and not talking to anyone." As he said this, Ranulfo imitated himself driving with a long, sad face.

"Pure silence," I said.

"Exactly. And my wife says to me, 'So now you're not talking? You must have lost money.'"

I laughed, knowing how much Ranulfo still hated losing money.

Finally, in late June, Ranulfo openly admitted that the car accident had caused him to cut back on the casino. "Because of the accident, I decided there's no reason to put your family at risk."

With the casino out of the picture, everything seemed to be proceeding smoothly with the restaurant plan—until Ranulfo had an ominous dream.

I got caught up in the library that warm July morning, so I called the store around noon to let Ranulfo know I wouldn't be coming in. I expected the call to end quickly, as it always did when Ranulfo got busy with lunch-hour customers, but he surprised me by quoting this proverb out of the blue: *Pobre del pobre al cielo no va. Lo chingan acá, lo chingan allá.* "Pity the poor person who won't get into heaven. They fuck him here, they fuck him there."

Holy cow. I'd never heard Ranulfo use such a negative proverb. I'd almost never even heard him swear. Something was clearly wrong. Right there in the college's parking lot, a few feet from my car, I stopped in my tracks.

When I asked Ranulfo to repeat the proverb, knowing that the authority of proverbs hinges on their exact wording, he cleaned it up a bit, substituting the euphemism *fregar*, screw, in place of *chingar*, fuck.

"But doesn't the Bible say the poor will be fine in heaven?" I asked, still shocked and trying to make sure Ranulfo really believed what the proverb said.

"Yes, but these proverbs come from *la gente*, regular people, not the church. They're saying the poor will always be poor. They'll even screw you in heaven."

"Wow, that's rough," I said, still wondering what had brought this on. Ranulfo agreed, then, without any segue, he announced, "Last night I dreamt I challenged God. I asked him for a third arm."

Another first. Ranulfo had never before mentioned any of his dreams. But without hesitating or slowing down for questions, he launched into a full description of the dream:

In the dream, I was back in La Palma [his village in Mexico], and I saw this man walking along by the stream, so I asked him, "Who are you?"

And he said, "You don't know who I am? I'll show you." He pointed to the water, and it was all dirty. Then all of a sudden it was clear.

Then he said, "What do you want to know?"

I said, "If you're really an important person, I want another arm."

He said, "You ask for too much. But we'll have a running race. If you beat me, you can have a third arm."

"And then I woke up," Ranulfo said. "I was *asustado*, frightened, and a little *arrepentido*, repentant, because I challenged God." This was the first time I'd ever heard Ranulfo say he felt afraid, much less repentant.

Then he said, "I'm worried I'm going crazy, like Don Quixote."

At first I thought he was kidding, or maybe viewing Don Quixote the way most educated Americans did, as a loveable, half-admirable character. But Ranulfo wasn't laughing. He was dead serious.[3] The only thing I could think to ask was, "So when did you read *Don Quixote*?"

"In a comic book in Mexico," he said. "Plus, later a friend lent me a copy of the real book, but I didn't read all of it. Cantinflas also made that movie, *Un Quijote sin mancha*."[4] He was referring to a Quixote film adaptation by a legendary Mexican comedian who goes around Mexico City as a law clerk defending the poor, accompanied by a goat that keeps eating his books. But Ranulfo didn't find any humor in the comparison with his own life. He confessed, "I just remember Don Quixote was a crazy guy fighting against windmills, and I don't want to go crazy like that."

This was getting bigger by the minute, much more than we could resolve on the phone, so we decided to talk more that night.

A few hours later we were back at one of our usual meeting spots, the park where Ranulfo's son Mauricio had soccer practice a couple nights a week. Despite the summer heat, the grass was still green and beautiful, filled with Latinos playing soccer and Anglos playing baseball. When Ranulfo pulled up with his whole family, his daughter Laura greeted me with an adorable smile and little-kid wave, even though I was only standing a couple feet away, next to her open car window. After Mauricio ran off to practice and Lupe and Laura went over to walk the track, Ranulfo and I set up folding chairs along the side of the field. Ranulfo was happy to report that the nursery gave him the chairs after his Safety Committee led the workers through three straight months without any accidents. Feeling safety-conscious myself, I suggested that we sit far enough from the baseball field to avoid the foul balls.[5]

The slight breeze and sunshine felt good on my bare legs. Even in July, I rarely wore shorts at the store, since none of the Mexican-American men did, but the soccer field was fair game. Ranulfo wore his usual jeans and collared shirt.

Returning to the dream, Ranulfo repeated that he didn't believe in "superstitions," then admitted that he still maintained the belief in his village that dreams can intuit and predict the future. His tone had significantly changed since we talked on the phone. Instead of sounding worried, he now talked in a subdued, almost serene, way.

To reduce his self-consciousness about sounding "superstitious," I said I'd heard that most cultures have a belief in the predictive power of dreams. Then I asked what he thought his dream predicted would happen in the future.

He said he didn't know, but that you can intervene, like a bridge, between the dream and the future. "In Mexico they say if you've had a bad dream, you have to tell it to someone the next day, so it doesn't happen in real life. And that's what I do, I tell Lupe, and she just says, 'Ah, you're crazy,' and that stops the bad dream from coming true."

"Other than that, I don't tell anyone my dreams."

"Not even your siblings? Or your parents?"

"No, we don't talk about our dreams. And they say if you have a good dream and you tell someone about it, it won't come true, so I only tell my wife about the bad ones, like one where a friend dies."[6] Ranulfo probably chose to tell me about his dream because he knew he could count on my usual eagerness to listen without judging. Plus, I'd walked past the exact place in his village where the dream transpired. That made me enough of an insider to understand what he was talking about, but I was still an outsider from different social circles, so the standard dream rules did not clearly apply to me. Whatever the reason, Ranulfo's divulgence was an act of great trust, which I wasn't going to betray by asking him why he was telling me all this.

"But this was a bad dream, so you told Lupe about it, right?"

"No, no. For me, this was a *good* dream. Because even though I offended God, I had the courage to speak to Him."

Instead of expressing regret about challenging God in the dream, as he had a few hours earlier on the phone, now he saw the dream as an accomplishment.

Continuing to speak calmly, he said, "I like to enter into *lo desconocido*, the unknown, to not have fear. Well, a little fear, but at the same time to be strong and go further into *el más allá*, the beyond. The bad thing was that in this case I woke up, so I never got to find out what happened."

Ranulfo reminded me of Kalimán, a Mexican comic-book hero with extraordinary powers of the mind. Wearing a white turban and fighting for justice in the name of the Indian goddess Kali, Kalimán vanquished his enemies through telepathy, meditation, levitation, hypnosis, astral projection, and encyclopedic knowledge. He made Superman look like a simpleton, and had no need for Batman's fancy car and gadgets. As Kalimán often said, *No hay fuerza más poderosa que la mente humana, y el que domina la mente, lo domina todo.* "There's no greater strength than the human mind, and he who conquers the mind, conquers everything."

Growing up without television and reading the new Kalimán comic book every Saturday, Ranulfo absorbed these teachings, and he sometimes passed them on to me, like when he told me, *Serenidad y paciencia, mucha paciencia.* "Serenity and patience, lots of patience."

When Ranulfo first taught me that Kalimán dictum earlier in the summer, I thought it was odd for a superhero's watchwords to be "serenity and patience," instead of something about flying up into the sky or crushing the bad guys, but now, as Ranulfo spoke to me in quiet, reverential tones, it made sense. Kalimán comics were at the height of their popularity during Ranulfo's formative years, selling five times as many weekly copies as the nearest competitor in the 1970s, read by doctors, lawyers, university students, and others, especially rural and working-class males like Ranulfo.[7] Ranulfo hadn't read comic books in many years, but he found in Kalimán an enduring model from his childhood of inner strength, mental discipline, and spiritual adventure, made all the more respectable by Kalimán's allegiance to Western science and rational skepticism.[8] For my part, I found in Solín, Kalimán's young sidekick, a model of pure faith, attentive listening, and undying loyalty.

A few minutes later, I declared, "I'm going to help you get this restaurant, or the bakery, if the owner changes his mind. You can count on me."

I wasn't exactly sure what I had pledged. I hardly knew anything about restaurants or bakeries, let alone fighting God.

Nonetheless, I was all in.

Ranulfo repeated what he'd often told me, that everything he did was for his family. "The fear I have is that you arrive at a certain golden age, and you have a lot of success, and later your kids ask you, 'Where were you when I graduated? Why didn't you come to my soccer practices?' That's what I want to avoid."

Looking at Mauricio on the soccer field, he said, "I'm here to give my support...I think the family is the foundation for everything."

"And, Pete," he said with a smile as kids played all around us, "I hope that 30 years from now we'll still be talking together.... It's like we're honoring life with these talks."

I was touched by Ranulfo's vision of our friendship stretching into the future. But I was also worried about his determination to enter the beyond, the dream world.

Notes

1. Rather than claiming Ranulfo's store was unique, I see it as an example of what Collins (2004) calls "interaction ritual chains," expanding the definition of ritual beyond formal settings and synthesizing perspectives from other major writers on ritual, from Durkheim to Goffman. Collins aptly calls this synchronized ritual experience "emotional entrainment" (2004, 47–101).
2. Douglas wrote: "Money provides a fixed, external, recognisable sign for what would be confused, contradictable operations; ritual makes visible external signs of internal states. Money mediates transactions; ritual mediates experience, including social experience" (1966, 86).
3. To understand why this dream scared Ranulfo so much, it helps to look at Lohmann's cross-cultural dream paradigm (2010a), which clarifies the major implicit theories of dreams found in cultures around the world. Starting with this "God dream," we can see that Ranulfo's theories slide between several of Lohmann's categories. In saying that dreams might predict or intuit the future (or be a *guía*, guide, to the future, as Ranulfo put it), Ranulfo was subscribing to what Lohmann calls "Discernment theory," that is, the belief that "dreaming entails an enhanced capacity for thought and awareness" (Lohmann 2010a, 231). Yet, as seen in this God dream, Ranulfo's view also encompassed "Message theory," defined by Lohmann as "communications, in linguistic or imagistic form, between or within minds" (Lohmann 2010a, 231). That is, Ranulfo saw this dream (and others) as potentially being a message from the mind of God, whom he also sometimes referred to as time (*el tiempo*), as discussed further below. Ranulfo's view is similar to what Foster found earlier in nearby Tzintzuntzan: "God, says MH, puts dreams in one's head so they will know what is going to happen" (Foster 1973, 111). But Ranulfo's final, overlapping dream theory raises the stakes even higher, as if communicating directly with God were not high enough. As he told me later, Ranulfo was also partly thinking that his dream could have a direct, causal effect on the future, i.e., what Lohmann calls "Generative theory": "In order for something to exist, according to these theories, it must first have been dreamt" (Lohmann 2010a, 231). Entertaining this Generative dream theory was unnerving to Ranulfo at this point because he knew such a view

violated basic scientific notions of cause and effect, and it made him wonder if he was being "superstitious," maybe even going crazy.
4. *Un Quijote sin mancha*, Director Miguel M. Delgado, 1969.
5. Lately, David Sutton and I had been thinking about the way foul balls play havoc with the out-of-bound lines, analyzing such ritual details in sport as reflections of American ambivalence toward authority. See Sutton and Wogan (2009, 47–70).
6. Similarly, Stewart (1997, 879, 2012, 121) reports that modern Greek dreams of treasure are supposed to be kept private, or else people say the dream won't come true; instead of gold, for instance, one who has revealed the dream too soon to others will only find ash or coal. Somewhat like Foster, Stewart says that such treasure stories reinforce a norm of keeping business matters and wealth aspirations private. However, moving away from Foster, Stewart sees such treasure tales as ultimately more focused on creating an emotional connection with local places (Stewart 2012, 121–123).
7. These Kalimán reader statistics come from surveys carried out in Mexico in the mid-1970s (Hinds and Tatum 1992, 33). It's important to note that Kalimán is a subject of debate among academics. On the one hand, some critics have argued that Kalimán trucks in pernicious stereotypes and power dynamics. See, for example, Butler Flora (1984), Fernández L'Hoeste (2009), and Sotres Mora (1973). By contrast, other academics have argued that Kalimán provides an inspiring Mexican figure for political action and cultural pride. See Campbell (2009), Rubenstein (1998), Sánchez and Parker (2007), and Stavans (2000, 169–175). Rather than trying to resolve or intervene in this debate, I just want to note that Kalimán can be viewed from various angles. Naturally, my main focus is on how Ranulfo himself views Kalimán.
8. Kalimán's adventures invert and play upon class and racial hierarchies that overlap in complex ways with tensions between science and "superstition," as Patricia Varas and I have argued ("The Appeal of a Mexican Superhero: Kalimán, El Hombre Increíble." Western Social Science Association conference, Portland, Oregon, April 9, 2015).

CHAPTER 8

Searching for The Key

August, 2006

After that conversation in the park, I decided to focus my research on Ranulfo's dreams. If I was once again heeding the call of the coyote, Ranulfo was the best kind of coyote—one with a business plan.[1] Plus, the shift away from movies, my initial focus, wasn't such a big leap. Movies are just dreams on a larger projection screen, which is why cinemas in the early 1900s were called "Dream Palaces," and the percentage of Americans who reported dreaming in color more than tripled after the advent of color television and movies.[2] I had simply switched the location of the Dream Palace, from Mexican cowboy movies to the dreams Ranulfo had at night and chose to tell me about the next day.

The real change was that now I had to get more personal. Anthropologists usually work with a range of "research subjects," so as to make generalizations about entire social groups.[3] I wasn't interested in those group-level abstractions anymore. Finding the common denominator in the dreams of 50 Mexican-Americans struck me as a sure way to kill off their meaning and mystery. Instead, I wanted to understand the dream interpretations of *one* person: Ranulfo.[4]

Only within this intense focus on Ranulfo would I look at larger patterns, such as the way his dream interpretations partly came out of the local culture he grew up with in rural Mexico. In fact, I could already see overlaps between things Ranulfo was telling me and reports from a famous anthropologist who had studied dream interpretations in a village less than 50 miles away from Ranulfo's hometown in Mexico, above all, the same belief in prescient dreams that predict the future.[5] For that matter, the basic belief that dreams can predict the future has been found among diverse cultures around the world, from indigenous South Americans to Greeks, Puerto Ricans, and other Americans.[6] In a national survey, 74% of Americans said they believe dreams can predict the future, and in one study at a Boston train station, commuters told social psychologists that they would be more likely to change their travel plans if they dreamt of a plane crash than if in real life they received an orange-level warning of a terrorist attack from Homeland Security.[7] Clearly Ranulfo wasn't the only one who believed dreams can predict future events. I was interested in these comparisons, but, most of all, I was interested in finding out what specific dreams meant to Ranulfo and how they could help him get the bakery.[8]

Another big change from the anthropology I had done in the past was that now I had to include myself in the analysis. I couldn't erase myself from the picture, writing in the passive voice and pretending there is a pure Archimedean point for something as subjective as dream interpretation. If Ranulfo had told his dreams to someone else—a close sibling or aloof friend, a quiet Gestalt therapist or extroverted fireman—the questions, answers, and interpretations would have been different. As an integral part of Ranulfo's interpretive process, I had to write about myself.[9]

This wasn't going to be easy. I had to take the risk that I'd be seen as self-indulgent or what anthropologists call a "confessional" writer, a coded, derogatory term for an anthropologist considered to be too personal and subjective. I remembered what Ruth Behar, the foremost advocate of "vulnerable anthropology," said about the risks with this approach: "when an author has made herself or himself vulnerable, the stakes are higher: a boring self-revelation, one that fails to move the reader, is more than embarrassing; it is humiliating."[10]

Ouch. Obviously it would have been safer to stay out of this book, to minimize my vulnerability, but then readers wouldn't get to evaluate how my personality and moods and biases influenced my interpretations. I wouldn't get to explore what Behar calls the "connection, intellectual and emotional, between the observer and the observed," nor the other theoretical insights that, as Behar says, "take us somewhere we couldn't otherwise get to."[11]

It also wouldn't be fair to Ranulfo. If Ranulfo was going to share his secrets in public, I had to join him. I couldn't hide behind the veil of impersonal social science.

Like wide-eyed Solín, I also had to listen well because everything Ranulfo said and did potentially related to his dreams. I noticed, for example, that he talked a lot about turtles. At the store he told me, "When I first got to the U.S., I was like a rabbit or sheep—lots of fur, easy prey. But I've gotten tougher. Now I'm like a turtle."

I laughed, partly because of the way he imitated a turtle—head down, feet slowly rising and plopping down one at a time—and partly because I had expected him to choose a more majestic animal.

"But wouldn't you rather be a lion or something?"

"No," he quickly said. "I don't like lions. They're lazy."

I should have remembered that survival depended on hard work in Ranulfo's world, so the disdain for laziness applied to animals as well. This had come up before when Ranulfo saw my cat lying on her back, looking up at us as we talked in front of my house, hoping to get her belly scratched. Ranulfo stopped the conversation and brusquely said, "Is the cat lazy? It looks to me like it is."

I defensively rushed to explain that my cat had only started lying on her back very recently, now that she was getting older, but she'd always been a good hunter and the other cats in the neighborhood were still afraid of her.

Ranulfo said, "Oh, I'm impressed," and I knew he meant it because he didn't give out compliments easily. He had just told me I wasn't properly pruning the roses in my garden.

Back at the store, Ranulfo explained his interest in turtles with a serious, philosophical tone. "You learn so many things in this life, Pete. You're creating a turtle's shell, like a shield, a coat of arms. And you're in a race against time. You're slow, but you're going to make it."

The turtle's shell made sense as an image of the hardships Ranulfo had overcome, not just in the U.S., but also Mexico. He said a poor person in Mexico gets used to being humiliated. All those abuses just bounce off the turtle's back.

Ranulfo learned about turtles through a geography textbook, which fired his imagination with thoughts of a world beyond the village. In the U.S., he increased his knowledge through science documentaries and visits to the zoo, but never owned a turtle as a pet. The turtle remained an animal of the imagination, another reason why he was so fascinated with them lately.

What I couldn't understand, though, was why Ranulfo liked the turtle's slow pace. When we had talked about the Albany restaurant, Ranulfo had distinctly stated, "I'm in a hurry to make money." Yet now he admired the turtle's slowness, quoting a proverb to drive the point home: *Al pasito pero llegamos. No hay que aflojarle.* "Slowly, but we'll arrive. You can't slack off."

He also told me a joke about a turtle who was trying to get to a party in a house with a lot of stairs. Imitating a turtle struggling mightily, he said it took the turtle hours to climb about 15 stairs. Then, when the turtle got to the very last one, it lost its footing and tumbled to the ground.

The turtle sighed, "See, that's what I get for rushing."

I wrote this joke down because (a) I liked turtle jokes; (b) I wrote everything down; and (c) I knew Ranulfo's jokes might someday provide insight into his dreams, given their uncanny similarities, with all the rapid scene-shifting, unconscious symbolism, and sudden reversals.

When I asked Ranulfo why he didn't write down his dreams, he immediately laughed and rejected the idea. "No way. If they see you writing down your dreams, they're going to say, 'This man is crazy.' In Mexico, if you tell someone your dream, they'll say, 'Here comes the crazy guy. He's no good at working, just dreaming.'"

Publishing dreams was different. Ranulfo gave me permission to put his dreams in any future publications, which at that point I still envisioned as journal articles, at best. He liked the idea of helping scientists and the public understand the dream process, comparing it to the way scientists eventually figured out how electricity and rockets work. With a self-deprecating laugh, he joked that someday scientists might say about him, "That crazy guy actually knew something." As for possible criticisms from fellow Latinos, he was willing to take that risk, especially since he could point out that he shared his dreams for the benefit of others, including immigrants looking for practical clues to getting ahead in America.

He said he had been studying his dreams more than ever since he got the store, and especially now that he was thinking about buying a second business. Before, when he worked at the nursery, he was too tired to remember or think about his dreams, but now that he had more time to relax, vivid dreams flooded through him almost every night, filling him with tantalizing images, questions, and ideas.

His interpretations partly drew on the principles he'd learned in Mexico, hearing comments made in passing by older family members like his grandmother. Above all, he retained the village belief—*lo que dicen por allí*, what they say over there—that dreams predict what will happen in the future. He was less sure about the standard interpretations of specific symbols, such as the belief that a dream of a dead person means you'll gain money, and a dream of raw meat means someone will die.[12] He thought these equations might be "myths," but he didn't want to dismiss them, either. The old beliefs often contained an element of truth, so they were worth testing out.

Aside from these basic guide posts, he was breaking out on his own, investigating his dreams through trial and error, looking for patterns and meanings, analyzing the connections between his dreams and waking life. Day and night, his mind kept drilling below the surface.

"The thing I want to know," he said, is, "What is a dream? Why do we dream every day?"

His search also had a definite material dimension. He believed he wouldn't obtain true business success until he found *La Formula*, The Formula, or *La Llave*, The Key.[13] The Formula or Key apparently would contain insight into his entire life and soul, not just his business, but since it was different for each person and he hadn't found it yet, he couldn't describe it in detail.

The Key sounded to me like what some psychologists call self-integration and self-actualization, or what the alchemists and mystics trying to turn lead into gold called the Philosopher's Stone. Ranulfo, too, wanted gold, but he couldn't get it until he achieved higher self-understanding.

"Maybe only 10% of people ever find it," Ranulfo said. "Somebody is knocking on the door, but you don't want to open it."

He sensed that someone was knocking on the door in his dream about God (if that's who it really was—he was no longer sure), but still hadn't come to any firm conclusions about its meaning. He just felt that this dream was more important than others, and that its results might unfold over and affect the course of the next 10 or 20 years, maybe the rest of his life. It was a mystery.

Within this purely speculative realm, I, too, had started developing some theories about the dream. I didn't presume to know the ultimate meaning of Ranulfo's dreams or anyone else's, my own included, but I reminded myself that others sometimes notice things that the person directly involved doesn't, providing new angles worth thinking about.

According to my tentative interpretation, the dream represented Ranulfo's fears of over-reaching. In reference to his request in the dream for a third arm—a good metaphor for what Ranulfo would need to operate the restaurant in Albany, 35 miles away from Salem—God explicitly stated, "You ask for too much." Even Ranulfo had admitted earlier that having a second business in a distant, unfamiliar city would stretch him thin, possibly to the breaking point. To buy the restaurant equipment, he would have to spend all his savings from the store, leaving him without any funds to cover the other initial costs or a buffer zone in case sales dropped at the store or restaurant. He had long ago learned not to expect help from the banks. Years earlier, when he tried to borrow $3,000 to buy a car, the bank said they would only loan him $300. Ranulfo joked, "Did they think I was going to buy a car or a go-cart?!" When he applied for small-business loans to start the video store, they wouldn't lend him a single dollar. Unwilling to cry discrimination, Ranulfo pointed out that banks don't like lending money to *any* small business, since the majority of them fail, including the ones run by white people. Plus, he didn't look good on paper. He only had a GED and no credit history, never having taken out a credit card or major loan other than his mortgage.[14] Without any help from the bank, he started the store by doing what other poor immigrants do: he cobbled together his personal savings and loans from family and friends.[15] But he couldn't do that again to start the restaurant, so he had little to fall back on this time, and much more to lose.

He'd also have to stay in Albany for long hours, taking time away from his family. And his brothers and sisters, who worked in nearby nurseries and canneries, probably couldn't make the commute, so he might end up hiring strangers, workers without the same level of trust and commitment.

The dream forced him to admit to these fears about the restaurant. I'd never heard him express fear before this day, yet he suddenly did four times while discussing the dream. He confessed on the phone that the dream left him "afraid," then in the park he said he had "fear" that someday his kids would ask why he hadn't been there for them, and admitted he had fear (albeit only a little fear) about going into the beyond. Without any prompting from me, he also volunteered that he got scared when Lupe and the kids went to Mexico without him. "One time they were gone for five, six weeks, and I was afraid to sleep at night. I had a fear of being alone. Sometimes I went out to sleep in the living room, alone."

Then he confessed, "When I'm with people, I'm strong because that's the way I am. But when I'm alone, I'm weak. Or like when I'm with

Laura. The other day we were watching TV and she wanted something to eat, and I said no, and she said, 'Daddy, you don't love me.' Ooof, that killed me."

He'd rejected all fear as he plowed ahead with the restaurant plan, but fear came back with a vengeance at night, in this dream about an angry God who rebuked him for asking for too much.

And God had another big reason for being upset: Ranulfo continued throughout this period to call himself a Saint of the Casino, pushing religious limits to the extreme. Even though he'd cut back on his visits to the casino, he hadn't given up on his more dangerous efforts to canonize himself. On the trips he did make to the casino in late spring and early summer, he continued praying to San Ranulfo...and recruiting his wife as a co-believer.

Lupe wasn't convinced. With a chuckle, Ranulfo reported one time, "And the saint failed her, too. On the way back to the house, I found out she lost $30 at the casino. She said, 'You know what? Your saint...'"

"...doesn't work," I said, as we both laughed. I didn't usually finish Ranulfo's sentences, but his slight pause and smile in mid-sentence invited me to complete the joke.

Ranulfo was serious, though, when he professed faith in San Ranulfo a few minutes later, and still hoped Lupe and others would eventually join him. "Pete, for anything, you have to have that great faith. Above all, you have to understand that when you start something, it's a slow process. A process where, out of ten people, one will be on your side, but nine will be opposed. But you have to convince them, and not with words, with deeds."

"But in terms of San Ranulfo, you didn't convince Lupe?"

"No, no, it's going to take a long time. Until the day that she wins big. There will be a correct day and correct moment."

"So you're going to continue with the saint?"

"Yes, you have to continue, you have to make history in one way or another. You have to create new traditions. You have to develop them."

These bold ambitions, the restaurant and the Saint of the Self, put Ranulfo on a collision course with God, and not a happy, cheerleading God, more of an angry, punitive God, the one he'd known back in Mexico through popular proverbs like *Uno hace, Dios deshace*. "What one does, God undoes."[16]

The same anthropologist who studied dream beliefs in the village near Ranulfo's hometown argued that this fatalistic view was tied to the limited options available in the 1950s in a subsistence-agriculture economy.[17] Ranulfo seemed to agree when he said, "Lots of people think, 'I have to be poor because God wants it that way.'"

Ranulfo had flatly rejected such thinking. "People like that create their own *barreras*, and that's what's holding them back. What they need is to break down the barriers. Like me, that's what I'm doing. I'm going to get a robot that can just drive itself and break down barriers even when I'm not there. The robot just needs a little gasoline."

Yet at this critical juncture, when he was about to expand his business, this negative outlook had reappeared in his dreams, a return of fear and the cultural repressed in the form of an angry God.

At least this interpretation seemed plausible, but then I started to wonder, *What if I had gravitated toward the "anxiety" interpretation because it matched my own penchant for doubting?* This would explain why I, an academic, someone paid to doubt and critique arguments, saw dreams as expressions of anxiety, whereas Ranulfo, an immigrant filled with optimism, saw dreams as guides to concrete, future actions. It's not that Ranulfo lacked skepticism, as his frequent questions and rebuttals on all topics demonstrated, but he did value decisive action, especially in the realm of business. One of his favorite phrases was, "You have to take action." By contrast, I subsisted on anthropology publications filled with caveats and hedges, anticipating the critiques to follow. My heroes were philosophers like Descartes, who tried to get back to first principles by doubting everything, including his own existence, and Nietzsche, who questioned knowledge itself, like when he made this loaded joke about Socrates and science: "An issue that has been resolved stops mattering to us.—What did that god who counseled 'Know yourself!' really mean? Was it perhaps: 'Stop letting anything matter to you! Become objective!'—And Socrates?—And the 'scientific man'?"[18] I liked that kind of doubting.

Ranulfo noticed, too. One time in early August, after I explained that it took me all morning to fix his external hard-drive because I kept double-checking every step, scared I'd erase something, he said, "Pete, you've got a big problem—you live with doubt."

He was right. I'd even applied my doubtful nature to movies, viewing them as giant dreams that play upon collective anxieties and conflicts. Yet now I questioned whether the anxiety theory matched my own proclivities too conveniently. Maybe I was like those thinkers who, as Nietzsche said, rationalize theories that actually grow out of an urge, vague conjecture, or "some fervent wish sifted through and made properly abstract...."[19]

It's not that I was giving up immediately on doubt and anxiety. I wasn't *that* confused. I just had one more thing to worry about now.

As a respite from all this worrying, I became drawn to the more uplifting theory that dreams crystallize our thoughts and emotions, leading in dramatic cases to creative breakthroughs. Most famously, a dream led James Watson to discover the double helix DNA model, Paul McCartney to find the tune for the song "Yesterday," and Jack Nicklaus to develop his trademark golf grip. And such dream crystallizations were not limited to a chosen few. In brain-imaging tests and laboratory research, psychologists showed that dreams help ordinary people solve puzzles and master music, motor skills, and other challenges.[20]

From this perspective, I could say Ranulfo's dream helped him clarify his thoughts about two elusive, interconnected subjects: time and money. The Albany restaurant forced him to project himself into the future, to calculate where he and his business might be in 10 or 15 years. Such calculations pushed Ranulfo into studying the prescient dimensions of his dreams, viewing them like money itself—as a contract with the future, a form of time travel.[21] The restaurant brought out something taken for granted in ordinary life: money's inherent orientation toward the future, what anthropologist David Graeber called its potential for future action, and what sociologist Georg Simmel meant when he said money is "never a conclusion but only a transitional point...."[22] Even economists, not exactly known for their mystical talk of time travel, refer to individual purchase decisions as "intertemporal choice," a lovely term that calls to mind the documentaries about "intergalactic" space travel that Ranulfo loved to watch.

Dreams functioned, then, like wins and losses at the casino: as guides to his future, indications of whether the universe loved him. The casino environment was fittingly dreamy, an altered state of consciousness brought about by the blocking out of sunlight, time, and the outside world, replaced with flashing lights, blasts of noise, and persistent cycles of anticipation, fear, regret, and reward.[23] Dreams and the casino offered glimpses into the future.

Ranulfo took inter-temporal travel to another level. Thinking so much about the future made him want to understand time itself. If it doesn't seem like time appeared in his dream, that's because time is invisible, ubiquitous, and in charge—like God, who did appear in response to Ranulfo's summons. By challenging God in the dream, Ranulfo confronted time, no easy feat.

Then, in the aftermath of the dream, Ranulfo turned more than ever to turtles because they, too, struggle with time, here on earth. As Ranulfo stressed, the turtle feels like he's moving fast, battling time with every step. He can only arrive at his destination when he learns to be *un aliado del tiempo*, an ally of time.

Ranulfo was expanding his mind, looking at everything from different perspectives, from that of God above to the turtle below. As he said right after mentioning the turtle's race against time, "Your life is like a camera. You have to use it to see from many different angles." Through science and art, dreams and jokes, metaphors and fantasies, he kept viewing the world from multiple angles.

I didn't dare pass these interpretations on to Ranulfo at this point, for fear of tainting his thinking, saying something that he wouldn't be able to get out of his head, even if he didn't fully agree with it. This was his life, his dream-world, his scientific adventure, and I wasn't about to muck it up with my view of dreams as unconscious symbolism and expressions of anxiety. He looked to dreams as guides to the future, not the past. He didn't need me to heighten any self-doubts he might already have. He needed me to help him reach the future.

If anything, I already exerted too much influence through my questions, body language, and rejoinders, all the subtle cues that gave away my perspective. By this point I used a tape recorder more often than written notes, so that my opinions wouldn't be revealed by variations in my pen movements, quick scribblings indicating strong interest in what Ranulfo had just said, a motionless pen revealing confusion or absorption in the moment (disinterest was never a possibility). Yet the tape recorder freed me up to look more directly at Ranulfo, perhaps revealing even more through the way certain topics made my eyes twinkle, others causing a look of surprise or confusion to cross my face. Everything I asked about—and everything I did *not* ask about, everything I let pass—potentially had an effect on Ranulfo. A time would come to find out what Ranulfo thought about my dream interpretations, but this was not it.

In any event, Ranulfo had already provided the best possible explanation for his dream: it was a mystery.

Ranulfo wasn't going crazy like Don Quixote. He was going on a journey into a land of mystery, to find The Key. I felt like Sancho Panza, packing the saddle bags on his donkey, confident in Don Quixote's courage and vision. Ranulfo had already proven himself by giving up a secure income at the plant nursery to start his own business, the kind of bravery you don't often find among professors with lifetime employment. I believed he could reach the next level. Of course, I had a Quixotic streak myself, what some might have seen as an overactive imagination caused by reading too many books. But I wasn't in charge of this vision quest, Don Ranulfo was, and I was just glad to be joining him.

Notes

1. As Simmel said, we're naturally attracted to both similarities and differences: "The contrasting element complements us; the similar element strengthens us. Contrast excites and stimulates; similarity reassures" (Simmel 1912, 218).
2. In 1942, 71 % of respondents said they rarely or never dreamed in color, whereas only 18 % said the same in 2003 (C. Clairborne Ray, "Technicolor Dreams," *New York Times*, Science Q & A, January 27, 2004). For more on the anthropology of movies from a social-level anxiety perspective, see Sutton and Wogan (2009); for excellent use of movie associations to flesh out anthropological dream interpretations, including ones that could be considered anxiety-focused, see Mageo (2011); and for anthropological interpretations of anxieties in modern Greek dreams, see Stewart (1997, 2012).
3. Making typologies and generalizations about social patterns has been a central goal of anthropology and the social sciences since the late nineteenth century, so that, as strange as it might sound, real people are often absent from the disciplines most dedicated to studying people. As Nigel Rapport put it, "In short, it is almost as if, for much of its history, actual people have been incidental to the Durkheimian project—irrelevant, if not departicularized: generalised into one impersonal (defining, limiting) category or another" (1997, 25). Such impersonalism is particularly strange considering that, as Rapport reminds us, there can be no social institutions without individuals and personal relations.
4. By focusing on just one individual, I was following through on what Barbara Tedlock said in 1991 when sketching out the methodological parameters of what she rightly called "the new anthropology of dreaming": "Labeling certain dream experiences 'prophetic' or 'precognitive,' however, does not explain how these and other dream experiences are used both individually and culturally within a society. In order to learn about the actual use of dreaming, researchers cannot simply gather examples of different types of dreams by administering a questionnaire but instead must interact intensively for a long period of time" (1991, 164). I believe that Tedlock and other anthropologists (e.g. Crapanzano 1980; Hollan 2003; Mageo 2003) are right: to understand the ambiguities and contextual meanings of dream beliefs and practices, we

need long-term research with a small number of individuals. However, focusing on a single individual is still often viewed as a questionable approach in anthropology at large, an issue I'll return to shortly below and, once more, at the end of this book.
5. George Foster (1973) wrote about dream customs in Tzintzuntzan, a town located only about 45 miles (72 kilometers) from Ranulfo's village. For example, Foster wrote, "Most informants believe that dreams may foretell the future, and instances are related in which subsequent events bore out the warning of the dream" (1973, 111). Many of Foster's findings matched up with what Ranulfo reported, yet many did not, as is to be expected, since Foster was writing about older generations in an indigenous town, whereas Ranulfo came from a more recent generation and a village that did not speak indigenous languages or see themselves as indigenous. Ranulfo said there were no speakers of indigenous languages in his *rancho*, village; by contrast, Foster reported that 11.4% of Tzintzuntzan's population in 1960 spoke Tarascan/Purépecha (Foster 1979, 35).
6. On the prevalence of beliefs in "prescient" dreams that predict or intuit the future in various cultures around the world, see Basso (1987), Lohmann (2007, 42), Tedlock (1991, 164). Such beliefs, broadly conceived—below I will make further distinctions and employ Lohmann's (2010a) framework for cross-cultural analysis of types of dream interpretations—are also common among non-indigenous persons in the West, such as modern Greeks (Stewart 2003, 2012) and Puerto Ricans (Jacobson 2009). Jacobson, for example, found in interviews with 60 Puerto-Rican Americans that by far the most commonly reported dream type was "prescient dreaming" about numbers—*soñar números, hacer combinaciones*—that are later used to play the lottery.
7. Chapman University Earl Babbie Research Center, 2014 Social Reality Index, Wave 1. http://www.chapman.edu/wilkinson/_files/new%20research%20centers/babbie%20pics/social-reality-index.pdf. Accessed January 20, 2016. For the Boston commuter study, see Morewedge and Norton (2009).
8. Given how prevalent beliefs in prescient dreams are and how much effect they have on people's actions, they clearly warrant scholarly attention, yet despite the excellent anthropological work done on dreaming, only a portion of which can be cited here, we still have virtually no studies of how such dream beliefs affect pragmatic

business decisions and actions in modern Western economic contexts. This is unfortunate because, in a monetary economy, prescient dreams are likely to highlight and play upon the inherent future orientation of money itself. As Graeber succinctly put it, "Money is the potential for future specificity" (2001, 114), and as Simmel said, money is "never a conclusion but only a transitional point…" (1907, 212–213). Graeber explores the money–dream–future nexus in his analysis of Iroquois dreams, wampum, and social creativity (2001, 117–150), but that's obviously not a modern economic context, nor does he have the historical data with which to investigate the more contextual, subjective uses of dreams by individuals. I see *Corner-Store Dreams* as trying to address this gap in the literature, even the many sections not explicitly about dreams, which are still needed to understand the complex, ambiguous, shifting contexts for Ranulfo's dream interpretations.

9. These are some of the major anthropological works that convinced me I had to include myself in the analysis, and that paved the way for me to do so: (a) Vincent Crapanzano's book *Tuhami* (1980), with its intensive focus on dreams, a single research subject, and interactive, dialogical meanings; (b) Ruth Behar's poignant, honest anthropological writing, focused intimately on herself, her family, and one or two research subjects and friends (1993, 1996, 2013); (c) Renato Rosaldo's *Culture and Truth: The Remaking of Social Analysis* (1989), which called attention to the value of writing about emotion, fieldwork dynamics, and humor; (d) Deborah Reed-Danahay's edited volume *Auto/Ethnography: Rewriting the Self and the Social* (1997), which opened my eyes to the wide-ranging possibilities and value of "auto-ethnography." Again, these sources raise large issues that get to the heart of anthropology and what I'm doing here, so I'll return to them much later, toward the end of the book.
10. Behar (1996, 13).
11. Behar (1996, 13).
12. Similarly, Foster said this about nearby Tzintzuntzan: "Dreams are not emotionally neutral experiences, and most people do not like to discuss them, or even admit that they dream"; and a dream of raw meat portends death (1973, 110–111).
13. Here, too, Ranulfo's underlying dream theories start to enter into Generative theory, according to which a future event (economic

success) couldn't exist without a preceding dream, that is, finding The Key or Formula in a dream (Lohmann 2010a, 231).
14. Studies suggest that racial discrimination likely plays a role in denials for small-business loans. A study by Cavalluzzo and Wolken (2005) found that Hispanics were turned down for small-business loans at twice the rate of white applicants, a difference that could only partially be explained by differences in home equity. While suggestive, Cavalluzzo and Wolken do not claim their study conclusively demonstrated discrimination because they did not get to examine the internal application documents that the banks used in making their loan decisions; they're only saying that discrimination was a plausible explanation after other factors were controlled for in their statistical analysis of the 1998 "Survey of Small Business Finance." More concretely, Wells Fargo, one of the major banks in Oregon, agreed to pay at least $175 million for charging higher mortgage rates to Latino and black borrowers from 2004 to 2009 (Charlie Savage, "Wells Fargo Agrees to Pay for Mortgage Loan Bias," *The Oregonian*, July 13, 2012).
15. On the common pattern of ethnic immigrants' reliance on relatives and other sources of non-bank credit, see Light and Gold (2000, 115–116) and Krohn-Hansen (2012).
16. Similar proverbs are found in Foster (1970), including some of the same proverbs cited by Ranulfo about divine will and the poor getting "screwed" (1970, 314–315). Though with slightly different translations, Foster says these proverbs convey the idea that God has the final word and that one "should not want anything too much" (1970, 314). Similar proverbs and translations are also found in other collections, such as Glazer (1987). However, as discussed later, for any given situation, there are usually multiple proverbs with varying angles to choose from, so that ultimately the individual speaker has the authority, not the proverbs per se. For a good discussion of the main functions of proverbs—censure, teaching, union, and rapport—and their flexibility as used by transnational Mexican-Americans from Michoacán, the same Mexican state where Ranulfo grew up, see Domínguez Barajas (2005).
17. Foster (1979). Foster's notion of the "Image of Limited Good" has been heavily debated and it certainly drew an overly sharp contrast between cultures, but there is no doubt that it was accurately identifying important aspects of an egalitarian ethos in certain cul-

tures. See, for example, Charles Stewart's recent analyses (2003, 2012) of Greek dreams of treasure, which use Foster to good effect. What I'm discussing here are lingering elements of Foster's original model that overlap with the outlook that Ranulfo sees himself as rejecting. I think of these lingering elements as a general social norm against openly talking about wanting money, and would compare them to what Ordóñez found recently among Latino day-laborers: "…in many cases men are simply weary of others who talk too much about their own economic gains" (2015, 140). For that matter, among many college professors in the U.S., I see a similar reluctance to ask for and discuss large economic gains.
18. Nietzsche (1886, 60).
19. Nietzsche (1886, 8).
20. On the connections between creativity, puzzling-solving, and dreams, see Barrett (2001), Lohmann (2010b, 229), Rock (2004, 77–100), and Stewart (2012, 216). It's worth emphasizing Ranulfo's creativity to counter any lingering assumptions that prescient dream interpretation is a simple, unthinking matter. In Latin America and elsewhere, dream dictionaries and websites provide written versions of stock, formulaic dream interpretations. Ranulfo had heard of such dream books being sold in the big cities in Mexico, but said that's not where he got his interpretations. Even with the interpretations that he'd heard about growing up, he always remained skeptical and made up his own mind about what a given dream symbol meant in a given context. In short, he was a creative thinker, working with multiple cultural traditions and creating his own theories.
21. This time dimension comes through even more strongly in one of Ranulfo's later dreams about a garbage truck. When I get to that dream below, I will bring in Stewart's (2012) anthropological application of existential psychology, looking at how the fusion of temporalities, past, present, and future, affects the dream interpretation.
22. Graeber (2001, 114) and Simmel (1907, 212–213). It might seem strange to keep putting Graeber and Simmel side by side, given the way Graeber dismisses Simmel as nothing but a "free market Neoliberal" (2001, 31–33). These disparaging remarks are unfortunate because Graeber is otherwise so good at breathing new life

into classic texts, and his analysis of value dovetails in interesting ways with Simmel's. For example, Simmel talked about the way degrees of abstraction depend on the perceiver's perspective and desires, which Graeber somewhat similarly addresses (citing Marx, not Simmel) in his interesting chapter on beads (Graeber 2001, 91–116). However, to take advantage of Simmel's vantage points, Graeber would have to proceed with what he elsewhere characterizes and celebrates as an open-minded, "anarchist" approach, as opposed to the "sectarian" approach of academics who constantly try to dismiss others by carrying around a list of the 32 most common ways to be wrong (Graeber 2005, 191). Certainly other scholars have found Simmel complementary to Marx in key regards, especially on alienation, and, like them, I see Simmel as more interesting than a simple "free market Neoliberal."
23. Again, Ranulfo's experience of the casino environment was not completely idiosyncratic. See, for example, Reith's excellent interpretation (1999, 127–155) of the "experience of play" and the way it alters perceptions of time, space, and everyday life, an interpretation that synthesizes a wide range of authors, from Goffman, Huizinga, and Caillois to Kant, Dilthey, and Baudrillard.

CHAPTER 9

A Moon Shot

September–October, 2006

Apparently not all older white men in Salem were bad people. Mr. Hanning, the gray-haired white man who owned the building that housed El Palmar, quietly agreed in September to sell his building to Ranulfo and Pablo—and he agreed to finance it himself. Without any bank loans or down payment, Ranulfo and Pablo just had to make monthly payments directly to Mr. Hanning over the next 15 years, until the total cost of the building, more than $200,000, got paid off. Having faith that they would make the payments and eventually own the building, Mr. Hanning agreed to let them start remodeling anytime now, to make room for the bakery in the back of El Palmar. Forget about the restaurant in Albany. The bakery had the green light. Mr. Hanning saved the day.

Ranulfo wasn't sure why Mr. Hanning was being so good to them (Ranulfo always respectfully referred to him as *"Señor* Hanning" or "Mister Hanning," even when he wasn't present). Maybe Mr. Hanning's kind move was preordained by their first meeting years ago. On his way to work at the nursery that day, Ranulfo noticed a man about 70 years old in the parking lot of a small store at the end of the street, struggling to get a table out of a truck by himself. With his usual respect for elders, Ranulfo pulled over and helped this stranger move the table. When the stranger, Mr. Hanning, explained that the renters had just decided to vacate his building there, Ranulfo remembered his discussions with

Pablo about their fantasies of opening their own business someday, so they wouldn't have to keep working under the thumbs of the nursery supervisors. Seizing the moment, Ranulfo asked Mr. Hanning if he could rent the building himself, and Mr. Hanning said yes, based on nothing but his good instincts about Ranulfo's character. Mr. Hanning hated lawyers and bureaucracy, so without requiring a large deposit or credit check, a few days later he drew up a simple rental agreement for Ranulfo and Pablo to sign. Just like that, the brothers were suddenly the proud new renters of the building, trying to figure out how to buy Mexican videos and launch a small business. Ranulfo wondered whether the good will from that initial meeting in the parking lot still burned bright and set in motion Mr. Hanning's present decision to sell them the building.

Ranulfo also wondered if his dreams had helped. For the last two or three years, Ranulfo had gone to sleep at night praying that Mr. Hanning would sell him the building. He called this *un sueño creado*, a created dream, or sometimes *un sueño de fe*, a dream of faith, and believed that it might have impacted Señor Hanning. But as soon as he threw out this idea, he quickly added, "You can't just have a dream you're an astronaut and call up NASA and say, 'OK, I'm ready, I had a dream.'" Ranulfo didn't just pray and dream. He had proven himself through his actions, always paying the rent on time, as well as the loan that Mr. Hanning later provided so they could buy the washing machines in the laundromat. So it could very well have been Ranulfo and Pablo's reliability as business partners that convinced Mr. Hanning to sell them the building. Yet it seemed to go beyond that. In his quiet whisper, Mr. Hanning once told Ranulfo he liked "people who came here with nothing and try to get ahead." Maybe Mr. Hanning saw something of himself in Ranulfo and Pablo. Maybe he just liked hard workers. Ranulfo couldn't be sure what motivated Mr. Hanning to sell the building, but he was immensely grateful that he did.

Ranulfo also felt confident that buying the building was a smart business move. He knew sales at the store remained steady and the new monthly payment would actually be lower than the rent had been. What Ranulfo didn't realize at the time was that Mr. Hanning had saved him from the predatory loan agents crawling all over the country, and, worse, the higher-ups who gave them their marching orders: investment bankers on Wall Street. Ranulfo avoided Wall Street bankers for now, though he'd have to deal with their minions soon enough, to get a loan for the bakery remodel and equipment.

Toward the end of September, Ranulfo called me at home to ask me to review Mr. Hanning's contract, once again over-estimating my skills, just as he did when he assumed I could fix printers and computers because, after all, I was a professor. But it's one thing to hack your way through a printer repair in order to live up to someone else's stereotype of the gringo professor, and quite another to serve as legal counsel on a major purchase of real estate, so I tried to beg off…until I realized Ranulfo distrusted lawyers as much as Mr. Hanning. I always had a soft spot for Ranulfo's trust in me, the closeness it implied, so I accepted my newest role.

A few hours later we were meeting at Mauricio's soccer practice, sitting at a picnic table on the sidelines. As a beautiful crescent moon rose in the sky, I pored over the ten-page contract, doing my best to translate the English legalese into plain Spanish. I went so slowly that I still wasn't done by the time it got dark and the soccer practice ended, so we decided to drive over to the store and finish there. On the way to the parking lot, I caught up with Mauricio's coach and let him know which dates the soccer field at my college would be available for practices. The college had recently agreed, after I argued with the insurance company about our liability coverage, to lend its coveted turf field to Mauricio's team during the school year when the rain came and the parks got muddy.

The store was buzzing, with Pablo at the register, surrounded by Ranulfo's brother-in-law and a couple other guys standing around chatting after a long day working in nearby fields and yards. I loved being out on a school night, standing behind the counter, on the side of the owners, reading the contract to Ranulfo while everyone joked and chatted around us. So help me, I felt like Tom Hagen, the adopted son and family lawyer in *The Godfather*.[1] Just like in the movie, I was a trusted adviser to an immigrant family trying to make it in America without dancing like a puppet on the strings of some big shot. The only difference was that Hagen was German-Irish, while my ancestors were Irish, English, Welsh, and French—and Ranulfo just wanted a bakery, not a mafia empire.

Whether or not anybody called me *consigliere*, I was in deep. When I stopped by the store on Monday morning, for a quick visit before heading off to class, Ranulfo told me to wait right there; he had just gotten a new letter from Mr. Hanning and he wanted me to read it.

"I'll be right back," he said. "I'm just going to my house to get the letter."

"And what do I do?"

"You'll be here, in charge of the store."

"But..."

"You can do it, don't worry. You know how to ring up customers. Just do it, and I'll be right back."

After giving me a quick review of the register keys—I had only rung up a few customers, and that was months ago, in the middle of summer—Ranulfo left. I wasn't just standing in the Inner Sanctum now, I was managing its most essential ritual. I was nervous.

Luckily, the first customer to arrive was Pancho, one of the regulars, a young guy with a wide face and a silver cap on his front teeth. He worked in landscaping and liked to chat on his breaks, teaching me Spanish puns and double-entendres once he found out I was interested in Mexican comedies. Today, though, he had something else on his mind: a dinner he had gone to recently with the owners of the landscaping business. Amazed to find himself in such company, he exclaimed, *¡Puros güeros...y encorbatados!* "All white people...and all wearing ties!"

As he described the dinner, I realized this was the first time he'd ever gone to dinner with a white person, despite having worked for, with, and around them for over ten years, his entire adult life. He hadn't gotten close with his white supervisors the way Ranulfo did. For Pancho, the workers and the owners were so close, yet so far apart. They could work together, even develop mutual respect and affection, yet still remain invisible to each other in the parallel worlds of Hispanics (variously referred to in the store as *mexicanos*, *Hispanos*, and *Latinos*) and the whites (*gabachos*, *güeros*, *Americanos*, and *gringos*).

The necktie wasn't helping either.

"Can you tie a tie?" he asked.

I admitted I could, then added, "But I don't like them. I feel like, '*Oye*, someone cut off my oxygen!'"

Pancho laughed and confessed, "I know, I couldn't even turn my head with that damn tie on."

Then he explained how he overcame the tie problem. "I got a friend to tie it for me. And when I got home, I just pulled it over my head, then put it away, all tied up, so it will be all ready if I ever need to use it again."

When a middle-aged female customer approached the counter with a bottle of laundry soap, I greeted her and braced myself for the transaction, while Pancho stood there without batting an eye, apparently assuming that because I always stood behind the counter, next to Ranulfo, I knew what I was doing. The customer assumed the same, or at least she didn't act surprised to find a gringo running the register.

I managed to ring up the customer without incident, then Pancho went right back into his story. "Yeah, I got my tie at Walmart. And you know what's crazy? It's the *same* as these white guys' ties. One guy told me he spent $200 on his tie, and it was the *same* as mine!"

I agreed he got a good deal.

When Ranulfo returned a few minutes later, I told him everything went fine, feeling like a nervous shaman's apprentice who just passed another test.

I also confirmed Ranulfo's reading of the letter: documents would be arriving soon from the title company, and the closing was set for Monday, October 30.

Ranulfo smiled and said, "This is why I wake up every day with *ganas*. I have so much energy, I feel younger and younger. One of these days I'm going to wake up and find out I've turned into a baby."

On the morning of the closing, I arrived at the real estate office 15 minutes early, to make sure everything was ready to go for our 10:30am appointment. The office was located in a tall, square building with minimal windows and landscaping, less than a mile from the store, next to the interstate. I walked down a few stairs, spotted the empty room where the closing would take place, then turned around and returned to the lobby, as if I had just scouted out an airplane landing.

When Pablo and Ranulfo arrived a few minutes later, I escorted them to the office downstairs, and shortly afterward the escrow agent arrived, a blonde woman in a black skirt and business attire. I secretly hoped she'd ask about the sale, so Ranulfo could talk about this moment being like a moon shot or whatever new space metaphor had gripped him that morning, but she got right down to business, pulling out her pile of documents and asking them to sign "here and here, and initials here."

She was probably in no mood for chit-chat because she had a busy day ahead, stamping documents and getting customers out the door. She was just a polite, hard-working employee on a fixed income, the lowest level of the food chain. None of us realized that the entire housing market was about to explode in a year or two. Ranulfo and Pablo just kept signing papers, most of which I had already reviewed during the previous weeks. No marching band, no trumpets, just multiple signatures, all executed in the neat print letters that Ranulfo and Pablo had learned in Mexico. Ten minutes later we were out in the parking lot.

There was no way, though, that I could let this important moment pass without marking it somehow.

I asked, "Do you know what sparkling cider is?"

Ranulfo nodded yes, while Pablo remained silent.

I said, "Let me show you something," then led them over to my minivan, slid the door open sideways, and pulled out a thick green bottle of bubbly apple cider.

"I know you guys don't like to drink, so I got this instead. It's basically champagne, but with apples and no alcohol."

They laughed and both said, ¡*Órale*! "Right on!"

We took the bottle over to Ranulfo's Ford Explorer because it had a wide bumper, where we could set everything down. I opened up my black laptop case and pulled out three small glasses, taken that morning in a hurry from my kitchen cabinet. The glasses had a gold rim around the top, a clover in the stem, and green lettering that said, "Irish Coffee."

With big smiles, we raised our full glasses and clinked them, as I pronounced a simple toast. "Congratulations…cheers."

Then I made them laugh by joking, "They're going to see us drinking in the parking lot and call the police!"

We did look like tailgaters, standing there in the parking lot, drinking on a Monday morning, feeling giddy. Ranulfo's truck was parked directly in front of the building, but it didn't matter. We were exercising our American right to celebrate in the parking lot.

Nobody wanted to leave, so we just kept pouring more sparkling cider, marveling at the goodness of life.

I said, "This is the beginning of something great…."

Pablo started to say, "This is the step of…", and while he paused, I couldn't resist interjecting, "the step of a dinosaur."

When Pablo complimented me, "Pete, you've said it very well," I had to credit Ranulfo for teaching me the phrase *un paso de dinosaurio*, another sign of how much time I had been spending with him, to the point where I was unconsciously imitating his way of talking.

Ranulfo said, "Pete, we need to take you on a trip to Mexico and show you everything. It will be like *Caminos de Michoacán, Parte Dos*."

Pablo added a correction. "No, Part III, because they've already made Part II." They were referring to the sequels to a low-budget movie shot in their home state.

Having become U.S. citizens long ago and now owners of the store, Pablo and Ranulfo seemed to tingle with the possibilities opening up before them, but rather than talk about future plans for the bakery, they wanted to review their beginnings and thank everyone who helped them along the way. Ranulfo recalled the inauspicious opening of the store in

1998. That first day he only sold one piece of candy, bought by an elderly Asian woman—*one candy*, after an entire day standing around in his new store, waiting with Pablo for customers to arrive.

After buying candies for the next couple days, the Asian woman never appeared again, but over time Latinos in the neighborhood started showing up, and they were on their way.

We toasted the mysterious woman who had brought them good fortune.

As we sipped and chatted, I thought of Ranulfo's struggles upon arriving in the U.S. in 1981, 19 years old with nothing but hopes and dreams and a white cowboy hat. I scanned through my memory of the stories, trying to think of one that Pablo, who wasn't with Ranulfo at the time, could jump into with just a quick reference. There was Ranulfo's first night in Salem, spent sleeping under a bridge with homeless men because he ran out of money. Then there was his arrival at his friends' apartment in Hillsboro, west of Portland, and his shock when he saw carpeting for the first time. He stood frozen at the door, unsure what to do, until his friends said, "It's OK, you can walk on it." And there were those tough early years when he moved in with his friends, 14 guys in a two-bedroom apartment. They got potted plants from the nursery where they worked and peed in them on the balcony when the bathroom was full in the morning; he only had access to the shower after midnight; and the guys packed together in one room on the weekends and drank beer and listened to *ranchera* music, tears running down their faces because they missed their families in Mexico. When it got too noisy, Ranulfo slept in the closet with the blanket pulled up over his head.

I couldn't think of a way to reference these stories without getting bogged down in details that didn't include Pablo, so I just let them go.

Pablo, however, recalled another arrival story. He reminded me of the first time I came in the store, asking him to recommend a Mexican video. Pablo said, "I saw you walking around with your little backpack and I was thinking this man must be a…"

"*un vagabundo*, a vagabond!," I interjected, again completing Pablo's sentence, this time because I knew he wouldn't crack a joke at my expense.

Since Ranulfo and Pablo were laughing hard, I kept the joke going. "What's this gringo doing watching a video in the middle of the day?! Doesn't he have a job, *¿o qué?*"

Pablo admitted he thought I might have been a police detective or immigration officer, and, after we laughed about that for a while, Ranulfo asked, "So how did you know about the store?"

"The Yellow Pages," I answered.

"Oh, right," said Pablo, "we got the ad that year because it was free."

Feeling my fingers getting cold on the cider glass, I noted that the cold weather was coming soon, but instead of accepting my clichéd lament, Ranulfo said, "I like changes. That's something I like about America—the changes in the weather, so many kinds of changes."

I thought of the baseball players I'd seen on TV a few days earlier, trying to warm their hands while playing the World Series in Detroit and St. Louis. The Cardinals had won the Series, so the season was now over, even for the boys of summer. They had carried summer as far as they could, into the last exquisite days of fall. Ranulfo, Pablo, and I had also extended the season as far as possible, standing outside in Oregon on what could be the last sunny day before the rains came.

I wanted to spend the whole day tailgating in the realtors' parking lot—reminiscing, toasting, admiring the sun and sky and life's stunning possibilities—but we'd finished the cider and it was time for me to get to class. I told Ranulfo and Pablo to keep the Irish glasses as a memento, and congratulated them one last time.

Happiness is greatest when you get more than you ever expected. Feeling that way about a sunny fall day, I could only imagine how good Ranulfo and Pablo felt at that moment. I could no longer see extreme gratitude and optimism as potential dangers.

Note

1. *The Godfather*, Director Francis Ford Coppola, 1972.

CHAPTER 10

Visit to Campus

January–April, 2007

Tim, a lanky student in my spring "Latin American Cultures" class, wrote something so beautiful that I had to do something about it. In response to my request on the first day of class for a description of something interesting that the students had recently learned, this is what Tim wrote about the monarch butterfly's migration every year from central Mexico to the United States and back again:

> It has been proven time and time again that each generation of monarch butterfly, when migrating in the cold season, returns to the exact same spots, the exact locations that their ancestors travelled to, down to the exact trees. Genetic testing and alterations of the trees themselves have no effect on these simple beautiful fluttering wonders.

This paragraph got me so excited that I broke all the usual rules. During the next class session, I read Tim's description out loud, repeating the last line: *these simple beautiful fluttering wonders.*

I looked up from Tim's paper, eyes wide open, and said, "Can you stand it?"

A quick burst of laughter ripped through the semicircle of roughly 20 students, maybe because they suddenly feared they had a butterfly fanatic on their hands. After Tim acknowledged he'd written this paragraph

(I had read it out anonymously because I didn't have time to get his permission before class) and others added interesting details about monarch butterflies, I decided to tell a story or two, borrowing time from the scheduled lesson plan, a close reading and critique of an anthropological theory about Latin American gender roles. I marveled at how these butterflies follow the same paths as their human counterparts, immigrants from Mexico, many of whom come from central Mexico and end up in Oregon, including Pablo and Ranulfo, my friends in Salem. I explained that the monarch butterfly is the mascot for the professional soccer team in their home state, Michoacán, at which point a student named Julio said his family was from there, too, and he was a *huge* fan of the *Monarcas*. I think he was a little surprised to hear a professor talking about his favorite soccer team, and wanted to take this rare chance to swear his allegiance.

I suddenly wanted to tell the students all about the store, but didn't know where to begin. Should I tell them about Pancho and his Walmart tie? Or the heavy-set, white salesman who reminded me of Willy Loman, always worried that his international phone cards weren't selling well? Or Ranulfo and Pablo toasting with the sparkling cider? As the proverb said, there were so many places from which to cut the cloth.

The best I could come up with was a Beatles analogy. I explained that Ranulfo, the older brother, is hard-driving, like John Lennon, and Pablo is like sweet George Harrison. Smiles told me that the students got the reference, that the Beatles had reached another generation, making me grateful all over again for music's capacity to transcend differences, the way the sounds of Chuck Berry and Buddy Holly reached the shores of the United Kingdom, only to come back across the water in the form of the Beatles and Van Morrison, still rocking people's souls all these years later. I wished I could call on Mexican counterparts, artists like Vicente Fernández or Los Tigres del Norte, but such allusions might have only resonated with the three or four Latino students in the class.

In any case, I was eager to get back to the day's scheduled textual analysis. I told myself that focusing on the assigned readings was the best way to put the students back at the center of the discussion, establishing proper expectations for the rest of the semester, but that textual shift was also safer for me. I had never told stories in class that felt so personal. When I occasionally illustrated with fieldwork anecdotes in previous classes, it had been about indigenous people in Ecuador, a far-away country. Now that I was speaking about Ranulfo and Pablo, everything felt more real.

Since we spent the rest of class ripping apart the readings, I couldn't tell whether students took the butterfly discussion as a digression, but after class a few students stayed behind, eager to talk more about butterflies and the store. A shy student whom I'd had in two previous classes, a young man with a Dutch-Boy haircut and puppy-dog eyes, hung back and listened to the other students, then quietly asked, "So is there any chance you could get the brothers to come talk to us?"

"Sure," I said. "Let me see if I can work something out." That was how my two worlds, the store and the classroom, started to intersect.

In April I finally found an opening in the syllabus for a guest speaker, during a unit on the linguistic structures of *corrido* music. Knowing Pablo would not be interested in public speaking, I only invited Ranulfo. Fortunately, he quickly agreed, saying that it would be a "pilot project," one of his favorite English phrases. But he added two conditions: First, he would only speak for a half hour, and, second, he would speak in Spanish.

"But you speak great English," I protested. And it was true. He could understand and say just about anything in English.

"Well, I just feel more comfortable in my own language."

Given his preference, naturally I agreed. Translating would use up more class time, but it had a couple advantages. I had long ago noticed Ranulfo used more metaphors—those portals to culture and creativity, like daydreams—in Spanish than English. Plus, most people who aren't used to public speaking get nervous the first time. Ranulfo had spoken many times in front of large groups at the plant nursery, but never in a college classroom. Spanish was the safer bet.

We had another partnership, this time with Ranulfo as the teacher.

On the appointed Tuesday morning, I met Ranulfo in the parking lot at the back of campus, next to the soccer field. With the few minutes we had before class started at 9:40, Ranulfo walked over and felt the turf with his bare hands. Confirming that the surface hadn't soaked up water, despite the steady rain the day before, he said, "See, this is why it's great for Mauricio's team to practice here."

Then we walked the few hundred yards across campus to my building, past the library and music halls.

"What do they do here?" Ranulfo said, pointing at the quad.

"Oh, they play this game called rugby, like football, or talk and study when the sun's out, things like that."

"That's excellent. A good way to relax. And how many years are they here for?"

"Four years," I said, an answer I would have to repeat twice more before the end of the morning, explaining that the students would still not be lawyers or doctors when they finished their four years at the college.

When the class started, Ranulfo and I stood together at the front of the room, with the whiteboard a couple feet behind us and the students a few feet away, sitting at their desks. Through the tall windows behind the students, Ranulfo and I could see the white marble State Capitol, topped with a giant, gold-plated man, the "Oregon pioneer," clutching an ax.

As I translated, Ranulfo started off with a joke about being a poor immigrant, then launched into a long narration about his first trip from Mexico to Oregon, at age 19, with a friend of a friend who gave him a ride from Los Angeles in his Ford Pinto.

The first problem, Ranulfo said, was that the Pinto's tires were so bald that they couldn't drive more than 55 mph, and the friend had never been to Oregon before and didn't have a map, so he grossly underestimated the distance, and they ran out of both gas and money somewhere in northern California.

Seeing Ranulfo and me chuckling, the students realized it was all right to laugh.

Ranulfo continued, "Then we got hungry, so we had to look for food. We didn't know what to do, so we went to the dumpster at the back of a McDonald's on I-5."[1]

Knowing where this story was headed, I started to worry it wouldn't translate well. I assumed many students hated McDonald's—the unhealthy food, the corporate imperialism, the whole greasy mess—and that would make it hard for them to get into this story. But Ranulfo wasn't stopping.

"Then one of the McDonald's workers came out and asked what we were doing back there. He was a young guy, a Mexican-American, and he ran inside and brought out a garbage bag with food that had been thrown out that day. So we got a lot of food from that bag—Big Macs with a few bites taken out, lots of French fries."

With a smile and look of contentment, as if he were reliving the greatest meal of his life, Ranulfo said, "It was delicious."

Seeing Ranulfo's smile, a nod to the irony of treating McDonald's garbage as a sacramental meal, we all laughed.

What Ranulfo didn't explicitly explain was that he had conquered huge barriers, first in eating the Big Mac and fries, and now in talking openly about it with strangers, college students, no less. Nobody in his family had ever been forced to eat garbage, but if they had, they would have been ashamed to sink to that level of abject poverty, the level of people who live on the street or in garbage dumps, the poorest of the poor.[2] College represented the other extreme, the apex of the class system, the height of professional achievement. Ranulfo had the resourcefulness to eat garbage in a pinch, and the strength to present it later to American college students *as a triumph, something to laugh about*. The whole McDonald's story was a good example of what Ilan Stavans said: "Jokes are one of Mexico's most effective weapons to battle adversity."[3] Ranulfo went out on a limb in telling his McDonald's story, and, to my relief, the students laughed with him.

Ranulfo's humor reminded me in that moment of the film comedian Cantinflas, the way he constantly turned the world upside down and made fun of both himself and the powerful, an underdog who somehow maintained his dignity. Charlie Chaplin called Cantinflas "the greatest comedian alive," and Stavans said Cantinflas "still typifies, at least for the masses, Mexico's true heart and soul."[4] Ranulfo and his customers constantly rented Cantinflas films (including the one about Don Quixote), yet, like most cultural humor, these films were exceedingly hard to translate, so they never did well at the American box office. A Harvard-educated, native bilingual speaker once took upon himself the unenviable task of providing a simultaneous translation during the screening of a Cantinflas film in New York. It just couldn't be done. The translator couldn't keep up with Cantinflas' double and triple puns and lightning-quick riffs, all incoherent rambling on the surface, but stunningly logical and insightful when you thought about it. According to Stavans, this poor translator was completely deflated by the time the movie was over: "He was empty of all energy, humorless, completely mute."

My translation skills weren't any better than those of this deflated Harvard scholar. Far from it. I would never speak Spanish with the nuance of a native speaker, whether from Harvard or anywhere else. The difference was that I didn't have to translate the verbal pyrotechnics of Cantinflas. Ranulfo constantly paused to give me time to translate, and he held back on his usual puns and metaphors, sticking, instead, to stories that he knew the class could easily follow.

He also spoke from the heart. In a sincere tone of gratitude, he concluded his story by saying, "Nowadays I don't usually eat hamburgers, mostly just Mexican food, but once in a while, I go to McDonald's, to remember. I lift up my Big Mac with both hands, and I say, 'Thank you,

McDonald's.'" The students smiled as he raised an imaginary Big Mac, solemnly saluting McDonald's for giving him new life.

Ranulfo moved on to other stories about the nursery and the store, then he answered the students' questions, so we didn't get the chance to discuss the commentary his McDonald's story made on abundance and waste and the American dream, or the assumptions it turned upside down. Later I considered assigning a *Harper's Magazine* article about the opening of a McDonald's in Zacatecas, the last state in Mexico to get Golden Arches. The extra reading would have been worth it just so students could see the excitement this event generated. At the Grand Opening, television and newspaper reporters packed the restaurant, as well as politicians and a select group of gifted schoolchildren, hand-picked by their teachers. The regional Economic Secretary literally wept tears of joy—"'*Perdón!*' he cried, dabbing at his cheeks with a blue hanky"—and the Governor told the fervent crowd, "This day… is of great importance for all Zacatecans, and for all of us who form the great McDonald's family, nationally and internationally." Looking at the crowds inside, the electrician who wired the McDonald's told the other construction workers, "We're the anonymous heroes out here, like the workers that built the pyramids at Tenochtitlán." A young man named José, who fondly recalled working in the U.S. as a bricklayer and being treated well by the gringos, said, "Having a McDonald's here will be a beautiful thing, because it will remind me of the United States."[5] Far from an evil corporation, these Zacatecans saw McDonald's as a lifeline to the wider world.

I could have also assigned an article by Conrad Kottak, an anthropologist who argued that the appeal of McDonald's' lies precisely in its standardization—the familiar, unchanging phrases, settings, and behaviors that are the hallmark of any ritual. Through these rituals, he says, McDonald's provides comfort, and, ultimately, communion with millions of other people. Even those disgusted by McDonald's might have appreciated his comparison with Australian aborigines who made religious totems out of lowly animals and insects. Kottak asks, "If frogs and grubs [worms] can be elevated to a sacred level, why not McDonald's?"[6]

For the clincher, it would have been perfect to cite the first-generation Vietnamese man in Texas who, when asked by an anthropologist about his self-identity, replied, "When I do feel most American? When I'm in McDonald's eating a hamburger or eating a big steak."[7]

But I just let it go. I wasn't up for more McDonald's lessons or the risk that one too many would finally disgust the class and require a time-consuming discussion about the pros and cons of this mega-corporation.

Though Ranulfo had said he'd only stay a half hour, the full hour and a half flew by, sped along by the many laughs and questions. On the way out of the room, students came up to Ranulfo, shook his hand, and said a few words of thanks in a combination of Spanish and English.

Then I took Ranulfo upstairs, through hallways filled with students, past other classrooms, to my office on the fourth floor. When he saw my bookshelves and stuffed chair for students, he used the same phrase he'd used for the quad—*Bueno para relajarse*. "This is a good way to relax." I considered pointing out this was actually where I *worked*, but decided against it. Even other Americans, professionals who never worked in a plant nursery, couldn't see what I did as real work, mistakenly assuming that I "have the summers off" and that anyone having this much fun couldn't really be working.

Ranulfo caught me up short when he stated, "I wish I could go to college."

I immediately insisted that he still could, but he just repeated what he'd told the class a few minutes earlier—"I hope someday my kids can go to college here."

On the way back to the parking lot, I showed Ranulfo the botanical gardens, next to the stream that ran through campus.

Ranulfo asked, "You know what I like about this college?"

Before I could offer a guess—the cozy atmosphere? the flowers? the soccer field?—he declared, "The bridges."

He was referring to the foot bridges over the stream, the one we'd crossed in front of the library before class, and the one we were standing on at that moment, a few hundred feet upstream.

I had forgotten how often Ranulfo talked about bridges—bridges in dreams between the present and the future, bridges between cultures, bridges to success. We were standing on top of one of his favorite metaphors.

A few minutes later in the parking lot, still not ready to let the visit come to an end, Ranulfo said, *Me sentía en casa aquí, muy cómodo*. "I felt at home here, very comfortable." Then he added, "I thought the students were going to be *barbones*, all hairy and bearded, but they were really good students. They liked to laugh."

He summed up the visit by saying, "We're a good team, Pete. We worked well together, like water pouring from one glass into the other. We understand each other. It was like we'd done this hundreds of times before."

I had never heard that water-pouring image before, but I did get the uncanny feeling during class that we were mirror images and extensions of each other. Something about the setting brought out this weird sensation, perhaps the constant translating and shifting of perspectives, matching Spanish words with their English counterparts, imagining how Ranulfo viewed the students and the students viewed us, two middle-aged men standing side by side, at the intersection of different worlds.

In fact, we were both exactly 44 years old—and we had the same name. When I started talking about Ranulfo during the first week of the semester, I didn't know how he would feel about me using his real name, so I instinctively called him Pedro, the name he used when answering the store phone. He said he called himself Pedro to give the slip to the annoying salespeople trying to sell him something, but, as usual, there was probably more to it. He once referred to Pedro as his *nombre artístico*, his stage name. Although I introduced Ranulfo by his real name during the class visit, his "stage name" had stuck by that point with the students, so Ranulfo and I stood there as Pete and Pedro, English and Spanish reflections of each other. The refractions were a momentary illusion, but they felt real while the moment lasted.

In class I had asked every student to pick out one thing Ranulfo said that they found interesting or meaningful, and to write it down on a 3x5 card. In my kitchen that night, after putting the kids to bed, I read highlighted Ranulfo quotes like "If you can believe it, I love the rain," and "If I could measure how the U.S. is treating me on a scale of 1 to 10, I'd say it's a 9.9." Another card recalled Ranulfo and his friend raising their hands in triumph after arriving at the first rest stop in Oregon, while some elderly Oregonians looked at them like they were crazy.[8] On the back of her card, another student wrote, "Just listening to him makes you like life more."

I was especially glad the students got Ranulfo's humor because that was a key missing ingredient in the anthropology publications we'd been reading all semester. Américo Paredes, a famous Mexican-American folklorist, once said that he finds anthropological accounts of his culture to be unreal because the people portrayed in them "are not only literal-minded, they never crack a joke." Paredes identified a gaping omission, because, as another scholar said, Mexicans use humor all the time: "Mexicans constantly use verbal puzzles that demonstrate the cleverness of the speaker and challenge the wit of the audience...[including] riddles and brainteasers, often obscene, as well as proverbs, unexpected rhymes, humorous naming, folk poetry, and shrewd puns."[9] Searching for jokes in anthropology books, though, was like searching for water in the desert.

This wasn't a minor oversight, like wishing anthropologists had said more about a certain species of Mexican artichokes, interesting information for those who love artichokes, but not a deal breaker for most anthropologists. By contrast, humor goes right to the heart of culture and cognition. Sammy Basu summed it up this way: "Humor finds ambiguities, contradictions and parables in what is otherwise taken literally. The comic is itself a form of contingency, novelty, re-creation, re-description."[10] More recently, experimental psychologists have been confirming the insights into humor's cognitive agility that Basu finds in many philosophers, from Aristotle to Descartes and Kant. In one experiment, subjects who first watched stand-up comedy performed significantly better at solving creative word puzzles than subjects who watched a boring or scary video.[11] When you cut out the jokes, you lose all this culture and creativity.

To my surprise, though, Ranulfo wasn't laughing as much as usual when he told me about reading the quote cards. A couple days later, he said, "Very good comments. They really impacted me. Reading some of them, suddenly I couldn't move. It was like I was paralyzed for a few seconds. I said to myself, 'What's happening to me?!'" As I understood it, he was saying that, after all these years, he'd finally told his story in public, at college, and the validation literally took his breath away.

Once he'd finished stocking the detergent, we went behind the counter, and Ranulfo pulled out the stack of cards, which he'd placed in an envelope for safekeeping. He said, "There's a lot of wisdom at that college. If I kept going there, I think I could become wise. I showed my kids the cards and said, 'Look, your father talked to important people, college students.'"

That comment, like the one about wanting to go to college, took me aback. My first impulse was to point out that wisdom comes in many forms, not just the book-learning that goes on at college. I could have quoted the proverb that says, *Más enseña la adversidad que diez años de universidad.* "Adversity teaches you more than ten years of university."[12] Or I could have repeated what Ranulfo himself had once proclaimed: *profesionales*, white-collar workers, are no better than people like him, *artesanos*, artisans and craftsmen. Usually we didn't have much trouble reconciling our two worlds, but, in a sad irony, his visit to campus brought out our differences, at the same time that it brought us closer together.

Ranulfo had to resist the widespread bias in favor of higher education, as difficult as that might be, especially now that the economy had moved away from manufacturing toward service jobs that required more and more titles and diplomas. Without denying power dynamics and differences, I preferred seeing our relationship the way Ranulfo had often put it before: *como un intercambio*, as an exchange. Built into the English language was an elitist presumption that an "educated" person referred to someone who'd gone to college or graduate school, without recognizing that you could get an equally valuable education in other places—like at home, or at a corner store. Spanish made more sense. Saying in Spanish that someone's *bien educado* doesn't refer to formal, higher education; rather, it means the person has good morals, that they've been raised (educated) well by their parents. I decided a little envy between Ranulfo and me for what the other had wasn't the worst thing, as long as it was mutual, and, in our case, the feeling was definitely mutual, starting with my huge admiration for Ranulfo's business ventures and creative imagination.

We were back on more familiar terrain when Ranulfo declared, "The visit was like a landing strip, and now I'm ready to fly. I'm ready to make it to the sky this time."

Ranulfo was cleared for take-off. The paperwork on the sale of the building had all been finalized over the course of the spring, so now we could begin working in earnest on plans for the bakery. The dream was about to unfold its butterfly wings.

Notes

1. The dialogue here is reconstructed from notes I jotted down after the class visit.
2. For an account of garbage pickers in a Mexican dump, see Urrea (1996). Urrea's account is devastating, humane, inspirational, and poignant, all at the same time.
3. Ilan Stavans, quoted in Stavans and Aldama (2013, 12). Stavans is specifically referring in this section to Cantinflas' "revolutionary dimension: in the face of adversity, even apocalypse, he makes the audience laugh" (Stavans and Aldama 2013, 11).
4. The Stavans quotations, including the one from Charlie Chaplin, are found in Stavans' essay "The Riddle of Cantinflas" (Stavans 2000, 192–210).
5. Although the article author, who spent a year in Zacatecas, views this McDonald's opening as an act of American imperialism, he makes it clear that most Zacatecans don't agree with him (Jake Silverstein, "Grand Opening: Ronald McDonald Conquers New Spain," *Harper's Magazine*, January, 2005, 67–74).
6. Kottak (1978). The behavioral standardization of McDonald's, however, does not necessarily lead to cultural homogenization, as shown, for example, by ethnographic accounts of how McDonald's has been re-imagined and localized by cultures in Asia (Watson 1997). But keep in mind that not all anthropologists are as culturally relativistic about McDonald's as Kottak and others. For example, practicing anthropologists Sunderland and Denny report that when they sent around a job offer for a project on finding *health-food* options for a fast-food chain, an anthropology graduate student retitled and forwarded the email to fellow graduate students with a subject heading that said, "Selling yourself to the devil for a few days," and Sunderland and Denny's usual video editor, someone with an MA in anthropology, refused to take the job (2007, 31). As Sunderland and Denny note, these other anthropologists refused to believe that "the corporate goal was *truly* to create healthier options....Thus, when we tell people that the clients with whom we worked on these fast food projects have been among the nicest, most thoughtful, most cuisine-interested we have come across, they find it difficult to believe" (Sunderland and Denny 2007, 31–2).

7. Brettell and Reed-Danahay (2012, 60). Of course, from a strict chronological perspective, I couldn't have cited this man's quotation in my class that day in 2007 because Brettell and Reed-Danahay's book wasn't published until 2012. However, including this quotation in the main text doesn't violate the chronology of the narrative because it's fair to assume that the food-identity sentiment expressed in the quotation also prevailed in 2007.
8. This is the same "quote card" system I always used (and still use) to capture good classmate quotes. At the end of every three or four weeks, we review the best quotations, giving credit where due and recalling the various class discussions.
9. The Paredes quotation, as well as Rosaldo's amplification of Paredes' critique, can be found in Rosaldo (1993, 50). The Stavans quotation about Mexican humor comes from Stavans (2000, 201).
10. Basu (1999, 388). For further discussion of Basu's analysis and the philosophy, psychology, and anthropology of humor, see Wogan (2006).
11. For a summary of this and other psychological research on humor and cognition, see Weems (2014).
12. This proverb and English translation appear in Treviño-Hart's powerful memoir (1999, 25).

CHAPTER 11

Confronting the Enemy

May–June, 2007

We ran into a big problem in the summer of 2007: a proposed bill in Congress to reform the immigration system stirred up an angry backlash throughout the country. One typical (misspelled) comment online stated, "Illitterate find a new home!" After the bill passed the Senate on May 24, the AM radio airwaves lit up with callers expressing outrage. One seriously suggested that the U.S. should annex Mexico and impose martial law there.[1]

These people weren't anomalies. According to national polls, 45% of Americans at the time said immigration hurt the U.S., 48% said it threatened traditional American customs, and 34% claimed it was taking away jobs. Perhaps most alarming of all, 35% said "illegal immigrants" should be deported to their native country.[2] It felt like civil war had broken out.

Who were these people and what got them so worked up? I hadn't wanted to get too political, but now I had to worry about these questions, to know whether immigration politics would hurt Ranulfo's customers and kill off the bakery.

Statistics weren't much help. Studies showed that desire for lower immigration levels correlated with both perceived economic self-interest and cultural prejudice, but it was hard to know which came first, or what "prejudice" and "self-interest" even meant in real people's lives.[3] Underlying motivations were too complex and murky to be discerned from statistical analysis of brief answers to nation-wide surveys carried out by telephone.

I turned, instead, to more direct, personal experiences, starting with the Dairy Queen across the street from Ranulfo's store. Although located only a couple hundred yards away, the Dairy Queen was another world. When I stopped there some mornings, to finish marking papers or review my research notes, I was surrounded by white senior citizens thoroughly familiar with each other, the breakfast specials, and the free coffee refills. They made me feel young, as the only person in there besides the waitress without gray hair, and I couldn't help overhearing their conversations—about the weather, the news, the Bible, their grandkids, their aches and pains. When they got around to discussing government wastefulness, I thought complaints about Mexican immigrants would be coming next, but they never did. These senior citizens were more interested in comforting each other with camaraderie and easy-going humor. Seeing another elderly couple shuffling through the door, someone at a middle table would say, "Uh oh, here comes trouble," and everyone would laugh, as if it were the first time they'd heard this joke.

The most direct contact I had with anti-immigrants occurred almost a full year earlier, in July of 2006, when I helped Roberto, a landscaper and friend of Ranulfo's, get his car fixed.

Roberto had one seemingly simple problem: an electrical issue that intermittingly prevented his Honda Civic from starting. I agreed to help Roberto find a mechanic, thinking I would just make one or two phone calls and be done.

But it wasn't that simple. The mechanic I found through the Yellow Pages, a white guy in his 30s at a garage in town, seemed nice enough, but he couldn't fix the problem. Worse, he charged Roberto $200—and the car wouldn't start anymore.

Though usually agreeable, Roberto got upset, convinced the mechanic was ripping him off, and asked me to intervene. I called the garage, hoping there had been a simple misunderstanding, but it was worse than I thought. The mechanic immediately started complaining about the guy who came with Roberto to question the bill. "Yeah, Roberto brought some guy with him, some guy with gold chains around his neck, you know, the typical—"

He had been on the verge of saying "the typical Mexican" or something even more derogatory, but he caught himself before completing the phrase. I was so unprepared for this insult that I didn't call him on it, or point out that the other man was Roberto's brother, an honest, hard-working guy wearing a dainty gold chain with a Virgin of Guadalupe pendant.

I also didn't correct the mechanic when he went on to say that Roberto's brother didn't speak much English. The brother's English was actually fairly good, but the mechanic was one of those Americans who makes no effort to understand someone who speaks English with an accent.

I did point out that $200 was a lot to pay for a car that wouldn't start anymore, but the mechanic insisted that was the minimal charge any time they looked under the hood, and denied having agreed to call us before the charge went over $100. The situation was messy—bad, but not quite outrageous enough to refuse to pay.

That's the difference, though. When I'm getting ripped off, I don't suspect it's because of my race. I kept thinking of my own mechanic, this chubby white man with a shaggy black beard who always called me "bro" and kept my old Nissan Sentra running at a reasonable price, which I appreciated, since I loved that car the way Sancho Panza loved his donkey. My mechanic probably would have just called Roberto "bro'," fixed his car, and made another loyal customer. Instead, we had a broken car and broken race relations on our hands.

Not knowing what else we could do, Roberto and I went back to the garage in my car, paid the bill, jump-started Roberto's car, and drove away.

I was going to let the fiasco end there, but then a few days later Roberto himself managed to fix the problem for a grand total of $1.95, the cost of a single wire. Roberto and a friend with a standard electrical tester found the short and replaced the wire. We took this simple repair as more proof that the mechanic wanted to rip us off, since he had said it would cost $1,500–2,500 to pull out the entire electrical system and find the short.

I couldn't let this go anymore. Knowing the mechanic had refused to change his mind, Roberto didn't want to return to the garage, but he finally agreed to let me go on my own to register a complaint.

At the store, Pablo joked, "Pete, you're going to be like Padre Trampitas," referring to a 1980s Mexican comedy about a priest who fights street thugs.[4] Pablo, Ranulfo, Roberto, and I laughed at the incongruity of me, a college professor, going toe to toe with a surly mechanic, who clearly outmatched me with his powerful build of about six feet, three or four inches and 200 pounds, compared to my six feet, 170.

Ranulfo, who hadn't said much during the whole episode except to discourage me from getting too involved, suddenly said, "Pete, what if he punches you?" Ranulfo knew how physical it could get. When he first arrived in the U.S., angry white guys sometimes gave him the middle finger as he crossed the street or played soccer in the park. Ranulfo ignored those incidents, but he also knew some working-class guys like to settle problems with their fists.

Laughing off this possibility, I said, "No, no, that's not going to happen. Don't worry, it'll be fine."

Later that night I thought of Ted Conover's *Coyotes*, a vivid book about young Mexican guys crossing the border, looking for work in the U.S. During their first night in Los Angeles, Conover, a white American, spent hours in an all-night donut shop with his Mexican friends, quietly playing games with pen and paper while waiting for a ride. Without any provocation, a young, drugged-up white guy in a leather jacket stumbled over and asked, "White guy talkin' to some Messicans, huh?"

Caught off guard and stung, Conover curtly replied, "That's right... You got a problem with that?"

Apparently the guy did. A few minutes later, this leather-clad druggie walked up from behind and slugged Conover in the eye, knocking him to the ground.[5]

I sure didn't want to get punched in the face like that. I wasn't too worried about the mechanic, though, because I thought I was being careful, having used the past few days to assess my motives, triple-checking to make sure I wasn't over-reacting or being unfair to either side. At least by my reckoning, I wasn't in the wrong.

Plus, I had no choice but to see this through. Having led Roberto to this mechanic, I felt responsible for the ensuing mess. It didn't help that the mechanic was a white male. Despite our differences, I still felt strangely responsible for him as an affiliate of "my people."

It went beyond that. I always carried around a constant feeling of indebtedness toward American immigrants because I'd been showered with generosity, hospitality, and goodwill by people with very little means during my travels and studies in other parts of the world. People in Mexico had treated me with great kindness, not just Ranulfo's parents, but strangers in the streets and marketplaces, on buses and in stores. The same had happened when I lived in Ecuador, Sierra Leone, and Japan. Fleeting interactions with strangers—friendly greetings on mountain paths, spontaneous conversations in marketplaces, food and drink offered freely—exerted a disproportionate impact on me, almost equal to the long-lasting bonds I formed with my hosts. Despite or precisely because of their transitory nature, these passing interactions impressed upon me a sense of humanity's essential goodness. They were what anthropologist David Graeber called "the raw material of sociality, a recognition of our ultimate interdependence that is the ultimate substance of social peace."[6] The serendipity and ritual framing of these interactions—their clear beginning, middle, and end, like the interactions at Ranulfo's store—also helped imprint them on my soul. Such meetings, crossroads of humanity, left me with a feeling of debt, which I wanted to repay at every opportunity.

And then there was the guilt. In Ecuador, I lived with subsistence farmers and weavers who only made a few hundred dollars a year, living in simple houses made out of concrete blocks, eating potato soup every day. Back in the U.S., I tormented myself by looking at everything—peanut butter, toaster ovens, airplane tickets—and calculating how many sacks of potatoes that money could have bought for my friends in that Ecuadorian village. I had to accept that I couldn't fulfill every request for help, but I still felt bad about it, just as I felt bad about not resuming my ESL class in Salem that summer because I dedicated my time to the store.[7] I could never repay my karmic debts, but at least I could try to stop a mechanic from ripping off one Mexican immigrant.

Not that I expected the mechanic to share my outlook. I identified my impulses toward guilt, communion, and gratitude so I wouldn't project them onto others. I reminded myself not to expect the mechanic to open up a welcome wagon for immigrants, only to ask him to treat Roberto fairly, not to overcharge or demean him.

With this in mind, I drove over to the garage, and when the mechanic came out to the counter, I explained, as politely as I could, that Roberto had fixed the problem himself for less than $2 and wasn't happy with his bill or the way his brother had been treated.

The mechanic didn't take it well. Standing a couple feet from my face, he said, "Well, that's really *too bad*."

"I'm just letting you know how we felt about the service," I said, as if offering an innocent pointer.

Leaning a little closer, the mechanic countered, "This conversation is *over*," and his burning eyes and clenched teeth told me he meant it.

Having pushed the issue as far as I could, maybe too far, I walked out. It wasn't like the movies. No punches, no screaming match, no dramatic, edifying argument about race relations. It was over in a flash, before I had time to get nervous…or punched.

Thinking about it later, I decided he didn't get angry just because I was implicitly calling him a cheat, though that in itself was sufficient reason. He took my defense of Roberto as a personal betrayal, like the guy in the donut shop who punched Conover for being a white guy with Mexican friends. As much as I tried not to let it show, the mechanic could probably tell from the way I talked that I was middle class, and he knew that the wage gap between the middle and working classes had been growing for decades.

I had no sympathy for racism, but I couldn't dismiss the class tensions so easily. In middle school I had buddies from white, working-class families who felt like brothers, and it broke my heart to leave them for a new town and school. I got to know more working-class guys while working various jobs throughout high school and college, but it was never the same. I did everything from pumping gas and washing dishes to painting houses and building garbage dumps, and most of the time I got along well with my co-workers, but sometimes I sensed class resentments, like the summer after college when I worked as a furniture mover in Boston. I still remember the day when we did a big move in the financial district downtown. We were happy to be moving furniture in an air-conditioned building, protected from the oppressive humidity outside, and since we were surrounded by well-dressed office workers, we kept our voices down and our swearing to a minimum. But at the end of the day, as we headed back to the warehouse, packed like cattle into the back of the truck, the scorn for finance professionals came out. When the truck slowed down or stopped at a traffic light, a couple of the movers would scream, "Fucking suits!" at shocked men in white shirts and ties on the sidewalk. Seeing about seven of us guys hanging out of the open truck, the "suits" didn't dare respond. For a split second, it probably crossed their minds that this could be the day of class reckoning that everyone assumed would never happen in America.

I laughed along with all the other guys in the truck, but secretly wondered if they saw me as a future "suit." We listened to the same music, classic rock and Bruce Springsteen's newest album, *Born in the U.S.A.*, but I sometimes overheard movers in the other room refer to me as "the college kid." In their minds, I might have been working behind enemy lines.

Class issues surfaced again when we moved furniture into the dormitories at Boston University. During our lunch break in a warehouse near campus, one of the guys found a piano buried among the desks, dressers, and beds we had been moving all morning, and our foreman, Joe, sat down and started playing a few notes. As usual, Joe didn't say a word, he just led us with his stony silence and intimidating presence. His arms were so massive that they blocked my view out the driver's window whenever I got to ride up in the front of the truck, but now, with his head bent over the keys, Joe's strong arms and fingers softly tapped out Bob Seger's "Turn the Page," a simmering, melancholic song about a man on the road who's outnumbered and doesn't dare take a stand.

As always, Joe was accompanied by his sidekick, a short guy with a Napoleonic complex and a real mean streak. As if to translate Joe's silent glares, he regularly screamed at us, "What the fuck is wrong with you fucking idiots?!" But now he stood calmly next to Joe at the piano, and almost in a whisper, he started singing the Seger lyrics: "You pretend it doesn't bother you, but you just want to explode...."

After a minute, the rest of us, a pack of sweaty, young guys, joined in, while Joe silently worked the keys:

"Here I am, on the road again...

Here I go, turn the page...."

By the time the song was over, raw emotion hung heavy in the air, and I had no idea what would happen next. Cries of hurt? Confessions of stands not taken?

No, instead, one guy punched another in the arm and screamed, "Fuck you!" Then they wrestled on the dusty, concrete floor while the rest of us watched and laughed and shoved each other, until it was time to go back to moving furniture for college kids.

You don't forget days like that. All these years later, I got to reconnect with my memories of movers and childhood buddies by hanging out at a Mexican store, surrounded by guys in jeans and baseball caps who worked with their hands and watched action movies. The store was as close as I could get to recovering my lost home.[8] Maybe I had gone back to confront Roberto's mechanic because I wanted to turn all the guilt for my bountiful, middle-class life into something physical that I could taste and feel, like a bloody lip. Maybe I wanted to put myself on the line, to take a risk, like Ranulfo. Once gratitude, nostalgia, and debt get deeply inside you, anything is possible.

In the midst of the anti-immigrant rancor of 2007, the car incident from the previous summer didn't feel like a victory. I wished I could have spent more time hanging out with working-class whites, trying to understand their perspectives, maybe in some minor way helping to reduce the distrust and hurt on both sides of the Anglo-Latino divide. Even without doing that, I could guess that opposition to immigration was tied up with decades-long shifts in the economy, away from agriculture, timber, and manufacturing toward a globalized, high-tech, information and service economy. Wages had been stagnant for decades, especially for people with only a high school diploma, and personal debt was rising and income inequality was shooting off the charts.[9] As a college professor, I was part of that rising class inequality. Rather than focus on gradual, structural changes, though, it was easier for the working class to focus on what they could see with their own eyes: the sharp increase in the Latino population in Salem, up to almost 21% of Salem's roughly 150,000 residents by the 2005 census.[10] Overpaid elites and abstract economic trends were hard to visualize, so, instead of railing against them, the working class fought among themselves over a $200 repair on an old Honda Civic. Meanwhile, the middle class pulled into their two-car garages, closed the door by remote control, turned on the TV, and assumed everything was fine.

I didn't like battling with white working-class guys, but if the two worlds collided again, I would stand by Ranulfo and his customers. I envisioned myself as a football player defending Ranulfo as he carried the ball downfield on a long kickoff return.

It wasn't easy, though, because the other team was hard to see. After the car incident, I didn't personally encounter any more people in Salem expressing anti-Latino sentiments, but I knew they were out there, judging by the nasty comments on local and national radio shows and websites.

The news on June 12 definitely got my attention. That day Immigration and Customs Enforcement officers raided a Del Monte food processing plant in Portland, an hour's ride from Salem, detaining 165 ordinary line workers for possible deportation to Central and South America. Parents who had dropped their kids off at school before going off to work—to cut, wash, and pack fruits and vegetables—didn't come home that night, and didn't know when they'd see their families again. The raid sent shock waves throughout the state of Oregon. Families prepared wills, so that if one or both parents were taken away, instructions would remain on who should take care of their kids. Some churches offered themselves as sanctuaries, while others debated what to do.

It was happening—neighbors dragged away, lines being crossed. I remembered what a boatman in Ireland said to my mother and me, after we explained that our ferry tickets had gotten mixed up, so we had to take separate rides to the Aran Islands, our tourist destination. The boatman, a burly man who had been staring ahead like a military guard, immediately lifted up the gate and let us both pass, categorically stating in an Irish brogue, "A mother and son should never be separated." He was right.[11] I wished a boatman could lift the gate now and reunite these Latino families.

All these events led me to draw a few conclusions:

1) Watch out for the sucker punch.
2) Getting the bakery is going to be harder than I thought.
3) Prepare for battle.

NOTES

1. The online comment was posted by "Buckle Up" on Snopes.com, on March 21, 2007, under a thread titled "Immigrant Go Home!" (accessed roughly in June, 2008, but the url is no longer available.) This post came out before the bill was proposed in May, but it illustrates the type of comments that appeared at that time, which I didn't think to record, for reasons discussed in the main text. Likewise, I didn't note the title of the AM talk show.
2. These figures come from a Pew Hispanic Center review of major polls: "The State of American Public Opinion on Immigration in Spring 2006: A Review of Major Surveys," May 17, 2006, http://www.pewhispanic.org/2006/05/17/the-state-of-american-public-opinion-on-immigration-in-spring-2006-a-review-of-major-surveys/ (accessed October 4, 2016).
3. On the point that racial prejudice mattered more than economic self-interest, see, for example, Burns and Gimpel (2000). For greater emphasis on economic self-interest, see Kessler (2001). As made clear by these and subsequent studies, as well as the 2016 presidential election season, it's not easy to separate the two factors, economic self-interest and racial prejudice.
4. *El Padre Trampitas*, Director Pedro Galindo, III, 1984.
5. Conover (1987, 80–83).
6. Graeber (2011, 99).
7. For candid, thoughtful discussions of the ways such inequalities affect fieldwork dynamics and friendships, sometimes in a gut-wrenching way, see Behar (1993), Senders and Truitt (2007), and Shostak (2000).
8. If the comparisons can be allowed, I would say I was experiencing something akin to the homesickness that anthropologists like Walley (2013), Kane (2010), and Behar (1993, 1996, 2013) have insightfully written about in other contexts. Walley doesn't just capture the dignity and hurt of Chicago steelworkers like her father who were devastated by the closing of steel mills, she gives a sense of the way her own higher education, a Ph.D. in anthropology, caused her to feel split over her own identity and to experience longing for a home that could never quite be recovered. Kane (2010) writes beautifully about her anthropology education and working-class family, drawing out the contrasts while paying

exquisite tribute to her parents. Within the context of the Cuban-American Jewish diaspora, Behar also writes lovingly, honestly, and heartbreakingly about her family and ongoing search for a home and wholeness that can never be quite realized. As for the guilt of leaving people after an intense fieldwork experience, Crapanzano writes poignantly about "the wanderer who comes and leaves" (1980, 150), forever after haunted by the "sadness, the guilt, the feelings of solitude, and the love that come with departure" (1980, 140).

9. On the stagnation of wages and rise of personal debt, see Bellamy Foster and Magdoff (2009). On the hollowing out of the manufacturing sector and working class, see Walley (2013).
10. According to the 2005 U.S. Census, 21.64% of Salem identified as Hispanic or Latino. See U.S. Beacon, "Salem, Oregon," http://www.usbeacon.com/Oregon/Salem.html. According to the census, Salem's population in July, 2005 was 147,114. See "Public Data, Population in the U.S.," https://www.google.com/publicdata/explore?ds=kf7tgg1uo9ude_&met_y=population&idim=place:4164900:4105800&hl=en&dl=en. Both sites accessed September 5, 2016.
11. I can never forget that Irish boatman's line about a mother and son never being separated because my mother still likes to pull it out whenever she can, like when I ask her to wait in the car for a minute while I run into a store to get something.

CHAPTER 12

Mysteries of Money

May–June, 2007

Ranulfo followed the legislative maneuvering and anti-immigrant news, but he didn't let it get him down. When I went on a rant about these nut-jobs, he told me, "People born here like you get upset with these critics, but for an immigrant like me, it's just something you ignore. It's just another barrier, something that makes you stronger, like a turtle's shell." To survive and move forward, he stayed positive, like other first-generation Hispanic immigrants, the overwhelming majority of whom said in polls that they had never personally experienced discrimination in the U.S., though others, including their U.S.-born children, would say they had.[1]

Having been poor all their lives, Ranulfo and Pablo also didn't share other Americans' guilt and neuroses about money. They didn't worry that increased profits might make them "greedy," or fear that money is "the root of all evil," exaggerating money's power by treating it as a force in its own right, separate from human society. Instead, Ranulfo and Pablo saw money as a practical medium of exchange and something that tied together the local community, Mexican-Americans, Anglos, and all. Their view was closer to that of Simmel, who said desire for money is like Platonic love, caught halfway between desire and possession, a state that Simmel viewed as "the true human condition."² At least to Ranulfo and Pablo, money tasted sweet, and the anticipation of future profits tasted even sweeter.

Most anthropologists, on the other hand, didn't talk about the sweetness of money and profits. Instead, they published reports about the oppression and hardships of poor and disenfranchised groups, whether indigenous farmers in Nepal or drug addicts in New York. And they weren't wrong. They were accurately exposing harsh conditions that needed to be brought to light and changed. My own first book was entirely about the oppression of an indigenous group in Ecuador and their resistance to white Ecuadorian power structures.³ It's natural. When you live and work with disenfranchised people, you end up siding with them.

Not surprisingly, then, anthropology colleagues advised me to focus my research on the exploitation of Latino manual laborers, rather than Ranulfo. They worried that publishing anything about Ranulfo's success, however moderate, would just confirm the pernicious myth that anyone who works hard in America can get ahead. One colleague said flat out, "You've got to be more critical of capitalism." These were friends giving me good professional advice, and they weren't wrong about Latino suffering, as I could have shown if I'd focused on the poor, hard-working Latinos struggling in and near Salem, in hops and onion fields, cherry and apple orchards, groomed backyards and sweaty kitchens. It wouldn't have been hard to find them, either: most of Ranulfo's customers fell into this category, and good books and articles had been written about other Latino workers on the West Coast.⁴ But I chose to focus on Ranulfo and Pablo, instead, a couple immigrants buying their own store and just maybe getting slightly ahead.

They were giving it everything they had. Every day I found them hard at work preparing for the big remodel—throwing away old washing-machine parts in Pablo's pick-up truck, raking the small strip of grass that ran along the chain-link fence behind the store, crawling around on the roof, checking out wiring and heating vents. They reminded me of what novelist Denise Chavez said about the Mexican men she knows: "They're always busy working outside, fixing the roof or cleaning...."⁵

After I complimented Ranulfo and Pablo on their handiwork, they smiled and almost simultaneously replied that they were like *El Mil Usos*, The Man of a Thousand Uses, a reference to a favorite 1980s film about a poor peasant who works every job he can get, from selling flowers on the streets of Mexico City to bricklaying and dressing like Santa Claus. They identified with *El Mil Usos* as an ironic hero—a chump, yet a paragon of versatility and endurance in a tough world.[6]

I wish I could have been as versatile as *El Mil Usos*, but the best I could do was throw out bumbling questions about the construction plans, always a step or two behind Ranulfo and Pablo's rapid-fire discussions. It didn't help that construction terms like "joists" were not part of my Spanish vocabulary, and Ranulfo was moving around with the brisk purposefulness of a paramedic in action. I could see now why Ranulfo had been so successful at the nursery, overseeing 10 or 20 guys at a time. The man could move.

One time, seeing me in the back of the store, mopping up bottles of liquid laundry soap that were leaking, Ranulfo said, *Pete, trabajas bien*. "Pete, you work well." That was probably the best compliment he ever gave me. I reminded him that I did a lot of mopping while working in a convenience store during high school, and started joking about being like Cantinflas, dancing with his broom as he sweeps the streets of Mexico City in his last film and one of my favorites…but by then Ranulfo had left to do something else at the front of the store.[7]

Ranulfo didn't need me for my mopping and sweeping skills, anyway. He wanted me to serve once again as his liaison with the outside world, translating and dissecting the stilted legalese of the licenses and permits required by city officials, as well as the blueprints and letters of the architect they'd recently hired.

I loved being useful, but tried again not to get in over my head. When I reminded Ranulfo I wasn't an architect, he said, "It doesn't matter. You're from here. You'll understand."

At least I knew where I'd be spending the summer.

I bit my tongue, then, when the estimate on the cost of the remodel rose from $75–100,000, plus another $75,000 for the bakery equipment. Even if I'd said something, it probably wouldn't have mattered. As Ranulfo once said, "Pete, you know teaching, but you don't know business." Happy to maintain this division and fully confident in Ranulfo's business acumen, I didn't second-guess his calculations.

For the same reason, I kept quiet when I met Antonio, the local Mexican man working as an intermediary on this project. For an unspecified cut, Antonio was going to line up a general contractor, loans, and the bakery equipment. The first time Antonio came in the store, in late May, he reached across the counter and shook my hand quickly, then jumped into a discussion with Ranulfo about amperage and electrical loads for the new wiring. He spoke with great deliberateness, choosing his words carefully, his light green eyes intensely focused as he moved from one point to the next, never pausing for jokes or asides.

Ranulfo respected Antonio, a fellow immigrant from rural Mexico who now owned a Mexican restaurant and a few other businesses in the Salem area, but Antonio never talked about himself when I was around. In fact, he didn't talk about anything other than the bakery. When Ranulfo and I occasionally went off on other questions, such as whether he should put grass or pavement in the area behind the store, Antonio looked away, and if we continued the tangent, he walked down the aisles, pretending to busy himself by checking out the inventory, then coming back to resume his point.

I tried to make Antonio comfortable by greeting him warmly, curbing my questions, and nodding in agreement when he spoke. The last thing I wanted to do was offend a Mexican friend helping Ranulfo, especially not at a time when white Americans were attacking immigrants.

Antonio was particularly important because of his access to bank loans, to be arranged through an associate of his, a white loan agent in Portland. These bank loans had to be better than the alternative, credit from other Latino business owners or loan sharks, the informal network used by immigrants who knew, based on past experience, that banks didn't like to offer loans to small-business owners, especially minority owners without the required paperwork. Ranulfo wasn't sure how high the rates would be, but, from what I'd read about Hispanic immigrant loans in other cities, they could be anywhere from 100% to 260% of the loan value per year.[8] Antonio promised to save Ranulfo from such a fate.

And the bank loans offered solace at an even deeper level. For the first time in his life, an American bank was willing to loan Ranulfo thousands of dollars for his business. Ranulfo took the bank's loan offer as a huge vote of confidence from the American business community, an act of acceptance even more exquisite than the messages of love and encouragement he had sought at the casino. Ranulfo was ready to experience "credit" in the original Latin sense of *credere*: to have someone believe in him.

By contrast, many Americans continued to take credit as a simple necessity, not a sign of trust worth celebrating. I'm not even sure the deep level of trust inherent in money was fully appreciated by the thousands of people who visited the Treasury Department in Washington DC that year, as tourists do every year, to see the place where money physically gets made.⁹ Those enthusiastic Treasury visitors seemed to think they'd be able to lift the veil on money, to glimpse its true nature, if they could just view its inner mechanics, the ink, paper, and rollers used to print it, yet the real magic was out in the lobby—the crowds of people in line together, a living, breathing, spontaneous microcosm of society, united in the faith that museums and stores all over town, all over the country, would continue to accept their dollars. When they looked at money being printed, they were looking at the sheer power of society. They weren't looking at an esoteric force, they were looking at themselves.¹⁰ Dollar bills could have been printed on bubble-gum wrappers and they would have still had the same power, if everyone believed they did. The biggest bureaucracies in Washington never could have made that happen. The social trust in money persevered because it got renewed every day through seemingly trivial rituals of exchange, the expenses charged and paid by millions of ordinary people, the money passed between Anglo farmers and Latino construction workers, little kids with piggy banks and senior citizens on a fixed income, janitors and engineers, all united by a quiet ceremony of trust.¹¹

Yet most tourists in the Treasury lobby kept their eyes fixed ahead, not talking to strangers in line, certainly not grabbing their hands and saying, "Isn't society amazing?!" To convey something of what Ranulfo felt about credit and money that spring, we should have gone to the Treasury Department and passed around a copy of *Moby-Dick* in the visitor lobby and asked volunteers to read it out loud, especially the passages where Melville uses financial imagery to convey the best of humankind, its communal bonds. The visitors could read that great scene where Queequeg saves a drowning sailor and then thinks to himself, "It's a mutual, joint-stock world, in all meridians," or the one where Ishmael says a "joint-stock company" is "the precise situation of every mortal that breathes." As a Melville scholar said, "Credit here is an economic metaphor for the trust on which all human relationship and friendship is founded."¹² Ishmael reminds readers that bankers are a key part of that circle of trust: "If your banker breaks, you snap." And even Captain Ahab uses financial imagery to refer to the common bonds of humanity, what he calls our "mortal inter-indebtedness."¹³ Money and *Moby-Dick* go so well together, we should have read out the entire book in the U.S. Treasury lobby, like the marathon readings of *Moby-Dick* that they put on every January at the New Bedford Whaling Museum, with more than 150 readers taking turns over the course of 25 hours, everyone from fishermen and clergy to professors and physicians.¹⁴ Treasury tourists could have come and gone, moving back and forth from the money-printing rooms to the *Moby-Dick* reading in the lobby, eating chowder and light snacks, talking about money, water, and anything else that binds them together. Antonio's loans were like the gold doubloon that tied Ahab's crew together, the centerpiece that made Ranulfo's bakery quest possible.[15]

Under Ranulfo's influence, at least that's how I now saw money, in blissful, Ishmael-style reveries and visions of communion. I rejected stories of doom and suppressed my inner cynic. I believed in the bakery.

But even in my most fervently optimistic moments, I still didn't trust Antonio.

Notes

1. By contrast, their children, U.S. citizens, reported discrimination at roughly twice this rate. Surveys from this time period found that, overall, about 20 % had experienced discrimination in employment, a number that is much lower among first-generation Hispanic immigrants (Fraga et al. 2010). Others would see these rates as being distorted by a downplaying of racial discrimination by minorities, that is, the view of "racism without racists" (Valdez 2011, 138–53).
2. The quote on Platonic love comes from Simmel (1907, 211). This section also draws on Marx's famous analysis of money "fetishism," and dovetails with Keith Hart's synthesis (2005, 28–32) of the founding figures in social theory—Marx, Simmel, Durkheim, Weber. I am alluding, for example, to Hart's point that Simmel saw "money as a symbol of our interdependence, locating its value in the trust that comes from membership in society" (2005, 31).
3. Wogan (2004a).
4. For an example of the best of this kind of research, see Seth Holmes' medical-anthropological account (2013) of the suffering endured by indigenous migrant farmworkers from southern Mexico on a farm in Yakima Valley, Washington. The situation described by Holmes is comparable to that of Ranulfo's customers, many of whom are migrant farmworkers, working with similar fruit products and often coming from the same region of Mexico (Oaxaca). Even closer to Salem, recent studies (McClure et al. 2015) have exposed the health costs to Mexican-origin farmworkers in the Willamette Valley, as measured physiologically by higher levels of blood pressure, cholesterol, and glucose. For in-depth treatment of historical, political-economic contexts, labor conditions, and gender and racial hierarchies among indigenous Oaxacans in Oregon and California, see Stephen (2007). One last, excellent, example from the West Coast, though dealing with a work environment more typical of urban centers like Portland than Salem, is Ordóñez's book (2015) on day laborers in the San Francisco Bay area.
5. Chavez (2002, 8, my translation). Chavez makes this comment about Mexican men by way of contrast with Pedro Infante, a

revered actor of the 1940s and '50s who lifted weights, an unusual form of physical exercise at that time. In the Spanish original, she uses a resonant word for "working" that often comes up in conversations at Ranulfo and Pablo's store as well: *jalando*, which literally means "pulling."
6. *El mil usos*, Director Roberto G. Rivera, 1981.
7. *El barrendero*, Director Miguel M. Delgado, 1982.
8. These figures come from moneylender interest rates among the Dominican immigrant community in New York City (Dexter Elkins, "In Some Immigrant Enclaves, Loan Shark is the Local Bank," *New York Times*, NY/Region, April 23, 2001). For more details on the struggles of small-business owners among Dominican immigrants in New York, see Krohn-Hansen (2012), who shows that most Dominican immigrants don't receive (or apply for) bank loans for the same reasons cited by Ranulfo: (1) Banks don't find it cost-effective to make loans to small businesses, especially not very small loans to people without a lot of credit history; (2) Many immigrants don't have the required documentation.
9. Bureau of Printing and Engraving, Department of Treasury, 300 14th Street, Washington, DC.
10. A somewhat similar view of market rituals as Durkheimian collective effervescence, rituals that offer images of society itself, is developed by Appadurai (2016), but in a less obvious context: namely, the pricing agreements of Wall Street derivatives traders, which Appadurai argues re-create the market and society.
11. Similar ideas about money are articulated by the founding figures in social theory: namely, Durkheim on collective representations of society, Marx on money fetishism, Simmel on money's basis in interdependence, and Weber on capitalist rationalism. For a synthesis of these theories, see Hart (2005, 28–32). For more on Simmel's point about economic interdependence, see the upcoming discussion about *Moby-Dick* in the main text.
12. Adamson (1997, 95).
13. Melville (1851), Chapter 13, "Wheelbarrow" (…"in all meridians"), Chapter 72, "The Monkey Rope" (…"situation of every mortal"), Chapter 108, "Ahab and the Carpenter" ("inter-indebtedness"). I agree with Donaldson (1973) that Melville's financial imagery is surprisingly ambiguous, especially in light of the condemnation of materialism in his other writings. Ambiguity

is present right from the first chapter, where Ishmael gives his motives for going out to sea: "The act of paying is perhaps the most uncomfortable infliction that the two orchard thieves entailed upon us. But *being paid*,—what will compare with it? The urbane activity with which a man receives money is really marvellous, considering that we so earnestly believe money to be the root of all earthly ills, and that on no account can a monied man enter heaven" (Melville 1851, Chapter 1, "Loomings").

14. Details on these New Bedford "Moby-Dick Marathons" can be found at http://www.whalingmuseum.org/programs/moby-dick-marathon. Accessed on February 4, 2013.
15. Susan McWilliams (2012) argues convincingly that Melville was bothered by American individualism in the nineteenth century, including Emersonian celebration of "self-reliance" and, as de Tocqueville said, the tendency in American democracy towards political indifference. While I agree with her overall argument about individualism among the crew and Americans in general, I don't completely share her view that Ahab's doubloon illustrates the crew's atomization. Although it's true that the crew doesn't speak directly to each other in their later, individual reflections on the doubloon's meaning, they are still united by their interest in it as a special object. Moreover, the doubloon unites the crew in their coordinated hunt for Moby Dick, a form of physical union, an intense synchronization of bodily movements, that can be more powerful than verbal discourse about the doubloon.

CHAPTER 13

Garbage Dream

June, 2007

The immigration debate got under Ranulfo's skin, after all—in a dream about crossing the border in a garbage truck.

Ranulfo had been studying his dreams more than ever, in search of clues as to how he should proceed with the bakery plan. Not that careful, pragmatic accounting was being thrown out the window, but dreams were needed to take that accounting to a deeper level. Ranulfo had used his cash-register software to compare sales figures for previous years, and he wrote out by hand all his revenues and costs in carefully printed columns, one sheet for each month. He studied all these figures like x-rays that could save his life. I had complete faith in Ranulfo's calculations. Without checking his notes, he could tell me exactly how high his water bill had been last month, and how much he made on phone cards. He was sharp as a tack, calculating figures in his head in a split second. And he was ultra-careful, motivated by permanent memories of his childhood poverty and ongoing distaste for losing money. He spent restless nights tossing and turning, worrying about the rising costs of the bakery, then rechecked all his cost calculations and projected outlays. His calculations continued to indicate he could afford the bakery.

The problem was, these calculations could only take him so far. Everything ultimately depended on projections about what might happen in the future—how much customers would like the bread Lupe baked, how long it would take before he could recoup his expenses, how well the economy would hold up. There were no guarantees. For daily operations, his success depended on hard-nosed math, but for this huge, long-range decision, success required something much more intuitive: insight into himself and others. To better understand these hidden realms, Ranulfo studied his dreams more intensely than ever in the summer of 2007.

Ranulfo shared a particularly important dream about a garbage truck with me in late June over burritos at a local Mexican restaurant, after joking about who was going to treat the other. I succeeded in paying this time, but Ranulfo got in the last joke. As I paid the cashier, who had been patiently waiting behind the register for us to make up our minds, Ranulfo told her, *Yo invito, pero él paga*. "I treat, but he pays."

At our table by the window, we talked about bakery plans and customers we hadn't seen for a while, then Ranulfo announced that he'd had a big dream last night. As usual, he poured it out rapidly, beginning to end, without any pauses for questions or comments:

In the dream, I was trying to cross the border, from Mexico into the United States, in a garbage truck. There was a group of about 50 of us, all from my village. We were getting inside the garbage truck so we wouldn't be seen. It didn't smell too bad inside, but it was dirty.

I said to this Mexican soldier, "Can you give us a ride to the border, so we can meet the garbage truck there and not have to ride in it the whole time?"

I figured this way we could stay clean longer, and then meet up again with the garbage truck at the border, and get back inside and cross into the U.S.

He said, "OK, but is it legal?"

I said, "Yes."

He said, "How much are you going to give me?"

I said, "A thousand pesos [about $100]."

We didn't want to spend all that time stuck in the garbage truck, from the village all the way to the border, so we did this instead.

There were about 50 people, all families. It was only me and Laura [his daughter]; Mauricio and Lupe [his son and wife] were already in the U.S. There were other families from various pueblos in the area, crossing the border for the first time.

And then we were going to sleep in some house, and the house owners wanted to charge $10 for each person. It was the house of a friend from my village. His sisters wanted to charge us, but he didn't.

We decided no, we won't pay; we already had arranged this stay-over with the brother for free. So then the sisters wanted to sell us cell phones, at $10 each.

We said, "OK, we'll need those in States." So we chipped in our money and bought ten, at $10 each.
  And that was it.
  I could tell this was a pivotal dream because Ranulfo kept rolling it over and over in his mind. For most of his dreams, he came up with an interpretation right away, often deciding the dream foretold the loss or gain of money at the store that day, and then he "closed the chapter" on the dream and moved on. But this dream was alarming and confusing, giving rise to multiple interpretations, some overlapping and some contradictory.
  In the restaurant that day, Ranulfo first said, "Maybe I had the dream because I read the other day about more immigration raids, and a friend of mine, this guy who works at the restaurant we went to last time, just got deported."
  On the surface, this sounded like a typical dream that recycled bits and pieces from recent waking life, just as most Americans say their dream images recapitulate their experiences of the last day or two, what psychologists call the "day residue." Ranulfo, too, sometimes subscribed to this view, recognizing that something he saw on TV or at the store showed up in his dreams that night, but he said even such seemingly insignificant dreams could still predict and alter subsequent events, and that's what he was more interested in, the dream's connection to the future, not the past. Knowing this, I fished around to see how his friend's deportation might relate to his own life.
  Ranulfo said somberly, "The U.S. is always changing its laws. They could still change their minds and take away my citizenship."
  What?! How could Ranulfo think this?! I almost spit my chips out.
  Ranulfo had been an American citizen for almost 20 years. They couldn't suddenly revoke his citizenship after all these years. He'd paid his dues. He'd done everything right. He was here to stay. It shocked me to hear him even consider the possibility of deportation. Those naysaying, anti-immigrant misanthropes had broken into his psyche and planted fear there, a drop of existential poison. Ranulfo loved America as much as any citizen ever had, and it repaid him with venom.
  It turned out Ranulfo hadn't been completely joking a few weeks earlier when he had said he could end up rejected by both Mexico and the United States, left in limbo, without any country at all. At the time I was sure he was joking because he followed up this suggestion by referring to a famous movie called *Ni de aquí, ni de allá*, "Neither From Here, Nor There," a comedy about an Indian woman who goes to work in

the U.S. as a maid, and, because of a mix-up in the Los Angeles airport involving chilies left in her suitcase, ends up on the run from immigration authorities and the FBI.[1] I took the reference as a joke because Ranulfo rarely identified with Indians. He respected the Mayas and Aztecs for their knowledge of astronomy, and felt sorry for contemporary indigenous people who suffered racism in Mexico City, but he saw those as other worlds, not his own. Nobody in his family spoke an indigenous language or wore a poncho. He also wasn't a big fan of this film persona, La India María (Maria, The Indian), a peasant Indian woman in pigtails. When he was young, he'd laughed at India María's wacky escapes, along with everyone else in his village, but hadn't watched her films much since then. Her comedy hadn't held up well over the years, at least not by comparison with Cantinflas. They both made fun of themselves and authorities, but while India María played a buffoon and country bumpkin, Cantinflas played his roles with more dignity, cleverness, and versatility, everything from a teacher named Socrates to a priest who fights bulls and a lawyer who defends the poor. In Ranulfo's favorite, *Por mis pistolas*, "By My Guns," Cantinflas doesn't run scared like India María. He enters America with fast-talking, irreverent humor. When the border patrol agent asks him if he plans to topple the American government, he retorts, "Ay, Don't be a clown, man. I'd need weapons, and you Americans took all of them," and with his sharp wit he proceeds to defeat the cowboys, make a fortune, and marry a pretty woman.[2] If Ranulfo identified with any film character besides "A Thousand Uses," it was Cantinflas, not an indigenous woman in braids, so when he said he might end up like India María, I assumed it was nothing but a joke.

And I made the same assumption when one day he lightheartedly mentioned a film about a Mexican man who gets sent back from the U.S. because he doesn't have a birth certificate, only to find the Mexican government doesn't recognize his legal status, either, and then spends the last 20 years of his life living under a bridge, stuck in limbo between both countries. Ranulfo joked that he'd end up like *El Hombre del Puente*, The Man of the Bridge.[3] But Ranulfo wasn't joking now. The garbage dream scared him and fused movies, jokes, and TV news into the same dirty psychological reality.

Ranulfo didn't want to accept that the dream literally meant he'd be deported, though, so he offered two other possible interpretations. Finishing up his burrito, he conjectured, "Maybe I dreamt about garbage because Hispanics often do jobs that other people don't want. Like just yesterday afternoon in the store I was talking to a friend who works in a recycling plant, pure Hispanics, pulling bottles and cardboard off the line. And they pay $11 an hour, so this friend was really happy." This interpretation was somewhat more positive than the first, but it contained a devastating implication for his future—he'd be working for an hourly wage because he had lost his store.

I was more relieved when Ranulfo added his next interpretation, and finally interjected some humor. He said that yesterday he thoroughly cleaned the house, as if he were *El Hombre de la Toalla*, The Man of the Towel, and he found his kids' trash behind the couch, so maybe that influenced the dream. Calling himself "The Man of the Towel" wasn't a huge joke, but we both laughed at this ironic play on the more common uses of the phrase "The Man" in names for superheroes, such as *El Hombre de Acero*, The Man of Steel (Superman), and *El Hombre Increíble*, The Incredible Man (Kalimán's secondary name). The humor depended on gender reversal, too. By saying, "The Man of the Towel," Ranulfo cast himself as a male superhero—for cleaning around the house, typically considered women's work. Ranulfo actually loved house cleaning, so the joke was ironic and self-deprecatory.

I was happy to see Ranulfo joking again and offering a "day residue" interpretation without any hints of possible deportation, but he didn't stop there. Looking for the dream's bridge across time, he said maybe the dream already came true that morning. "The dream already turned into reality because this morning I had to put out the garbage cans, and this was the first time I've ever forgotten to put out the cans the night before." Yet he wasn't entirely convinced by this interpretation, either. As in the God dream, he brought up his nemesis, Don Quixote, that icon of confusion. "I feel like Don Quixote, fighting against time. But you can't be an enemy of time, you have to be time's ally." Once again he wasn't laughing.

He speculated that this dream might also contain a positive message, maybe even The Key. "It could be a really ugly dream, a test, or maybe it contains The Key. I don't know." In saying this, he was following the logic of his village, which held that dreams often spoke in opposites, with bad images in dreams foretelling good fortune in real life. A dream involving a dead person, for example, supposedly meant you were going to make a lot of money in the near future. Yet the village didn't have a standard interpretation for garbage, perhaps because it was such a minimal part of their daily lives. They literally had no trash service or garbage trucks. Residents just burned the few pieces of trash they had, as his father and I did during my visit the year before, watching the flames rise and the smoke disappear under the grey, moonlit sky.

This dream was a true puzzle. Worn down by the many possible interpretations, Ranulfo sighed, "I wonder if turtles ever get headaches.... Probably not because they don't have stress."[4]

But he didn't give up. He had to keep pondering this dream because he knew it could make or break his business. On June 28, three days later, while we were back at the store, he declared he'd finally found the dream's true meaning. "I figured it out," he announced. "I think that dream means I'm going to end up homeless."

Another shocking interpretation.

"No, that's not going to happen," I immediately objected, but before I could finish, he said, "I was going to tell you that now I have a fear—a little fear—that the bakery won't work."

There it was again—one of his very rare uses of the word "fear." This was serious.

"I mean, what if we run out of money and can't finish the construction?"

I was sorry to see him interpreting his dream as an expression of anxiety, but relieved that he did so without any prompting from me.[5] I never even told him I'd been reading psychological studies that repeatedly confirmed the anxiety theory of dreams, including myriad reports of dreams about common worries, such as showing up unprepared for an exam, speech, or job interview, and pregnant women dreaming about their changing bodies and unborn babies, and, most intensely, soldiers and other trauma victims repeating the same nightmares.[6] Fitting this pattern, Ranulfo's dream anxiety might be healthy if it helped him see the connections between immigration politics and his business plans.

And he had good reason to feel anxious. If he went bankrupt, he'd not only lose the store, but also his house, which he hoped to use as collateral for loans totaling more than $100,000.

I couldn't help thinking of Ranulfo's father, whose own father died when he was nine years old, forcing his mother (Ranulfo's grandmother) to leave the village, to peddle oranges on the streets of Mexico City, one of the most insecure, desperate jobs in the country. It broke the nine-year-old boy's heart to hear his younger sister cry, "I'm hungry," when they ran out of tortillas at night. He couldn't do anything to help her, and that fear of hunger stayed with him his whole life.

That would be a terrible fate for Ranulfo to relive at any level. Not being able to feed his family ran against Ranulfo's deepest instincts of protection. Yet despite—or because of—his protective instincts, Ranulfo was ready to risk everything on the bakery.

To highlight the risks, Ranulfo told me about two cases of nearby Mexican businesses that recently failed: a restaurant that had to halt new construction in mid-stream, leaving the owner with loans he couldn't repay, and a check-cashing business that just went bankrupt, the owner recently begging Ranulfo to bail him out with thousands of dollars.

Ranulfo didn't want to end up like these friends, but he needed the large bank loans to start the bakery, and he needed the bakery so his wife could work with him. Citing a famous proverb, he said, *No hay mejor negocio que el que cae en casa.* "There's no better business than the one with your family."

Switching tack, Ranulfo joked, "I'm an optimist. I'm going to buy land directly from God, without any real estate agents."

After we laughed, he got serious again. "I'm thinking about the costs. We need a contingency plan. We have to go forward, but if we can't afford the construction, maybe Pablo and I will have to get extra jobs to make the payments." He punctuated the point about risk by quoting another proverb: *Del plato a la boca, se puede caer la sopa.* "From the plate to your mouth, the soup can fall."

Not being comfortable with such mental flip-flops, Ranulfo self-critically joked, "I'm like a new father who doesn't know how to change diapers. Like the first time I changed Mauricio's diaper: I put it on backwards and he peed right in my face!"

As confused as Ranulfo felt about the dream's meaning, he never altered his description of its contents during our various conversations. In fact, he had never altered any of the details in the hundreds of dream reports I'd recorded, even when I asked about them again weeks and months later. I pointed this out when a cynical English professor at a conference surprised me by immediately asking, "So how do you know he's not making up these dreams?" I never doubted Ranulfo was telling the truth about his dreams, though of course he creatively shaped them in the very act of putting them into words, like everyone else.

Definite answers arrived the next day, Friday, June 29. Ranulfo said, "I figured it out. The dream meant the immigration reform wasn't going to pass because that's what's on the news today. And now it's going to be like in the dream, many people are going to have to come here in all kinds of tricky, nasty ways. Some may even come in garbage trucks."

Yet even the failed immigration reform didn't fully resolve the dream's mystery. Within a week, Ranulfo switched tack yet again, deciding the dream might mean the opposite, that he would make *more* money.

"I have to think positive," he said.

After that he stopped talking about the dream, focusing, instead, on the practical plans for the bakery.[7] When I asked for his newest interpretation, he said he still didn't know, that only time would tell…if it chose to divulge its secrets. He had too much respect for the power and mystery of this dream to pretend he already knew its meaning. That was more than I could say for the academics who insisted that all dreams perform wish fulfillment or some other specific function, as if the incredible diversity, ambiguity, and complexity of dreams could ever be captured by a single explanation.[8]

Adding to this diversity, I came up with a few speculative interpretations of my own, starting with this one: *the garbage truck in the dream was a turtle, a motorized version of Ranulfo's favorite animal spirit.* Just like the turtle, this garbage truck was hard on the outside, a little beat up, but fully alive and moving forward, lumbering along in the dust, slipping under the radar of the American authorities. As Ranulfo had often said in other contexts, nobody stops the turtle because nobody notices the turtle. When in danger, the turtle pulls its head inside its shell and only remerges once the coast is clear.

Moreover, this motorized turtle offered a striking image of both death and rebirth. Ranulfo and his compatriots experienced a symbolic death when they entered the darkness of the garbage truck, but this darkness contained the possibility of rebirth. They seemed to be huddling in a giant womb, enveloped and consumed by a large, powerful creature, travelling along the border between two worlds, waiting to be reborn on the other side. The dream was like the Biblical story of Jonah in the belly of the whale, except this time it was 50 people in the belly of a garbage truck. You could even say there were two deaths in the dream. If all nighttime sleep is a temporary death, in which we die to the conscious world and then come back to life in the morning, this dream contained a death within a death: the darkness of the garbage truck enveloping Ranulfo from within the darkness of his sleep-death, like Jonah entering the belly of the whale after first entering into a deep sleep below deck, in the belly of the ship at sea.

Ranulfo never mentioned Jonah, but he was fascinated at this time with trash and recycling, both of which also contain profound life–death symbolism. One minute we buy something in the store and it has great value, then the next it's discarded and worthless, reminding us of the transience of consumer products—and ourselves. Garbage trucks seem outsized and clumsy, but they ride on the thin line between value and worthlessness, life and death. Robin Nagle, the official Anthropologist-in-Residence at the New York City Department of Sanitation (yes, that's her title, the best one an anthropologist could ever hope for), said that garbage reminds us of "the inevitability of decay, the absurdity of endurance, the lie of continuity."[9] Ranulfo's dream took this death symbolism, though, and turned it on its head, like people who create art or valuable antiques out of other people's refuse.[10] The garbage truck in his dream was filled with people yearning to start all over again on the other side of the border after passing through a harrowing ordeal. Instead of a symbol of death, Ranulfo's unconscious turned the garbage truck into a symbol of new life. Ranulfo created his own graphic version of the death–rebirth symbolism found in many rites of passage throughout the world, in which, as one anthropologist said, "the initiates die to their old life and are reborn to the new." [11]

Ranulfo himself explicitly connected the dream with recycling when he said it might have been related to his recent talk with a Latino friend who worked for $11 an hour in a recycling plant. This recycling symbolism could have gone either way, just as his life could have. It could mean he'd end up losing his store and working again for an hourly wage like this friend, or it could mean the exact opposite, that his bakery and business would succeed because most Americans tried to forget about garbage. Americans produced tons of garbage every day, but tried not to think about it once it went in a receptacle and out the door, whereas Ranulfo's friend got paid good money to touch garbage all day long. The first proverb Ranulfo ever taught me proclaimed, *De la lagartija en adelante, todo es cacería*. "From the lizard on up, everything is good for hunting." Ranulfo took this proverb to mean one should never neglect the seemingly worthless business opportunities that others pass over. Like a turtle or his friend at the recycle center, Ranulfo's store and bakery might make it if other Americans ignored him and his customers, allowing him to protect his family and compatriots.

From this more positive perspective, recycling is rebirth: you take something dead, like a discarded can or bottle, and give it new life. Such economic symbolism also contains religious undertones. As Hayden

White said, recycling is a capitalist tale of redemption, like the alchemist's dream of turning base matter into gold.[12] Although Ranulfo didn't stick for long with the recycling interpretation of this dream, he often thought and talked about trash and recycling. He even told my class that he arrived in America thanks to trash: the discarded Big Mac and French fries he ate in the back of McDonald's on his way into Oregon.

Trash seemed to both disgust and fascinate him for the same reason he searched through his dreams for The Key: he liked reversals, alchemy, transformations. He reminded me of those artists who make sculptures and paintings out of old bottle caps, flotsam, discarded metal, and other refuse, taking advantage of the creativity at play when solid forms get broken down and taken out of their normal contexts, like cans, papers, and metal shelving thrown together in a garbage truck or municipal dump. The garbage truck was visual art, an original and surprising juxtaposition of forms, images, and emotions.

Even more than all this, the dream enabled Ranulfo to review his entire life: his past, present, and future, and the relation between all three. The dream was about time, one of Ranulfo's other burning concerns at this point in his life. The dream was about the universe and his place in it. This was, in other words, one of those rare existentialist dreams where Ranulfo got to contemplate the meaning of his entire being.

The best source here is Charles Stewart, who, in a study of modern Greek dreams, managed to integrate anthropology and existential psychology. Stewart showed how dreams, especially in times of major world changes, can reveal personal and communal reflections on the fusion of the past, present, and future in a search for meaning in the present.[13] From this perspective, note that Ranulfo's dream wasn't just located on a spatial border, the national border line between the U.S. and Mexico. It was also located on a temporal border: Ranulfo's present moment, which was caught somewhere between the past of his Mexican village and the possible future of his life in the U.S. By taking dreams so seriously, he was contemplating the relation between his past, what he had previously rejected as "superstition" and "tradition," and his possible future, oriented around the U.S. and science, business, and modernity. He was contemplating his past and future to make sense of his present. In its turtle-like way, the garbage truck encapsulated this temporal and existential review of his entire life. As Ranulfo often said, the turtle is fighting time and will only succeed if he can make an ally of time. The turtle in the dream, the garbage truck, might have been such an ally, but its whispered message was confusing.

Ranulfo was being pushed toward these reflections on turtles and time because of the high stakes involved: a social death through the loss of his business, his role as family provider, possibly even the loss of his identity and sense of belonging as an American. He wasn't consciously contemplating his physical death, but that, too, was mixed in here somewhere. Up until this point in his life, Ranulfo had mostly focused on the near future: getting a job at the nursery, getting married, raising a family, opening the corner store. But now, at age 44, he started for the first time to contemplate the distant future, his retirement. He had told me that he wanted the bakery because he wanted to have enough money to support his family in retirement, to have his kids come live nearby, and this was his last chance to do this by taking a big financial risk, before he got old and scared to lose everything. He didn't have very definite plans for retirement—sometimes he said he wanted to get a mobile home and drive around the United States with Lupe, sometimes he said he wanted to open up a recycling plant outside Salem, so he could play with trash all day—but just letting the possibility of retirement seep into his thinking had changed his perspective. As Stewart says, drawing on Heidegger, contemplations of one's mortality lead to reflections on one's past and new possibilities for being in the present.[14]

This subtle, underlying shift in temporal orientation changed everything. For Ranulfo, contemplating the far horizon and the grand sweep of time subtly changed his vision of the close-up. He took the view from afar, like the photos of the earth taken from the moon, but also the one from up close, like the view of the turtle looking down at the road. As he said after the dream about the third arm, "Your life is like a camera. You have to use it to see from many different angles."

No wonder Ranulfo kept pondering this garbage-truck dream. Not only did it contain the key to his business, it gave him profound social and existential questions to think about. The dream confirmed what Mary Douglas said about dirt in general: "Reflection on dirt involves reflection on the relation of order to disorder, being to non-being, form to formlessness, life to death."[15]

But where did all this reflection leave him? One pressing question remained: Did the dream point to a solvent bakery or bankruptcy?

Notes

1. For a poignant exploration of the racial and class commentary provided by this particular India María film (Director María Elena Velasco, 1988), see Ruth Behar's description of the day she spent with Esperanza, a close friend and poor Mexican woman, as she makes the rounds selling produce to middle-class housewives in the city. One of the customers tells Behar that when she saw this latest film by India María, it reminded her of Behar and Esperanza: "Imagine you and your husband taking your comadre back [to your home in the U.S.], it was like that." The film, like the border itself, brought out differences in power and privilege, what Behar calls "that fundamental asymmetry—determining who can cross easily with a few dollars tip, as we do, and who has to put their life on the line simply to find a little back-breaking work" (1993, 241).
2. *Por mis pistolas*, Director Miguel M. Delgado, 1968. Adding to the ironic conquest symbolism, Cantinflas arrives at the border riding a horse named *Bucéfalo*, Bucephalus, the name of Alexander the Great's horse.
3. *El hombre del puente*, Director Rafael Baledón, 1976.
4. What added to the unusually high level of ambiguity and confusion were Ranulfo's belief that dreams can speak in opposites and symbols, as well as his mixture of multiple dream theories, including Discernment, Message, Generative and Nonsense theory, wherein dreams have "no useful relationship to reality" (Lohmann 2010a, 230). Ranulfo wasn't alone. As Lohmann noted more generally, "dream theories are plural and held with varying degrees of certainty" (2010a, 247).
5. Contrary to what you would expect from a functionalist view, these dream interpretations actually *increased* anxiety, rather than reducing it (hence, Ranulfo's mention of fear, confusion, and headaches). Confronting the possibility of homelessness and deportation induced a form of existential anxiety, a transnational migrant's anxiety about citizenship and belonging. Ranulfo was not alone in this regard, as shown by other anthropological work on immigrants in Europe and the U.S. (Behar 2013; Brettell and Reed-Danahay 2012; Flores and Benmayor 1997; Reed-Danahay and Brettell 2008). For example, Brettell and Reed-Danahay write, "Among those Vietnamese who had become citizens, 24 percent reported

that they 'rarely' saw themselves as American..." (2012, 58). And as indicated by the earlier example of eating at McDonald's, Vietnamese-American "identity is considered somewhat mutable and can change with the situation and also alter over time" (Brettell and Reed-Danahay 2012, 60). Ranulfo's garbage dream likewise showed just how much an immigrant's sense of identity can shift in response to changing events and contexts. Finally, I should stress that other prescient dreams, for Ranulfo and others, might have the opposite effect, providing a reassuring sense of control and meaning that reduces anxiety. Ranulfo seemed to feel this way when he found the result of a dream the very next day and put it to rest, or, as he said, "closed the chapter" on it.

6. Hartmann (1998), Mageo (2011), Rock (2004, 65–68).
7. The timing of Ranulfo's turn to his dreams follows what we would expect from other studies that show enormous dream creativity occurring when a culture is experiencing major politico-economic changes. Stewart (2012), for example, explores the way dreaming on a Greek island flourished in response to changes in the local economy because of the First World War and the Great Depression. And Graeber explores what he calls a "dream economy" among the Iroquois in the sixteenth and seventeenth centuries, which he compares with other revitalization movements and the Italian Renaissance: "remarkable bursts of cultural creativity that so often occur after many traditional societies are suddenly integrated into a larger world economy. If the conditions are right...the result can be a spectacular expansion and enrichment of existing cultural forms: of art, architecture, drama, ritual, exchange" (Graeber 2001, 147). Similarly, I would argue Ranulfo was going through his own cultural renaissance in 2007 and 2008. The offer of a bank loan for the bakery was a major turning point for him, a formalization and deepening of his connection with a larger world economy, that is, the system of national and global bank credit. On the cusp of being integrated into this world economy, Ranulfo rediscovered what he had previously dismissed, the dream system of his childhood in rural Mexico, and he selectively drew from it to create a novel, hybrid set of principles that would help him comprehend and to some degree control his incorporation into a larger economic system through a bank loan. The closest parallel in Graeber's writing on wampum and social creativity would be the experimental,

non-standardized "dream-guessing" reported in the Jesuit relations from the early contact period of the sixteenth century. As Graeber remarks, "In fact, the one thing that really jumps out at one reading the Jesuit relations and other sources from the same period is just how open-ended such things were, especially in comparison with the careful ceremonial etiquette of later times" (2001, 145).
8. As Crapanzano said, "We should respect in the Other the same mystery we expect others to respect in ourselves. This too is a social fact" (1980, 152). These are the final sentences and the ultimate lesson of Crapanzano's book.
9. Nagle also makes an excellent point about trash's liminal mixture of public and private: "Shifting assignments of value for this category of material culture [mundane, personal items purchased at supermarkets, convenience stores, and drug stores] point to the sometimes nebulous divide between private and public." Similarly, the garbage truck in Ranulfo's dream seems to mix together the public and the private, as people go into a hidden area inside the truck. See Robin Nagle, "Why We Love to Hate San Men," *Bad Subjects*, Issue 55, May 2001, bad.eserver.org/issues/2001/55/nagle.html. Accessed May 10, 2014.
10. In this sense, the truck is part of that liminal zone analyzed by Michael Thompson (1979), a former student of Mary Douglas, an anthropologist who opened many researchers' eyes to the social meaning of purity and dirt (1966), as will be discussed below. Thompson (1979) aptly shows how "rubbish," which gets defined in some contexts as worthless, can be rescued, converted, and recategorized as antiques or other valuables. Ranulfo was especially aware of the volatility of such categories at this point in his life. He felt he could be living the American Dream one day—and the next he could be bankrupt, homeless, and/or deported. Trash was an apt metaphor for this volatility, and it also fit with his view of dreams as often following the principle of opposites.
11. Douglas (1966, 118). In this case, Ranulfo seems to be envisioning the rebirth of his Mexican village into a transnational Mexican-American community. On an internal, psychological level, you could say his dream was doing what the U.S. Treasury visitors and Wall Street traders did on a more outward, group-wide level: create an image of the market and society (see Appadurai 2016). Hence,

in the dream there are two explicit economic transactions: cash payment to the soldier for a ride, and to the friend selling the cell phones. These transactions occur through the bargaining practices common in Mexico, yet they are both done with an eye toward entering and functioning in the U.S. market economy. (Ranulfo says they will need the cell phones in the U.S.) Taking place fittingly on the U.S.–Mexico border, the dream makes this transnational, market society psychologically real.

12. Hayden White, "Hayden White Talks Trash," *Bad Subjects*, Issue 55, May 2001, bad.eserver.org/issues/2001/55/white.html. Accessed May 10, 2014.
13. For example, Stewart wrote, "Heidegger's idea of temporality entailed the fusion of the future with the past and the present in human being. As Binswanger put it, '[the futurity of being] is through and through implicated with its past. Out of both of these temporal 'ecstasies' the authentic present temporalizes itself'" (Stewart 2012, 14).
14. See Stewart (2012, 14). See also the anthropologists who have viewed certain dreams in somewhat similar, existentialist terms, though without drawing explicitly on that literature, such as Hollan (2004) on "selfscape" dreams, Kirtsoglou (2010) on the "radical imagination" in dreams, and Mageo's "holographic" analysis (2011) of dreams about family and success.
15. Douglas (1966, 6).

CHAPTER 14

Crash Warning

July, 2007

It turned out we were looking for answers in the wrong place. Instead of studying the immigration bill in Congress, we should have been worrying about Wall Street. If we'd done that, we would have realized that a housing bubble was about to burst and drown the economy. But we had no idea. Almost nobody did, except for bankers on Wall Street and a few other groups who could see what was going on in the housing market. If you're one of those people whose eyes glaze over when others talk about high finance, I hope you'll keep them open long enough during this chapter to see what was going down on Wall Street in the summer of 2007, so you can understand Ranulfo's chances of surviving the year.

Contrary to popular belief, banking was not business as usual at this time. A housing bubble had arisen due to a radical innovation: "mortgage-backed securities," bundles of home loans bought up by Wall Street banks from diverse parts of the country, then sold off in packages to managers of hedge funds, mutual funds, pension funds, and foreign government funds.[1] This was a huge change. For the first time in human history, banks didn't care whether their loans could be paid back, since they were passing off the risk to someone else, investors like pension-fund managers.[2] By assembling these mortgage packages and selling them immediately at more than face value to investors, Wall Street firms—Merrill Lynch, Goldman Sachs, Citigroup, JPMorgan Chase, and others—hit upon a banker's dream: enormous profits, minimal risks. The bankers got paid as soon as they sold the mortgage bundles, so not only did they not care if the homeowners would later default on these mortgages, they didn't care about the investors buying them, either. The bankers intimidated investors with opaque mathematical models, and, worse, they lied to them about rising default rates and the debased standards being used to give out the mortgages to just about anyone with a pulse. After closing a deal, they boasted to each other about "ripping the face off" the investors and blowing them up with shotguns. One gleeful expression in the derivatives business was, "I just ripped that fucker's head off."[3]

Basically, it was a Ponzi scheme: get people to hand over their money now in exchange for promised future gains, give back just enough profits to keep hope alive and bring in new suckers, then take off with everyone's money before the whole thing comes crashing down like a stack of wine glasses that can't go any higher. It was a classic con game, executed on a mass scale. The ones who gained the most were the Wall Street bankers at the top, the ones who created the scheme and collected money up front. The ones who could lose the most were the investors and homeowners, the suckers who signed their futures away on mortgages that they couldn't afford, on houses that would eventually lose their value and sink into debt quicksand when the supply of new suckers at the bottom of the pyramid exhausted itself, which would inevitably happen because the real economy wasn't keeping up with these inflated house prices.

Like most bubbles, it seemed great while it lasted. From 1997 to 2005, house prices rose more than 80%, a meteoric rise by historical standards. Many homeowners were happy to take out huge mortgages, not realizing that the banks had thrown away their control system, so that when they said you qualified for a big loan, it wasn't because they actually believed you could pay it back, the way it had been for your parents, grandparents, and great-grandparents. Homeowners signed on the dotted line, and happily watched housing values continue to climb. Investors were also happy with the high returns and Wall Street bankers with the profits that came from skimming off the top of all these transactions. Not that the gains fit on the same scale of magnitude. Typical homeowners got incremental gains that would only be realized if they could manage to sell their houses in the future for a higher price. By contrast, bankers got paid millions of dollars at that very moment, year after year. From 2000 to 2008, the top executives at investment bank Bear Stearns each earned an average of $37.5 million a year.[4] One of Bear Stearns' fund managers,

Ralph Cioffi, owned a $2.6 million home in New Jersey, a $2.2 million home in Vermont, a $933,000 home in Florida, an apartment on 5th Avenue, and, for the coup de grace, a $10.7 million house on Long Island, with six bedrooms, a pool, a tennis court, and a separate guest house on 2.5 acres, as well as two Ferraris, each valued at more than $240,000.[5] Most Americans couldn't have afforded to live in one of Cioffi's *garages*, let alone buy one of his properties. And the lower-level employees at the banks, the young analysts, traders, and salespeople who did most of the hard work, also got well compensated within their pay grade, making roughly $500,000 each in 2006.[6] These bankers lived a fundamentally different lifestyle from average homeowners, one paid for with the sweat and tears of those same homeowners.

The fun couldn't last forever. The profits poured in only as long as new suckers could be found, people who would pay more than what the house had been priced at a few years earlier, but after a while they ran out of new buyers to pay the higher prices because wages among the working and middle class had remained stagnant for decades. By the early 2000s, banks started running out of buyers who could make their mortgage payments, even the interest-only kind. In just five years, from 2000 to 2005, risky subprime loans rose from 10% to 50% of all mortgages sold, and default rates, not surprisingly, started to shoot up.[7]

By the time Ranulfo was ready to buy the bakery, Wall Street insiders already realized their scheme was about to blow up. In early 2007 an official at Citigroup said, "we should start praying…I would not be surprised if half of these loans went down," and another said if his bank's models were correct, "the whole subprime market is toast." Even earlier, in 2006, a ratings agent exclaimed, the "'mailing in the keys and walking away' epidemic has begun—I think things are going to get mighty ugly next year!"[8]

As confidence sputtered, the market for mortgage-backed securities faltered throughout the spring and summer of 2007, most noticeably when two major hedge funds backed by powerhouse Bear Stearns went belly up. Bear Stearns had put these hedge funds up for sale in June, but nobody would pay the asking price because they didn't trust the mortgage-backed securities on their books, at which point creditors started demanding their money back in a classic "margin call." According to two respected business reporters, Bethany McLean and Joe Nocera, this was "the moment of truth."[9] The jig was up.

Or it should have been, yet most banks kept plunging ahead. What were they thinking? Why didn't they get out in the summer of 2007, before everything blew up in 2008? Most importantly, what were the chances that someone on the inside would break away from the pack, and in the process of saving their own hides, sound an alarm that Ranulfo, Pablo, or I might hear, a warning in the news about market tremors that might scare us enough to back out of the bakery?

The chances were slim. We were up against powerful forces on Wall Street, strong incentives to take wild risks and plow ahead.

First, unlike Ranulfo and other business owners, the bankers weren't betting with their own money, because in the 1980s and 1990s they had turned into public companies traded on the stock market. Previously, managers had a strong personal interest in the future health of the banks because they were putting their own money on the line, as co-owners. But once the banks got traded on the stock market, the managers became paid employees focused on short-term gains. In perhaps their most boneheaded move, the banks borrowed heavily to place bets on the stock market, to make even more astronomical profits. In 2002 banks kept roughly $1 in savings for every $20 they played with on the stock market, but by 2007 they had *doubled* their leverage ratio to 40:1. A mere 2.5% decline in their assets would wipe them out, and, in any market, it's only a matter of time before you hit a dip like that, if not worse. Only bankers gambling with other people's money would risk blowing up their entire firms like this.[10]

Second, the investment banks were all too aware that the U.S. government had effectively deemed them "too big to fail." In 1984 the government bailed out Continental Illinois National Bank, taking over $4.5 billion in bad loans and sending an implicit message to other banks that they, too, would be rescued by the government if they ran into trouble in the future.[11] The same message was delivered in 1995, when the government orchestrated a $50 billion rescue of the Wall Street investment banks that gambled and lost on foreign bonds, and again in 1998, when the government orchestrated a bailout of a large hedge fund that owed money to Wall Street. Of course, in the summer of 2007 the banks weren't trying to run their firms into the ground, but, feeling confident that the government would probably bail them out in the worst-case scenario, they continued to take daring risks in order to make unprecedented profits.[12] In the words of one trader, "You have all the upside when things go well. If you do poorly, you don't owe anybody money, so you might as well take as much risk as possible."[13]

Extreme risk-taking was also encouraged by high degrees of job mobility and low levels of company loyalty, with bankers easily hopping from one job to the next. As one Lehman Brothers associate explained, "People aren't scared of moving or being fired because you know you can get another job somewhere else...." Speaking about job cuts at Merrill Lynch a few years earlier, another said, "We had a lot of different people at a lot of different levels getting fired. Receptionists getting fired. They are crying. These people are not skilled people...*I don't worry about that because I am just like, I am going to ride this as long as I can.* If I am fortunate enough not to get fired, that will be great. If I do, well, you know what? I have made a lot of money...."[14]

And obviously the money wasn't incidental. The obscene surges in compensation noted earlier created a strong incentive to act recklessly. It might seem like the compensation factor goes without saying, that it's a permanent feature of the business, so it's worth stressing that this was *not* banking as usual, this was banking gone wild. Before the 1990s, banking profits had actually been relatively restrained.[15] From the 1930s until the 1980s, profits in the financial sector grew at roughly the same rate as the rest of the economy—then, from 1980 until 2005, the financial sector grew by *550%* more than the real economy. Along with that shift, compensation for bankers shot through the roof, so it lost effectiveness as a motivational tool; even if they made mistakes, they still got paid hundreds of thousands of dollars, sometimes millions.[16]

The underlying problem was a lack of personal responsibility. When people are not betting with their own money, when they're paid huge sums regardless of the likely outcome of their actions, when they sense the government will bail them out because they're "too big to fail," guess what happens? They get reckless. They get into an arms race with the competition and wring out as many profits as they can before the bomb goes off. Nobody expected Wall Street bankers to work for free, but even as profit deals went, the Ponzi scheme built on home mortgages was unusually aggressive, far-reaching, and destructive.

The contrast with Ranulfo couldn't have been greater. Ranulfo put his house and family savings on the line. He was ready to risk everything to get the bakery, prepared to suffer horrific consequences if he messed up. Though the bankers crowed about the free market's just rewards for those who took greater risks, they couldn't have held a candle to true risk-takers like Ranulfo. Their level of personal risk and courage couldn't have reached the ankles of Ranulfo or other small-business owners, yet they wielded a scythe that could cut everyone's head off.

Most bankers didn't pull out of the mortgage business in 2007 because they couldn't say exactly when it would crash—perhaps it would last another month, another six months, maybe even a few more years. The con game could continue as long as average Americans kept signing the papers for new loans and refinances, pushing the day of reckoning into the future. The bankers kept their tubes hooked into the credit market so they could siphon off every last drop of profit before the whole thing finally collapsed, like a giant piece of rotten fruit.

So nobody warned us about the impending crash. Wall Street was able to keep the credit machine going just strongly enough throughout July, 2007 so that the impending collapse didn't become public news. Even as late as the summer of 2007, the news media still relegated the rumblings on Wall Street to the business section, rather than front-page headlines. Ratings agencies like Moody's and S&P's continued to hand out AAA ratings on Wall Street's risky mortgage deals, even though they knew loan default rates across the country were rising steadily. And why wouldn't they? In a blatant conflict of interest, the ratings agencies got paid by the same investment banks that created these toxic deals, which was like having a criminal pay a judge's car, food, and utility bills, then asking the judge to rule on the criminal's case in court the next day. Not surprisingly, they let the criminals walk.

Government regulators were also useless, having been beaten down by politicians in both parties dependent on Wall Street campaign contributions, Republicans waving the flag for the free market and Democrats looking the other way as long as cheaper housing shored up the sinking working class. In the spring of 2007, three private investors met with the Securities and Exchange Commission, one of the main government regulators, and warned them about the impending crash in the housing market, but, as one investor said after the meeting, "they didn't know anything about CDOs, or asset-backed securities. We took them through our trade, but I'm pretty sure they didn't understand it."[17]

Nobody was going to warn us—not the media, not the government, and certainly not Wall Street itself. If I'd smelled the fuse burning in July, 2007, I would have screamed, "Pull out of the bakery and run for cover!" If Ranulfo had known what Wall Street was up to and what the impending crash would do to the economy, he would have reversed course immediately and dropped the bakery plan, so as not to take out loans that would drag him into bankruptcy in the coming months. But neither of us had any idea what was coming.

As crazy as it sounds, Ranulfo's best hope for salvation was his dreams. If just one dream could dissuade him from taking out the loans on the bakery, he could be spared from bankruptcy. It didn't matter if I or anyone else believed his dreams were truly predicting the future, and it didn't matter if he dreamed about garbage, stationary, walnuts, Don Quixote, or anything else. As long as the dream convinced him to back out of the bakery plan, it could save him.

Notes

1. As McLean and Nocera (2010, 7) note, it was actually the government, in the form of Ginnie Mae and Freddie Mac, that first started selling mortgage-backed securities in the 1970s, but that was on a limited basis, and they eventually turned to Wall Street for most sales. Tett (2009) provides a particularly good, detailed account of the historical development of mortgage-backed securities at JPMorgan Chase (including the merger of J.P. Morgan and Chase Manhattan Bank).
2. In Tett's words, "For the first time in history, banks would be able to make loans without carrying all, or perhaps even any, of the risk involved themselves" (2009, 45).
3. The "face ripping" and "shotgun" phrases refer to typical Morgan Stanley expressions in the derivatives business of the 1990s (Partnoy 1999, 88–91). According to Cohan (2009, 265), the quote about ripping "that fucker's head off" illustrates the contrast between the institutional cultures at Bear Stearns vs. Goldman Sachs in the early 2000s, with the Bear Stearns trader being more likely to use such violent imagery. As these examples suggest, there were obviously important differences between banks, as well as among the various types of workers in these large, complex institutions. As shorthand, in the main text I use terms like "investment banker" or simply "banker" as a convenient, but broad rubric, one that includes traders, salespeople, analysts, executives, and others. Unfortunately, I can't always go into these distinctions.
4. Figures cited in Roberts (2010, 18).
5. His boss, James Cayne, on the other hand, preferred his private jet and helicopter, which flew him to New Jersey to play golf a couple times a week, at a cost of $1,700 per ride (Cohan 2009, 283, 370).
6. Goldman Sachs paid such workers roughly $500,000 each in 2006, and that was for the 12,000 Vice Presidents that constituted about a third of the bank's workforce, almost all under 30 years old, according to a former VP (Smith 2012, 116).
7. The figures on the rise in house prices and changes in subprime loans come from Tett (2009, 125 and 95, respectively). Tett credits her Ph.D. in anthropology for her holistic approach and skepticism about elite rhetoric, which led to her reporting in the *Financial Times* in 2006 on problems with the credit world (2009, 252–53).

8. The quote about "praying" comes from Michael Corkery, "Citi Settles Mortgage Securities Inquiry for $7 Billion," *New York Times*, Dealbook, July 14, 2014. The "epidemic" and "toast" quotations come from McLean and Nocera (2010, 291 and 296, respectively).
9. These two hedge funds were called High-Grade Structured Credit Fund and High-Grade Structured Credit Strategies Enhanced Leverage Limited Partnership. The funds weren't technically part of the main Bear Stearns operation, but they were largely seen as connected. The quotation about these funds and the "moment of truth" comes from McLean and Nocera (2010, 294). Tett (2009) and Cohan (2009) also see the collapse of these two funds as the beginning of the end, though as these authors make clear, not everyone on Wall Street saw it that way at the time.
10. This argument obviously doesn't apply to the stock options that would be lost by major bank executives, but those losses were essentially made up for by the extravagant cash incomes discussed below. In terms of leverage risks, Princeton economist Alan Blinder writes, "With a 40-to-1 leverage, a mere 2.5 percent decline in the value of your assets wipes out all shareholder value. That's a pretty risky way to run a business. What were they thinking?" (Blinder 2013, 52). As Blinder and others show, the thinking and the risk calculus had been changed by certain incentives, especially once the banks went from being privately owned companies to ones that traded publicly on the stock market. For example, Steven G. Mandis, who worked at Goldman Sachs from 1992 to 2004 and later did extensive interviews with Goldman employees for a doctorate in sociology from Columbia University, writes, "With the change to a bonus culture [after Goldman became a publicly traded company], there was more incentive to take risks, and because the partners were no longer personally liable for covering losses, the constraints on risk-taking (not just financial but also reputational) were loosened....The incentive was to ask for and to invest as much capital as possible…" (2013, 162). Smith (2012), who worked at Goldman Sachs from 2001 through 2010, makes similar observations not only about changes in risk-taking, but also Goldman's entire, pre-IPO ethos of fiduciary responsibility, honesty, and long-term commitment to clients. Michael Lewis also has a good comparative perspective on these changes, having worked at Salomon

Brothers in the 1980s (see Lewis 1989) and then revisiting Wall Street after the Financial Crisis. Lewis put the changes from the 1980s to the early 2000s into perspective when he wrote, "No investment bank owned by its employees would have leveraged itself 35:1, or bought and held $50 billion in mezzanine CDOs [collateralized debt obligations]" (2010, 258). In short, when bank managers didn't have as much of their own "skin in the game" as they did when the banks were privately owned, they took increasingly reckless risks.

11. As Roberts (2010) notes, the key here is that they bailed out the *creditors*, the ones who are normally motivated to exercise market discipline because they don't share in increased profits, unlike shareholders. The goal of the creditors is to make sure the borrower stays solvent enough to pay back the loan, so they are particularly sensitive to previous rescues by the government and they calculate risk accordingly.

12. The effect of government bailouts can be hard to prove, since most bankers were not explicitly expecting to fail, nor imprudent enough to admit in public that they counted on bailouts. The primary evidence here comes from what was already noted: the widespread knowledge of these previous bailouts, coupled with the sensitivity of investment banks to market conditions. Other, supporting evidence includes the following: (1) the way insurance rates at Lehman Brothers dropped after the rescue of Bear Stearns, indicating the financial world's sense that Lehman would also be rescued, if necessary; (2) the remarkably low interest rates on Fannie Mae and Freddie Mac from 2000 to 2008, including years when they started to pile up on risky subprime mortgages; (3) the fact that Goldman Sachs pressured the government as early as 1991 to alter FDIC rules so that the Federal Reserve could lend to investment banks in times of crisis. On the first and second point, see Roberts (2010, 12–13). On the 1991 FDIC rule change, see Johnson and Kwak (2010, 152). On Morgan Stanley's manipulations of the Mexican bond market, which led to the $50 billion rescue by the U.S. in 1995, see Partnoy (2009).

13. Ho (2009, 291). Ho is an anthropologist who worked on Wall Street and interviewed many workers in the financial services industry well before the 2008 crash.

14. These quotations come from two financial analysts quoted in Ho (2009, 259 and 290, emphasis in original). Ho notes that some bank employees were let go during downturns, yet bonuses stayed high for those who remained; and there hadn't been significant job cuts for two consecutive years since the 1980s (2009, 267).
15. In calling these changes relatively novel, I'm referring to specific events that occurred in the latter half of the twentieth century, changes chronicled in Johnson and Kwak (2010). If you take a broader view, as Graeber (2011) does with impressive historical scope going back to ancient Mesopotamia, you could say the credit crisis was consistent with long-standing entanglements between central states and financial elites, and battles between rich and poor fought out in terms of credit.
16. Or compare pay scales: from the 1950s through the 1980s, bankers got paid roughly the same as their counterparts at big corporations, whereas by 2007 they were making *twice* the pay of corporate officers, who themselves had run wild with pay raises during this period (Johnson and Kwak 2010, 61–62).
17. The quotation about the SEC comes from Charlie Ledley of Cornwall Capital (Lewis 2010, 166).

CHAPTER 15

Stopping Time

July, 2007

To get Ranulfo to reverse course, he needed to have a dream that screamed at high volume to drop the bakery, but that wouldn't be easy because a lot had already been invested in this plan. Ranulfo and Pablo had spent a few thousand dollars on architect drawings and other preliminaries for the remodel. Antonio, I, and other people had invested time and energy in all the planning. Lupe wanted to work in the bakery with her husband. Ranulfo and Pablo were committed. It was the 11th hour—dreamtime.

Two particular dreams seemed to provide answers. The first one wasn't even a dream so much as a strong feeling after waking from a dream that Ranulfo couldn't remember. At the store in mid-July, Ranulfo told me that he had recently woken up with an unusual amount of energy, cleaning the house with extra speed and force.

Detuve el tiempo. "I stopped time."

Before I could ask what that statement meant, he continued, "Now I think superheroes exist because they nourished themselves with dreams. I'm even starting to believe in Kalimán. It's a myth, but it must have started from something."

With a smile, Ranulfo recalled a guy named Joaquín who used to love to read the new Kalimán comic book every week. When a fire started in the pharmacy where he worked in Ario de Rosales, a town near Ranulfo's village, Joaquín dragged the safe out to the sidewalk and asked two onlookers to watch it for him, then ran back inside to rescue one more precious item: his copy of that week's Kalimán comic book.

To Ranulfo, the funniest part of the story was the price Joaquín paid for this devotion. "When he got back outside, the two guys on the sidewalk had run off with his safe!"

Perhaps this story was on Ranulfo's mind because a man with the nickname of Kalimán had come in the store a few weeks earlier, a Mexican man in his 60s who still worked in the nearby fields and forests, picking berries and cutting down Christmas trees. The man was strong, like his namesake, the "real" Kalimán in the comic books, but he joked around and swore more than I imagined Kalimán would. He was also the first Mexican man I'd met with a positive nickname. Most nicknames were designed to bust guys down a peg or two, putting their egos in check by seizing upon a weakness. In his younger days, Ranulfo's buddies nicknamed him "Defect" after a girl said she couldn't dance with him since he wasn't from her pueblo, and his friends overheard him whimper, "What's the defect in being from another pueblo?" Others called him "El Loco" because he sang in the shower and had the hubris to predict that someday he'd buy a house in America. "Kalimán" got his nickname in similar circumstances—teenage buddies teasing him for acting too big, carrying more sacks out to the truck than they did—but the name stuck, and the man turned his nickname into a source of pride. I once heard him defeat one of Ranulfo's arguments by asking, "Don't you see who I am?" Ranulfo had to dutifully answer, "Kalimán," and drop the argument.

Whether prompted by that recent conversation with the "Kalimán double" or not, Ranulfo now seemed to be reaching out to the "real Kalimán," that Superhero of the Mind, because Ranulfo, too, was pushing the limits of the known world, reaching back into his past, including the years when Kalimán comic books helped him develop his nascent reading skills and imagination. Ranulfo earnestly said, "I wish I could remember what I dreamed the night before I felt all that energy like Kalimán. I'm still looking for The Formula, The Key. It's like a secret recipe, and the restaurant won't tell me what it is."

He hadn't found The Formula yet, but just a couple weeks after his dream about the garbage truck, which he took to mean he would end up homeless, his optimism was back in full force. "I have a lot of faith," he said. "I've got faith stored on my back, like a camel."

He wasn't excited about putting his house up as collateral for the bakery loans, but he accepted that he had no choice, this time quoting the proverb that says, *El que nada debe nada tiene*. "He who doesn't owe anything doesn't have anything." This pro-borrowing proverb urged almost the exact opposite of the proverb he'd quoted about a week earlier, in late June, when he worried about the bakery costs: *Del plato a la boca, se puede caer la sopa.* "From the plate to your mouth, the soup can fall." That's the beauty of proverbs: they seem so authoritative, but the real authority and creativity lies with the person who selectively decides which ones to use in which situations.

I was glad to see Ranulfo had recovered his optimism, but not sure where it would lead. The second major dream came toward the end of July, and it had a clearer message.

Ranulfo told me to come to his house for that afternoon's talk, and I welcomed the break from the store, where I had been spending many hours talking on the phone with city officials about the bakery plans, translating documents, analyzing architect drawings, and running other errands related to the bakery.

Meeting in the driveway, Ranulfo walked me to his backyard, a clean patch of manicured grass with roses and conifers along the side, and a cherry, pear, and maple tree, each about 20 feet high, in the center. Directly across the lawn sat Pablo's house, a narrow path connecting the two backyards. I could see into Pablo's kitchen, but there was no sign of him because it was his turn to work the day shift at the store.

Ranulfo directed me to a chair under one of the trees, then pulled over another chair from the small brick patio a few feet away, and went in the kitchen to get a drink of water for me and a Coke for himself.

When I complimented Ranulfo on how green everything looked, despite the bright summer sun, he reaffirmed his love for watering plants. He said, "It's a ritual, to clear my mind, like cleaning. It relaxes me." I thought of Oaxaca, where we had to pray the water truck would arrive to fill our well every week. Here in Oregon, water flowed freely.

Sitting in his chair looking at the yard, Ranulfo did seem more relaxed, more contemplative, not quite as hard-driving as he usually was at the store. He seemed comforted by the fruits of his labor, the flowers, shrubs, and trees he'd planted in his yard, applying the knowledge and love for landscaping he'd gained at the nursery.

His daughter Laura, ever-inquisitive, came outside to see what was going on. Holding a juice box in one hand, she plopped down in a chair next to us, and said, *Papi, ¿Por qué pusiste esa silla allí al lado de Pete, si hay un banco?* "Daddy, why did you put that chair there next to Pete, if there's already a bench?"

Chuckling, Ranulfo answered, *No, está bien, m'hijita. Estamos hablando...* "No, it's OK, sweetie, We're just talking...."

"Do you want to go on your swing?" Ranulfo asked, pointing to a sturdy swing in the middle of the yard that he'd made with wood, bolts, and spare parts from Home Depot.

Laura said no, then went back inside, satisfied she wasn't missing anything.

Smiling, Ranulfo remarked, *Es tremenda.* "She's really something else."

He said, "Now that I have kids, my dreams are different. Everything is more real because I have something to live for. Someone who lives alone has different dreams." As a supporting example, I could have added that he had more nightmares when Lupe and the kids went to Mexico, but I didn't want to disturb his peaceful mood.

After saying he'd have to leave in about an hour to pick up Lupe, Ranulfo recounted his latest dream about garbage:

I was walking where there's lots of trash. They were going to hire me to collect trash. There were four American supervisors and three Chicanos working with them, organizing the work groups. An American arrived and said in English, "What can I do for you?"

I said, "I want to work."

He said, "OK, you're going to clean a lot, there's a lot to clean, you can go wherever you like." And he gave me a lot of plastic bags.

So I chose to go to the football field because I remembered there's lots of trash there.

I just wanted to work hard. I was like an indestructible man, working really fast, with gloves on.

They said, "It's important." That's a phrase that they always used at the nursery, to make you work hard, to realize it matters.

I went to some field, like the football field at the school. And there were papers, all kinds of papers... And then I ended up cleaning in a parking lot, cleaning up papers in some parking lot of some big company.

They said they'd pay me $8 an hour. I said I just wanted to donate my time, for free. I wanted to donate my time because I like cleanliness.

I told Pablo, "Let's do this, work with pure trash, it's good business." But Pablo said, "No way." I said, "It's good business," because there at Monrovia, they were constantly cleaning, even cigarette butts.

The dream didn't just overlap with the previous one about the garbage truck—with trash again coming to the rescue, as he bordered on poverty—it overlapped with a major event in real life: his firing from

Monrovia, the plant nursery. Ranulfo had spent most of his two decades in the U.S. working at that nursery, starting two years after his first night in Oregon sleeping under a bridge with homeless men. Then, in 2003, he informed his immediate boss that he wasn't coming to work on Saturday because he wanted to watch his son Mauricio run in the Awesome 3000, an annual running race for elementary-school kids in Salem. The boss insisted Ranulfo come in that day to finish a big order of plants, but Ranulfo refused. "My attitude was," he told me, "If I have to choose, I choose my family. And they fired me."[1]

I figured that the nursery firing had something to do with this trash-picking dream. Even though Ranulfo was thrilled to be his own boss at the store, he didn't like being fired from the nursery. He still expressed tremendous respect, affection, and gratitude for the white supervisors he had worked with there. I thought Ranulfo might say the dream meant he'd end up begging them to give him back his old job at the nursery, or working somewhere else for an hourly wage, or homeless, picking up trash, as in the dream about riding in the garbage truck.

To the contrary, Ranulfo focused on positive, concrete results: he said the dream caused him to make money the next day.

"This friend came to the store just after I'd had the dream," he said, "and brought the money he owed me. A few years ago I lent him $4,000, to buy a house, and he went to Mexico without repaying me. Then two months ago he got fired from Monrovia, and they gave him a pension....That's when I asked about the money he owed me, and suddenly he showed up this weekend and paid me $1,000. I thought I'd never see that money again."

Ranulfo felt sure that the $1000 was what the dream had meant because it came out of nowhere. He said that a gradual change in store sales or other finances couldn't be the dream's meaning. The change had to be sudden, like this arrival of a $1000 out of the blue.

This dream had another effect. A month after dreaming about the garbage truck, Ranulfo reversed his opinion of it: he now believed trash in that dream and others signified financial *gain*, not loss. He took dream trash as the green light on the bakery. "Now I'm seeing that trash is a good thing," he said.

Trash also inspired more philosophical reflections. Sipping on his Coke and speaking with a quiet reverence that reminded me of our talk about the God dream, Ranulfo ruminated at length.

"People think that time is something natural, but somebody discovered it. Somebody had to work hard to think of those things, and now we just accept it. I'm not sure who first discovered time, but it must have been an advanced civilization, maybe the Maya. Like in Mexico the Aztec calendar was exact, perfect. On the basis of stone and sunlight, they knew what was going to happen in the future. And they told you the best days to do something."

While celebrating ancient Mesoamerican wisdom, Ranulfo still resisted traditions that bordered on superstition. He charted out his own path, the Way of the Turtle. "But I feel like I'm close to understanding time. We're going faster, so time must be getting tired. Maybe we're all going to live like turtles, for many years," he said, citing science documentaries he'd seen about turtles that lived more than 70 years.

Science was winning, but only up to a point. "I think technology is stopping time, by making things instantaneous. Like now we have fax machines, and when I was growing up we just had horses. So we're getting control of time. Still, we don't understand eternity. Nobody knows."

With time, the turtle, and dreams as his guides, Ranulfo renewed his commitment to the bakery. "I can tell it's a good moment to start a new business," he said.

Rather than saving him from bankruptcy, his dreams were pushing him headlong toward it.

Note

1. One of Ranulfo's former bosses told me another reason they fired him was that they felt Ranulfo was more focused on his store than the nursery at that point.

CHAPTER 16

Into the Mystic

Summer, 2007

As long as Ranulfo's dreams weren't putting on the brakes, I was probably his last chance to escape from the oncoming train wreck. If my ingrained trepidation rose to the surface, I might still be able to convince him to pull out of the bakery plan.

Any interventions on my part wouldn't come from simple math calculations. We were way past math by this point. The numbers checked out. Now it came down to intuition, guts, fear, emotional needs—the battle between my newfound optimism and fascination with risk-taking versus my long-standing tendencies toward timidity and skepticism.

Emotional forces, though, are mysterious, and at that time they seemed more mysterious than ever. I knew something strange had been going on below the surface because that whole year my eyes kept filling up with tears at unexpected moments, like while reading bedtime stories to my kids or singing "Yellow Submarine" with them in the car, which should have been joyous moments. What was wrong? Nothing like this had ever happened to me. I hadn't shed a tear in the last 25 years, my entire adult life, except during a couple funerals. Not that I wanted to be a tough guy. Sometimes I had even wished I could cry, but I just couldn't. Something about my male nature wouldn't let me. But within the last year, I suddenly found myself tearing up at weird, unpredictable times.

I never said anything about this to Ranulfo or other friends. "Yo, my eyes welled up when I was watching *Shrek* last night" wasn't a sentence I was prepared to utter. I guarded the tears like a secret music box, stashed inside my desk. The problem was that the music kept getting louder. By the summer of 2007, I didn't know if I could keep the lid on it anymore. I knew something was definitely wrong when I welled up with tears watching baseball players on TV clearing the benches and throwing punches to defend a teammate hit by a pitch. It didn't make sense. Unlike Ranulfo, I wasn't studying my dreams, but we were both receiving mysterious internal messages that summer, and they had to be deciphered before we could go into action.

Once I started following the threads back to their sources, I concluded that the recent death of my younger cousin was part of the problem.

My cousin, Andy Knipe, was the second-to-last child in a family of five, the tag-along. When our families got together at my aunt and uncle's house on Long Island, with eight of us cousins sitting around the table cracking jokes and poking each other, Andy was just trying to figure out where he fit in. We'd ignore him when he tried to say something, but every once in a while he'd crack us all up, usually by squeezing food through his fingers or reminding us about the toilet.

Over the years, I went off to graduate school and moved out to Oregon, while Andy stayed in New York and excelled at making funny TV commercials for companies like FedEx and Pepsi. His audience and humor had evolved. His jokes now cracked up millions of people all over the country. He almost seemed like an adult.

Then, in 2004, at age 37, with a wife, teenage daughter, and two little boys, Andy got diagnosed with Lou Gehrig's disease (ALS).

At Christmas dinner that year he couldn't make the salad tongs squeeze together, but otherwise he seemed fine, so I still thought there must be some mistake, some way out.

There wasn't.

ALS continued to destroy his nervous system, relentlessly. By my summer visit back to New York, he was in a wheelchair, hands propped on the armrests, unable to turn his head from side to side, barely able to swallow. His body was frozen in place, but he was fully alert, watching himself die.

In his final months, Andy and I connected over baseball. I had never been much of a fan, but now that my three young boys were playing it, and now that Andy, a true baseball fan, was dying, I wanted to know everything I could. Andy answered my questions with short emails, as pithy and tantalizing as Chinese fortune cookies.

It took a lot of effort to send those messages. Andy put on a headset that tracked his eye movements, looked ahead at a screen, and then clicked with his index finger—one of the only parts of his body with any sensation left—on the word or letter he wanted.

With his last ounces of energy, he didn't just send out Zen-like emails, though. He also got on websites for Red Sox fans and clicked out messages like this:

"R-e-d S-o-x = S-c-u-m-b-a-g-s."

Yes, he spent his final days tormenting Red Sox fans, the arch-rivals of his beloved Yankees. Some of Andy's Red Sox insults were so disgusting that baseball websites, not normally known for their sense of decorum, banned him.

Then the emails and rants tapered off, as the disease took over every last inch of Andy's body, including his internal organs. In August, 2005, he decided not to get an artificial respirator. At age 38, he wrote a final letter to his kids and got ready to die.

I couldn't get a flight in time, but I called to say goodbye. Andy couldn't speak anymore, so I did all the talking.

I said I loved him. I said I was sorry I ignored him so much when we were little. Pretty soon I was fighting through tears to complete my sentences, incoherent ramblings about childhood memories and wanting to see him again. Up until that moment, I hadn't been able to comprehend Andy's impending death, but now, realizing that once I hung up, I'd never talk to him again, the certainty and utter finality of his death sank in.

I didn't want to hang up, but Andy's energy was fading fast. I finally hung up, and Andy died a couple days later.

The funeral in New York was mostly a blur. Carrying Andy's coffin through the church with the other pallbearers, my cousins and younger brother, seemed too easy. We just placed our hands on the top of the coffin, to guide it, but the wheels on the cart below did all the work, rolling quickly along the smooth wood floor. How was it that we could walk so effortlessly, while Andy, the youngest among us, was dead and in a box beneath our fingers?

The greatest surprise came after the funeral, at the lunch reception. Standing around talking, suddenly my cousin Billy shouted, "Sick Bastard's here!" Looking over at the entrance to the restaurant, I didn't see anyone who looked sick or like a bastard, just a regular guy in his 30s. I found out that "Sick Bastard" was this guy's screen name. He was a Red Sox fan who had traded insults online with Andy for months, until Andy finally let on that he was dying of Lou Gehrig's disease. By that point, they'd spent so much time together, trying to reach new heights of creativity with their insults for each other, that they'd formed a bond. Sick Bastard, who had never met Andy in person, drove down from Boston to attend this funeral in the heart of Yankee territory.

This was like a soldier walking onto the middle of a battlefield during the American Civil War and screaming, "Shoot if you want, but that's my brother over there and I need to see him."

My cousins, all faithful Yankee fans, mobbed Sick Bastard, hugging him and treating him like a celebrity.

Even after his death, Andy was still making us laugh…and teaching us how to live.[1]

When I walked into El Palmar in September, 2005, a few weeks after the funeral, I thought I was just looking for Mexican movies and data for a journal article or two. Instead, I found Ranulfo, and it wasn't a coincidence that I stuck with him. My craving for Ranulfo's friendship had a lot to do with Andy's death and my confrontation with my own mortality. Apparently the philosopher Søren Kierkegaard was onto something when he asked if "everything in the world were a misunderstanding? What if laughter were tears?"[2] That would explain why I needed Ranulfo's jokes so much.

I also needed Ranulfo's extreme gratitude. We were both so happy to be alive, and he expressed gratitude better than anyone I knew. As one of my students said, "Just listening to him makes you like life better." Or as a Mexican-American vendor of phone cards once told Ranulfo, "That's why I like coming here so much. I always leave with more *ganas*, inspiration, hunger to succeed."

I assumed I would move on after Andy's death, as I had with other deaths in the family. But this one got through to me. For the first time, I had a visceral sense of my own mortality, and it changed everything. All the lines got blurred: home and work, inner and outer, cause and effect, Ranulfo, Andy, me. Everything felt connected…including the bakery. My natural instincts to worry about losing money were battling powerful counter-forces. Of course, if I knew the Financial Crisis was coming, I would have begged Ranulfo to drop the bakery and run for cover. But I had no inkling about the crash, and despite my habitual anxiety about money, I wanted to see Ranulfo brave the risks and triumph. I wanted to see him get the bakery, defeat the naysayers, and take gratitude into the stratosphere.

Somehow baseball was also caught up in the middle of all this. It didn't just connect me to my kids and Andy, it connected me to Ranulfo and risk-taking. Watching my kids play Little League, I kept thinking: this entire game is an exercise in humiliation, a public beat-down. They clear out this beautiful ritual space, put eight- and ten-year-old kids in the middle of it, slow everything way down, then make each kid, one at a time, fail in front of siblings, peers, authority figures, and strangers, right when they're getting old enough to understand public shame. The walk back to the dugout after a strike-out isn't even the worst of it, it's the ball that squeaks past your glove, the one you're sure you could have gotten to, the one you'll never see again all season, which is as far into the future as your young mind can see. As a Commissioner of Major League Baseball once said, baseball is "designed to break your heart."[3]

Baseball was my outdoor version of Ranulfo's casino and dreams: a completely beautiful or crazy game of chance, depending on the way you looked at it. And baseball allowed me to see great metaphysical significance in seemingly trivial details, the universe in a grain of sand on the base paths.

Of course, even in my most mystical moments, I still knew our risk-taking was fundamentally different. Ranulfo was literally risking his home, as collateral. I wasn't risking anything. No matter what happened, I would have two homes: the one I lived in and the one on the baseball field. But the emotional resonances with Ranulfo still felt real, and by this point cause and effect were getting harder to distinguish. All I know is that, by the summer of 2007, two years after leaving Andy's funeral and walking into Ranulfo's store, I was completely in love with baseball, and so were my three sons. Everything about it seemed bathed in a magical light: hitting soft line-drives at the park and watching my sons dive for them in the thick grass, playing catch with one son by the outfield fence while another played in his Little League game, getting ice cream at the snack bar on warm summer nights, consoling my boys after the painful strike-outs and cheering their big hits. If these were my last moments on earth, I was spending them exactly the way I wanted, the same way Andy would have with his kids. Baseball, like the corner store, allowed me to be with my family, yet part of something much larger than the suburbs. I had found risk-taking and transcendence I could believe in.

Everything was set in motion by the first real catch I had with my oldest son, Zach. Up until that point, the closest I'd ever gotten to having a catch with him was throwing a sticky ball directly at the Velcro in his tiny glove. Before that, he mostly played with toys and dressed up like Batman, and before that, he mostly got colicky and screamed his head off while I paced with him in my arms and begged him to stop. But when he turned six, we were finally ready to step outside and have a real catch.

On a spring afternoon in 2002, having broken in Zach's new glove during the rainy Oregon winter, we went in the backyard and I tossed him a rubber ball. To my amazement, he caught it almost every time, his little fingers squeezing the glove, a big smile spreading across his face.

I thought back to the time a few years earlier when Rich, my cousin and Andy's older brother, threw a beach ball to Zach, still a toddler, wobbling around in pajamas with attached booties and a zipper up the front. Zach instinctively reached out and clutched the giant ball, wider than his little body.

Rich's eyes widened. "Did you see that?!"

I hadn't thought much of it. I just assumed all toddlers could catch beach balls. Now, seeing Zach's catches in the backyard, I was starting to wonder.

Zach pleaded, "Daddy, throw it higher!"

I threw the rubber ball higher and higher, 30, 40, 50 feet straight up in the air. Zach and his brother Liam, five years old at the time, had recently been debating who was bigger, Godzilla or dinosaurs, a debate that Liam settled by saying, "Well, nothing's bigger than the sky."[4] Seeing that rubber ball silhouetted against the vast sky, I had to agree.

At times like these, I felt like we had tapped into the most elemental forces in the world.[5] Baseball didn't just have roots in America's agricultural era, or British rounders, or even the stick-and-ball games of ancient Egypt, played, fittingly, in honor of the goddess of love and joy. Baseball had roots in hunter-gathering, the very origins of humanity. As one of my graduate school professors liked to say, "Early hominids were friendly, stupid, and good to eat. How in the world did they ever make it?" The answer wasn't baseball, but close: sharing. Returning the ball to each other, back and forth, we were echoing that history of reciprocity, the key reason we hominids made it out of the Pleistocene. Just as I loved it when Ranulfo talked about understanding time and eternity, I loved being connected through baseball to something so universal and primordial. I saw in baseball the essential narrative of human history.

After that day, Zach dedicated himself to the game. If I had had more influence, Zach probably would have been a musician. One of his first words was "Cuna!", his garbled imitation of the Spanish word *cumbia*, the high-energy Colombian music I constantly blasted in the house. We later got Zach a guitar, but he didn't take to it. He took to baseball, instead, and his brothers followed his lead.

By the summer of 2007, all three boys lived and breathed baseball. Every night I read them bedtime stories from *Chicken Soup for the Baseball Fan's Soul*—all they had to say was, "Daddy, a little *Chickey*"?—then they'd sleep with their gloves and baseball cards under the covers, wake up, go to the breakfast table, pore over their baseball cards, move to the living room and read library books about baseball history, then go out in the yard and have a catch or play pickle, tagging out the player, usually the youngest brother, caught between two bases.[6]

Those little games of pickle replicated another essential aspect of humanity: the chase. As hunter-gatherers, chasing and being chased is what we hominids have spent more than 90% of our roughly 2 million years on earth doing. By contrast, agriculture is a very recent development, an innovation from the last 10,000 years, with industrialism even more of an aberration, a tiny blip in human history. As much as we've changed, as malleable as culture is, humans still remember the Great Chase, which is why to this day the single most commonly reported dream is the one where we're being chased by someone or something.[7] Similarly, in sports as varied as lacrosse, soccer, football, baseball, and basketball, the key excitement comes from seeing players being chased, running just one step ahead of their opponents. And Hollywood action movies wouldn't do so well, at home and abroad, if it weren't for high-speed chases, more images of humans fleeing the nearest predator, albeit a predator driving a 1000 cc motorcycle and equipped with high-tech gadgets.[8] As one anthropologist said, "Perhaps the most elemental fear for all humanity is to be trapped in an unbearable situation and unable to get away."[9]

Baseball takes these elemental aspects of humanity, the chase and sharing, and turns them into art. In Spanish the outfield is even called *los jardines*, the gardens. I love that. "Garden" is the perfect term because baseball is also about home, cycles, and cultivated beauty. I used to think that all the rapturous writing about baseball was poetic hyperbole, but when I started to play catch with my kids, I found out that the exaltation was entirely accurate and justified.

All my kids knew was that baseball felt right. Sometimes, during a game of pickle or a leisurely catch in the yard, they spontaneously broke out singing, "Rockin' around the Christmas tree!," or "Just hear those sleigh bells ringing, ting-ting-tingling, too!" Thanks to baseball, summertime felt like Christmas.

I myself listened over and over to Van Morrison sing about gardens and beauty: "Come in my garden…We can just sit and talk and feel…Till it's truth and it's beauty and it's grace." Van's rapturous trances sounded especially good at the end of another radiant summer day, doing the dishes while my kids played in the next room, drinking wine with my wife in the garden as the sun set, pulling her in close.

And the reverberations kept going after the lights went out. I woke up many nights with music running in the back of my mind, an elusive soundtrack for my dreams. I couldn't quite tell what the dream-music was trying to tell me. It might have been a warning, like the voice in one of Socrates' recurring dreams that exhorted him to make music and practice it. Of course, Socrates, being a stubborn, one-dimensional philosopher—what Nietzsche called a "rational despot"—ignored this dream, even though he had it over and over. He kept right on haranguing and antagonizing the citizens of Athens, until they threw him in jail and sentenced him to death. Then, shortly before he drank the fatal hemlock, the dream returned to Socrates in his jail cell, and he finally listened. In his last hours on earth, when it was too late, Socrates played the flute and composed poetry for Apollo. I had nothing in common with Socrates, except two things: I loved debate and I couldn't play the flute. Maybe the dream-music was telling me to stop spending so much time ripping apart the logic and evidence in academic arguments, to listen more to my heart, to resist the impulse to sacrifice myself by taking a final stand. I couldn't be sure. The answer seemed to be right there whenever I woke up, like a beautiful fish gliding past my feet in the water, darting away whenever I tried to grab it.

I wasn't frustrated, though. I was blissed out on gratitude. My wife and I had gone to the mountains of Ecuador and survived. I'd learned Quichua, which was like learning how to speak full sentences in multivariable calculus…backwards. We'd gotten by for years on scholarships and my wife's teaching salary, living in tiny apartments. We'd had three kids, and survived all the wailing and crying, the vomiting and sleepless nights. Despite the tough market for academic jobs, I got the job at Willamette, and then tenure in 2006. I didn't end up like the thousands of Ph.D.s who got downsized and shoved out of academia, as universities turned more and more to part-time workers, like Walmart and just about every other company in the early 2000s. I had a house, a close family...even this cute new thing called an iPod to store and play the family's CDs. We'd made it.

But if everything was so good, why were my eyes filling with tears at strange moments?

Maybe my gratitude at the goodness of life was pushing me in strange directions. Maybe I'd opened myself up too much, and my tears were the few raindrops that fall on your face just before a hurricane rips the roof off your house and destroys everything.

Fortunately, nobody suspected anything because I hid my tears in the dark, but on a trip to the baseball card store that summer, I got a glimpse of what my future might look like if I couldn't pull back.

For my boys, the card store was a magical place filled with mysterious possibilities. Its single room was jam-packed with cardboard boxes and plastic binders stacked up to the ceiling, each one filled with hundreds of baseball cards, tiny portals into other times and places, definitive proof of miraculous feats performed by giants who once roamed the earth. My kids studied the cards with great reverence and concentration, as if trying to crack a sacred hieroglyphic code. They had started to grasp the code's underlying logic—it stretched back in time and connected far-flung places like Seattle, Cleveland, and Atlanta with Japan, Venezuela, and the Dominican Republic—but many pieces were still missing and required more intensive study.[10]

As they worked through the cards, calculating how many they could buy with their quarters and crumpled dollar bills, two other customers took notice.

One man, about 50 years old, leaned in and asked Zach, "So why are you interested in Larry Doby?"

He'd overheard Zach talking to his brothers about Doby, which wasn't hard to do because the store was the size of a small kitchen, and we were the only ones in it.

With his delicate chin and eyes half hidden under his baseball cap, Zach shyly answered, "Because he was the first black player in the American League, and my grandfather really likes him."[11]

Zach was referring to my father-in-law, who taught the boys about important baseball moments, like when Lou Gehrig, forced to quit baseball because he was dying from a fatal disease, told a stadium of fans, "Yet today I consider myself the luckiest man alive." My father-in-law, like Lou Gehrig and Andy, had a disease that attacks the nervous system,

Parkinson's. The very last thing Andy whispered to me at his house, as I lingered at the front door next to him in his wheelchair, was, "I'm praying for your father-in-law."

I was actually surprised to hear Zach mention race. His classmates and friends were so uniformly white and Latino that I didn't even think he knew the word "black" could be used to describe another person. When I'd asked him why he liked Jackie Robinson, he simply stated, "Because he was so fast he could steal home." Race wasn't a factor in Jackie's greatness, nor was it when Zach and his brothers realized that some contemporary players came from other countries and spoke other languages. They were surprised when they first heard Ichiro Suzuki speaking Japanese on TV, and the foreign language added to Ichiro's mystique, but the only language that really mattered to my boys consisted of batting averages, number of steals, on-base percentages, and other measures of excellence. To them, Ichiro was just Ichiro, or, as Liam liked to say, "Ich baby."

And these two customers—the other one had by now looked away from the game playing on the TV mounted on the wall—spoke that language, too.

The first one ventured, "And what do you know about Steve Carlton? Or Ernie Banks?"

Zach mumbled each player's team and major feats from earlier decades, then looked back down at his cards, hoping the interruption was over so he could go back to work. But the older guys were just getting started.

"This kid knows!" the first guy said. All I could do was smile. If they had started testing me, they would have quickly realized that I hardly knew anything about baseball. I was just happy to be allowed a second chance this late in life.

The two men, total strangers, were so excited they started putting free stuff in my kids' hands, cards and posters of players from the under-$3 bin.

Now that they had all three boys smiling and paying attention, they peppered them with stories about players of old and more questions, to which the kids obliged with more succinct, correct answers.

When the men looked at me in amazement, I said, "I guess these cards really work."

As we left, the second man, Kenny, large and pudgy, followed us out the door and kept talking, imparting advice to my three little boys.

"Don't get into trouble. Stay in school. And don't drink," he said, standing on the sidewalk in front of the store.

Zach gave a quick little nod, though he probably didn't understand what Kenny was talking about. Drink what? Soda? How could anyone leave elementary school?

Liam and Petie had escaped by now to the car, parked a few feet away, already placing cards in their large, three-ring binders and discussing possible trades.

Kenny continued, "Because I was a drunk. And I lost my wife and I lost my kids...."

Suddenly Kenny's eyes filled up with tears.

"Uh oh, Kenny's going to cry," he said, wiping tears from his cheeks.

Zach stood there quietly, without moving or looking away, waiting for Kenny to continue or one of us to say he could leave.

Promising to show us the key to survival, Kenny took a printed card out of his wallet and read it to us. "God grant me the serenity to accept the things I cannot change...."

When we finally got in the car, I waited for Zach to say something to his brothers about Kenny's tears, and I started trying to think what I could say in his defense.

But Zach just went in the backseat and marveled at his new treasures.

Then, a couple hours later, while having a catch after dinner, Zach said to me, "Daddy, you remember Kenny at the card store?"

"Sure," I said, bracing myself for some awkward questions about divorce, alcohol, tears, fathers.

"Well, he told me he had a Mickey Mantle card," Zach said, then threw the ball back.

I just prayed I wouldn't end up like Kenny, even if he did have a Mickey Mantle card.

Either way, I was too enthralled with the goodness of life to try to stop Ranulfo from getting the bakery.

Between Ranulfo's garbage dreams and my tears, we were quite a team. All our defenses were down as we headed straight into the jaws of destruction.

NOTES

1. My mother was so touched when I told her what happened that she later sent an email to Sick Bastard to thank him for coming to the funeral and honoring Andy. This is how she began the email: "Are you the Sick Bastard? God bless you!" It cracked me up to see the way my 76-year-old mother respectfully and innocently addressed the email to "Sick Bastard"—and inadvertently added the word "the" in front of that nickname, turning him into "the Sick Bastard." His real name, we found out later, is Scott McCauley, and, in the years since the funeral, he has gone to baseball games with my cousins Billy and Rich, honoring Andy and continuing the healing. He may be a sick bastard, but he's a good guy.
2. Kierkegaard (1843, 44).
3. Giamatti (1998, 7).
4. These quotations come from my family journal.
5. On the Egyptian game, see Thorn (2011, 57).
6. Canfield (2001).
7. Rock (2004, 68).
8. I first became aware of this connection to our hominid past after reading Lee Drummond's discussion of Hollywood chase scenes, such as in James Bond movies. Drummond writes, "While any kind of chase gets our attention, we still display our keenest interest in chases of the sort that Bond movies have made famous: a nimble, quick-witted, dashing character eludes his powerful pursuer and turns to dish out a little misery of his own" (1996, 141).
9. Behar mentions the primacy of the chase in an essay about her son's leg injuries, and in making sense of her own concern with those injuries, she makes a connection with her relationship to Cuba: "As a child of immigrants who'd made a quick decision to leave Cuba, and as a child immigrant myself, I knew how important it was to be able to flee at a moment's notice, to escape danger, to escape countries in revolution, countries in the midst of strife, war, and suffering" (2013, 64–65).
10. There are a lot of great books about baseball, but, in my opinion, the best one about baseball cards is Josh Wilker's *Cardboard Gods* (2010). Mixing painful childhood memories with insightful ruminations on specific baseball cards in his collection, Wilker captures what those little cards can mean to a young kid.
11. Zach was referring to his maternal grandfather, William McIvor, who likes to teach his grandchildren about baseball history.

CHAPTER 17

Plan B

August–December, 2007

I only met the general contractor, Dave Hedding, once over the summer, when he breezed through the store late one afternoon. He had curly brown hair, medium build, tan arms, construction boots, well-worn jeans, an old pick-up truck, and a ready smile. What Dave didn't have were Spanish language skills or much time for Ranulfo's remodel. As I followed him and Ranulfo around the store, he told me he was in the middle of a big construction job down at the coast, a couple hours away, and he had some other things still going on around Portland, too. A few minutes later he was gone.

After the architect finished all his drawings in August, Dave said—actually, Antonio said it for Dave—that Ranulfo and Pablo now needed to hire an engineer, at a cost of $12,000, and once they had the engineer's plans, the construction could begin. The engineer part made sense, since knocking down walls would affect the structural integrity of the building, but I was alarmed when I found out Dave still hadn't given Ranulfo a written estimate for the total construction costs. Dave just had Antonio pass on a verbal message that the whole job was going to cost $140,000, which doubled his initial estimate, supposedly because of what he'd learned from the architect's drawings.

Once again, I tried to suppress my inner doubter. I reminded myself that Ranulfo and Pablo trusted real people more than legal contracts. They felt better with Antonio, a compatriot from the Mexican countryside, a fellow businessman in the Salem area, someone fluent in machinery, construction, and Mexican and American cultures, someone there to guide the process to completion. From this point of view, a written estimate was an unnecessary, legalistic custom for Americans who sue each other all the time, rather than rely on honor, reputation, and personal relationships. It was like when Ranulfo allowed an older Mexican man to set up his taco truck in the parking lot of El Palmar. No written contract was drawn up. They just talked it out, and did right by each other.

I thought I knew something about this alternative view, having spent ten years researching the ways people in Ecuador view writing.[1] But that research was the *problem*: it made me even more of a cultural relativist than I usually was, and, by most people's standards, I would have already been considered an extreme relativist, unwilling to condemn almost any cultural practices, at least while doing research. Sticking to this habit, I kept telling myself that I needed to see the lack of a written estimate and the dependence on one's word the way Pablo and Ranulfo saw these things within their cultural framework, so for many months I didn't intervene. It took me a long time to realize and accept that this situation could also be viewed from a more legalistic American angle. After all, Dave, as a professional contractor, not to mention a white guy, was part of the legalistic American system, so he should have already provided a written estimate and contract, whether or not Ranulfo asked for one.[2] To make the cultural lines blurrier, Ranulfo *had* finally asked for a written estimate in August, but never got one. At the end of September, Dave finally answered that he couldn't give a written estimate until Ranulfo got the engineer plans. So Dave was failing to follow the basic rules of his own culture and business, and Ranulfo was getting frustrated. This was my opening. My job was to defend Ranulfo whenever possible, so maybe I would be justified in intervening?

Seeing Ranulfo's growing frustration, I finally did. I suggested that he should get a second estimate, reminding him that doing so was common American practice on big construction projects. Of course, this was a risk. We both knew this move would probably upset Antonio and Dave by threatening to cut them out of the remodel after months of planning, but Ranulfo decided it was worth a try, reasoning that he didn't have to go with the new estimate, and just having it would motivate Dave to move more quickly.

I still wondered if I'd gone too far. Maybe Dave was right: he couldn't give an accurate estimate without the engineer's plans. Maybe my doubting instincts had spun out of control. I had vowed to defend Ranulfo on his long punt return, but maybe, like a confused Sancho Panza, I'd barreled into the sidelines and taken out one of the coaches on *our own team*. Maybe this mess would end up like Roberto's car problem, with hurt class and racial feelings all around. Maybe Ranulfo was right: I should just stick to teaching.

The search for a second estimate certainly didn't help my relationship with Antonio, who suspected my meddling was endangering his commission. When one of his visits to the store in November coincided with mine, he gave me an icy stare and barely mumbled a greeting.

But Antonio's reaction only confirmed my suspicions and emboldened me. Standing in my usual spot next to Ranulfo, with Antonio a few feet away, on the customer side of the counter, I asked Antonio point blank, "So when is Dave going to give us the estimate?"

Antonio repeated that Dave couldn't give the estimate until he got the engineer's plans, then sang Dave's praises at great length.

"You have to understand that Dave is a great guy, he's an expert, he knows what he's doing. I've seen it so many times before."

"I'm sure he is," I said as politely as I could. While Ranulfo rang up a customer, Antonio pretended to check something on the aisle with chilies and tortillas, then returned to the counter as soon as the customer left.

"And these other guys that Ranulfo is talking to now can't handle a job this big," Antonio continued. "They just don't have the experience that Dave does. But he's also not going to charge a lot like other contractors."

"Hmm, sounds good," I said, not admitting that, in fact, the Mexican contractors Ranulfo had contacted all said the job was too big for them.

Fortunately, Ranulfo came to the rescue.

"Pete," he said, turning towards me on his right, "we need to go to Mexico together. Lupe wants to go at Christmas time, but I'll be busy then, so how about we all go this March, instead?"

Órale, I said, always ready for another trip back to Mexico. We'd discussed this plan before, but I couldn't tell if Ranulfo was bringing it up now to defuse the situation, or to needle Antonio, who hated it when we went off topic, or both.

"If we go in March, we can see the pilgrimage for the Saint of Carácuaro," Ranulfo said, referring to a famous saint near his village, the one his parents venerate. "The pilgrims walk for days to get to the church, and then the last part they walk on their knees, and get all bloody. Can you handle it, Pete?" Ranulfo asked with a mischievous smile.

"Oh, sure," I said, not wanting to show any weakness in front of Antonio. "I can do the walk, but maybe I'll skip the bloody knees."

Antonio was the only one not laughing. I was facing Ranulfo by now, not looking across the counter at Antonio, but I sensed he wanted to bolt down an aisle again, until this nonsense had passed. Finally Antonio managed to say we should take a plane, since it would be faster, but Ranulfo and I preferred the idea of a slow road trip, like in that classic movie *Por mis pistolas*, where Cantinflas travels to the U.S. with a horse and donkey. While Cantinflas talks a mile a minute and dances circles around the border patrol agent, his trusty donkey quietly walks through the gate and starts grazing, which leads the agent to announce in bad, stilted Spanish, "I am sorry, but I am going to have to charge you a fine of one dollar for entering U.S. territory illegally." Cantinflas, as always, has the perfect response: "Then just charge the donkey—I haven't moved from my side of the border!"

And then there was *El Profe*, "The Professor," where Cantinflas rides into town on a cart pulled by two mules, but the cart driver calls them "horses," because they get insulted and won't move if he calls them "mules."

Antonio was getting worn out. Realizing we were going to keep joking around, he finally excused himself and left for the day.

* * *

As the weather got colder and more weeks passed, estimates still didn't materialize. Ranulfo couldn't find a second estimate, Dave didn't return phone calls anymore, and Antonio visited less and less often.

At first Ranulfo tried to maintain his good humor and faith in time. He said, "We have to hang on to time, you know? It's like Mexican people hanging onto the bottom of an airplane, the way they'll do anything to sneak into the U.S." But after a while he was ready to look for other options. Finally, in early December, he asked me to look for contractors in the Yellow Pages.

I immediately had flashbacks to the Roberto car fight, a fiasco that also started innocently enough with the Yellow Pages. I feared getting caught in the middle again. Worse, if I influenced Ranulfo's choice in any way, I would later feel terrible if the contractor over-charged or something else went wrong. I couldn't handle that kind of responsibility. I would make the initial phone calls, but that was it.

I opened up the telephone book to the contractor section, and asked Ranulfo with my eyes half-closed, "Should I just blindly pick one?"

Ranulfo said, "Yes, and remember, I want the three B's: *bonito, barato, y bueno*, beautiful, cheap, and good."

"Sure, no problem," I said, thinking to myself, *This could be a problem*.

The first guy I talked to said he couldn't do the job, but he recommended another company, Dalke Construction, so I called them and got into a conversation with the project manager, Jim Schiess, who said the job sounded manageable and, yes, he could give an estimate without any engineering plans.

When I told him he'd be dealing with Ranulfo, the owner, Jim asked how I knew him, the same question other officials and technicians asked whenever I made phone calls for Ranulfo. If I thought about it too much, as I sometimes did while waiting on hold, the question stumped me. What one word or phrase could describe what I was to Ranulfo? His friend and bodyguard? His liaison and personal anthropologist? His boxing trainer, as Ranulfo sometimes put it? I was tempted to say, "I don't know what you call it, but if you mess with this guy, I'll be your worst nightmare."

Instead, I said, "Oh, I'm just translating the Spanish, but you'll see Ranulfo has good English...."

Most people let it go at that point, but Jim followed up with another question. "So are you bilingual?"

"Yes, umm, hmm," I said, resisting the urge to call my Spanish level "fluent" and reserve the term "bilingual" for someone who has spoken both languages since childhood.

"I'm just asking because my son goes to a bilingual school in West Salem."

"Oh, really? Which one?" I asked.

"It's called West Salem Language Academy...."

"Mine, too!" I said, excited by the coincidence that we had kids at the same small, low-profile school in town.

When he reported that his son was in the third grade and I said so was my youngest, Petie, he said, "This is wild...Petie's coming to my house today for my son's birthday party."

That was all Ranulfo needed to hear. As soon as I hung up and described the conversation, he said, "It was destiny."

I tried to lower his expectations, pointing out I'd never actually met Jim in person, but Ranulfo said, "That's OK, it means there's *confianza*, trust.

He knows you live here in Salem, and your kids go to the same school, so you're not going away. That's what makes both sides do the right thing."

So much for not getting involved.

* * *

Monday morning didn't start out well. I had been up late the night before marking papers, so I slept through several snoozes on the alarm clock, which cut out the few minutes I had reserved to walk the dog before driving the kids to school. And when I walked out of my house, I discovered a bigger problem: I had no car. My neighbor was supposed to lend me his Honda Pilot that day, since our old Dodge minivan was in the shop, but he'd absent-mindedly taken his Pilot to work. I frantically called one of the moms, who agreed to come and get the kids. Then I had to get to the 9:30am construction appointment at El Palmar, so I hopped on the only transportation available, my wife's 20-year-old mountain bike from her college days, and pedaled like a madman across town, cutting through the park, past the hospital and my college, up some residential streets, along the sidewalks on Market Street, then left at the Dairy Queen.

Just as I was locking the bike in front of the store, a Dalke Construction truck pulled into the parking lot. Jim got out and headed toward me, the only gringo in sight. Hoping he didn't notice that my bike had no bar in the middle, I strode quickly over to meet him. He had light brown hair, and wore a clean, blue Gore-Tex jacket, jeans, and black leather shoes.

I introduced Jim to Pablo, who had just walked out of the store on his way to the laundromat next door. After Pablo greeted Jim in English, he turned to me and said in Spanish, "So this is the guy who will take care of us because he's your friend?"

"Yes," I said, not bothering to equivocate or point out Jim might turn out to be a bum like Dave, and if so, I couldn't take responsibility for him.

By this point Ranulfo had also arrived, and told Jim in English what he was hoping to do with the remodel. Jim got right down to business, circling the building inside and out, jotting notes on his clipboard, sometimes asking brief, pointed questions about the walls and our plans. Twice he told us, "This is a *big* job."

When Jim left, Ranulfo said, "I like him. He's honest. The first time Dave came here, he said the whole job wouldn't be that hard, probably only $60,000."

But now he was getting worried about the cost. He said he wouldn't be able to eat that afternoon, then laughed, recalling the way his daughter Laura always criticized his cooking. "No, Papi, you're no good!" he said, imitating her voice. "It's like when I sing and she comes in from the other room and tells me to stop."

* * *

A few days before Christmas we got Jim's written estimate—$392,000!

The price was double what Ranulfo had planned, but he wasn't prepared to take it as an immediate death blow to his dream. Studying Jim's detailed estimate line by line, he saw that if they only knocked out one small side wall, they could still gain about 800 square feet, possibly enough space to put in a small bakery for under $200,000. If everything were rearranged just right, there might still be a way to salvage the dream.

"I'm going to have to talk to Pablo. We're going to have to think really hard about this," Ranulfo said.

NOTES

1. Wogan (2004a).
2. As Sutton showed in an honest, probing account of his early fieldwork experience in Greece (1998), such seemingly minor issues—in his case, childrearing views and practices—are what tend to challenge the anthropologist's relativism, rather than more blatant cultural differences. As he says, such moments become even messier and challenging owing to the hybrid mixing of cultures through globalization. Having read Sutton's article multiple times, I should have known all this, but legal contracts were a blind spot for me for a long time.

CHAPTER 18

Mr. Success or Mr. Worthless?

January, 2008

Ranulfo faced a tough dilemma. The bakery costs kept rising, yet if he pulled the plug now, he'd be giving up his whole dream of baking bread with his wife, creating with his hands, nourishing his community the way his parents did with the tortilla mill, accepting America's embrace, the bank loans filled with trust and communion. Giving up now would mean all his hard work had been for nothing.

Ranulfo kept running the numbers over and over, but they had gotten so big that they seemed unhinged from reality. If he could afford $200,000 for the bakery remodel and equipment, then why not $225,000, or $240,000, or $302,877? Where exactly was the breaking point? He'd entered a surreal realm.

If only I could have contacted the ultimate source of economic mystery, Wall Street, I might have gotten some more direct answers. Throughout the fall of 2007, they had experienced clear signs of impending danger—spikes in mortgage default rates, banks like Citigroup, Merrill Lynch, and UBS reporting staggering losses of about $8 billion each on the value of their mortgage securities, traders betting more and more heavily that the mortgage market was about to explode.[1] But I never even noticed these problems in the mainstream press. And if I had asked a Wall Street investment banker his advice, he probably would have given me the same

"Everything is fine, nothing to worry about" line that banks fed in public statements to their investors and shareholders throughout 2007, even when they saw the values on mortgage securities sinking fast, the building caving in.[2] I stayed quiet and waited for Ranulfo's decision.

To make up his mind about the bakery, Ranulfo consulted his dreams, one last time in the first days of the new year, 2008.

Sitting in Ranulfo's car in the parking lot of Costco, just before heading inside to buy computer wires together, we caught each other up on recent news—my family trip to California, the presents our kids got for Christmas, the way somebody broke into the bill-change machine in the laundromat a few days ago. Then Ranulfo described the following dream, which occurred just a few nights earlier, on New Year's Eve:

I was working at the nursery, cleaning, raking up the leaves on the ground, and bringing in new plants to go out on the loading dock, and this friend of mine told me he had to fire me. But he was crying... And I said, "What's wrong?" He felt terrible. He said he didn't want to fire me, but the bosses said he had to. And I told him, "Don't worry, life is so beautiful." And there were these other two workers, guys I knew, who said, "¡Ese es el problema—se queja mucho! ¡Córrelo!" He's the problem—he complains a lot! Fire him!. I think they were mad at me because I'd been saying we have a bottleneck here, we can do better.

Although this dream recapitulated Ranulfo's real-life firing from the nursery, he took it as a sign that 2008 was going to be a *good* year. He said, "I liked it because this was the first time in a dream where I was *el villano, el inútil*, the villain, the worthless guy. It wasn't like the other dream where I was picking up trash and didn't know if I was working at the nursery or not. And I was flexible. I accepted my role as the villain, like a soccer player who can play multiple positions."

Then Ranulfo transformed the dream into a joke. "I'm going to get a tee shirt, and on the front it will say, *Mister Éxito*, Mr. Success, and on the back it will say, *Mister Inútil*, Mr. Worthless. And if someone comes up to me, I'll turn around and say, 'Who do you want to talk with, Mr. Success or Mr. Worthless?'"

I laughed, oscillating once again between Ranulfo's contradictory images. Even at this penultimate moment, Ranulfo used humor to consider all angles, to keep from burning up with his own ambitions. More like Ishmael than Ahab in this regard, he approached extreme peril with what Melville called a "genial, desperado philosophy."[3]

Yet even humor wasn't a completely safe harbor. In Ranulfo's hands, jokes often started as fantasies, then turned into serious plans. He could be joking about Kalimán one minute, then end up trying to fly off a cliff the next.

Ranulfo's dreams were like the gold doubloon that Ahab nailed to the masthead—open to wildly divergent interpretations. One sailor sees Ahab's doubloon as a series of zodiac signs, another as simply enough money to buy 960 cigars, and another as a prophecy of the future, leading Ahab to remark that "this round gold is but the image of the rounder globe, which, like a magician's glass, to each and every man but mirrors back his own mysterious self."[4] Or as Simmel said, money's limited vocabulary provokes one's imagination and gives rise to boundless "allusions, references, and psychological overtones," so that paradoxically its wealth results from its poverty.[5] Presumably the poet Wallace Stevens was getting at the same idea, how money's emptiness allows people to project an infinite range of meanings onto it, when he famously stated, "Money is a kind of poetry."

Ranulfo used dreams to grapple with his own poetic mysteries, but he kept getting divergent answers.

Smiling, Ranulfo concluded, "I'm realizing that sometimes you need to be *el tonto*, the fool. That's what makes the world run is *tontísimo*. They're running out of oil, but we'll never run out of idiots."

NOTES

1. On the reported losses at Citibank, Merrill Lynch, and UBS, see, for example, Tett (2009, 203–207). On the investors betting against the mortgage market, see Lewis (2010).
2. For example, Ralph Cioffi, the man with the two Ferraris and the head of the two Bear Stearns hedge funds that went bankrupt in 2007, misled investors throughout 2006 and 2007 about the nature of the funds' holdings and strategies, as stated by William Cohan, a business journalist: "Cioffi had not been avoiding residential mortgage-backed securities, as he had suggested to his investors on their monthly statements. Actually, he had done precisely the opposite and had started to load up on these toxic securities at exactly the wrong moment" (Cohan 2009, 312). Speaking about the firm in general, Cohan writes: "Of course, in terms of what the public was told, these problems might as well have been happening on Mars. In the firm's 2006 Annual Report, released in mid-February 2007, the theme was 'Eighty-three years of profitability' and 'Twenty years as a public company'" (Cohan 2009, 320). However, courts have not found that Cioffi's behavior was illegal. For an account of why Cioffi was acquitted in a federal criminal trial, including Cohan's analysis of how the prosecution blew it, see "Bear Stearns Trial: How the Scapegoats Escaped," Dealbook, *New York Times*, November 12, 2009, http://dealbook.nytimes.com/2009/11/12/bear-stearns-trial-how-the-scapegoats-escaped/. Accessed October 16, 2016. As for investors who trusted in the AAA ratings, they have to take a large share of the blame because they should have known that the ratings weren't very reliable, given that the investment banks paid for them.
3. Yet, even for Ishmael and others, Melville says this genial outlook was not permanent, but, rather, a "wayward mood" in a "time of extreme tribulation" (Melville 1851, Chapter 49, "The Hyena").
4. Melville (1851, Chapter 99, "The Doubloon"). Ahab famously interprets the doubloon as being a representation of himself ("all are Ahab"), but, by highlighting his line about "the magician's glass," I'm giving him credit for also holding a relativistic respect for the multiplicity of possible readings and the mystery of the individual. This relativistic view is usually associated with Pip (who says, "I

look, you look, he looks"), but there's also at least an undercurrent of it in Ahab, who has a special affinity with Pip.
5. As noted earlier, Graeber overlaps to a certain extent with Simmel in his discussion of money's future orientation, unlimited potential uses, and lack of specific content. I especially like the way Simmel sums up by comparing money with language and noting the paradox of emptiness leading to fullness: "As in the case of languages such as French, which have a limited vocabulary, the need to employ the same expression for different things makes possible a wealth of allusions, references, and psychological overtones, and one might almost say that their wealth results from their poverty; so the absence of any inner significance of money engenders the abundance of its practical uses, and indeed provides the impulse to fill its infinite conceptual categories with new formations, to give new content to its form, because it is never a conclusion but only a transitional point for each content" (1907, 212–213). Simmel's view also dovetails with the previous note's discussion of Melville's depiction of the doubloon as being open to so many interpretations, like a projection screen (Melville 1851, Chapter 99, "The Doubloon").

CHAPTER 19

Financial Crisis

January, 2008–January, 2011

A couple weeks later, in mid-January, 2008, Ranulfo made up his mind: he decided not to get the bakery, after all. He didn't know it at the time, but that decision saved him from certain ruin.

The decision didn't come from a dream, either. It came from Ranulfo's cost calculations and the advice of Jim Schiess, the general contractor. While inspecting the store, Jim told Ranulfo, "You're going to spend a lot of money just to get a little bit of additional space. If I were you, I'd just take that money and buy a separate building." Ranulfo had already been having second thoughts about the bakery, and Jim's comment tipped the scales.

Ranulfo trusted Jim not only because his son went to the same elementary school as mine, but also because he could tell Jim wasn't trying to rip him off. By encouraging Ranulfo to just buy a separate building, Jim had talked Ranulfo out of hiring and paying him about $200,000. Looking back later, Ranulfo said, *Es gente honesta, fue mi ángel guardián.* "He's an honest person, he was my guardian angel."[1]

He didn't say the same about Dave and Antonio, but in their own bungling ways, they, too, saved the day. If they had been more organized, the bakery construction would have started over the summer, and Ranulfo would have headed into the Financial Crisis a few months later with a fatal load of debt tied around his neck.

Of course, Ranulfo was deeply disappointed not to get the bakery. His dream was crushed. He wouldn't get to work side by side with his wife, making pastries together with their hands. But once the economy crashed, he would realize this decision saved him from ruin.

The crash unfolded over the next few months. The economy got shaken by the collapse of investment bank Bear Stearns in March, then went into a complete free-fall in September because of the bankruptcy of Lehman Brothers and news that AIG, a huge insurance company, was about to go under, too, removing the major safety net for the investment banks' toxic mortgage deals and setting off panic among money-managers and investors. Gillian Tett, an anthropology Ph.D. and reporter for the *Financial Times*, later wrote, "Around the world, stock markets collapsed, wiping $600 billion off global equity prices in just thirty-six hours....As investors confronted these triple shocks, many panicked to such an extent that they completely withdrew from the market. Almost overnight, liquidity dried up in a host of different debt markets."

It was like the bank runs of the Great Depression, except this time it wasn't ordinary citizens demanding their money back, it was fellow bankers. And, as big as they were, the investment banks couldn't pay up because they had only kept $1 million in cash or collateral for every $40 million they lent out or spent on the stock market, gambling recklessly in order to make themselves richer than any banks in U.S. history. This was a bank run of the highest order, the economic equivalent of a heart attack. Once the main arteries seized up, the trouble spread to the big investors and money managers, the ones who normally supplied blood to the heart. As Tett said, "A run on the entire system had started. As panic mounted, hedge funds and banks rushed to sell any assets they could. There were no takers. Markets went haywire, as prices of different assets spiraled upwards and downwards in a manner that appeared completely irrational based on a fundamental economic analysis....Nothing as brutal had been witnessed in the markets since the Wall Street crash of 1929."[2] In the coming weeks, banks with billions of dollars in assets and years of vaunted history suddenly disappeared.

The crash of 2008 proved Ranulfo right: credit is a delicate act of trust, an exquisite social achievement, not a given. Most people, from homeowners taking easy mortgages to investment bankers living on overnight credit markets, had taken credit for granted. If they thought about bank runs at all, they saw them as something out of old black-and-white movies or history books. But, like survivors of the Great

Depression, Ranulfo was acutely aware of the delicate trust that underlay credit. He thought so much about credit that he dreamt about it at night. Now investment bankers felt something akin to his anguish. They couldn't get "credit" in the original Latin sense of *credere*, to get someone to believe in them. They even experienced a form of Ranulfo's battle against time, begging creditors to give them another month or two before demanding payment, swearing they would be good for the money once the markets settled down. Like Ranulfo, they just needed time and a little faith.[3]

They got the time, but lost everyone's faith in the process. In 2008 the government bailed out the banks with $700 billion in taxpayer money. The Treasury Department asked the banks if they would take a loss, but they said "no thanks" and just took the money.[4] The banks only employed a tenth of 1% of the American workforce, whereas small businesses employed 49%, yet the half of the country with real jobs was left to rot, while the tiny mob that just precipitated the Crisis was put back in power and paid millions in bonuses with taxpayer money.[5]

The government bailouts saved the banks, but it was too late for the rest of the economy. The trust, goodwill, and optimism that held the economy together had been lost. Credit dried up and stock values plummeted, even on stable companies that had no connection to housing. Investors started buying gold again, the equivalent of putting money under the mattress. Consumers got scared and stopped purchasing, so companies pulled back on production and laid off workers, leading to a vicious cycle of unemployment and sales losses. Unable to pay their bills, millions of people lost their homes. It was the worst economic crisis since the Great Depression, leading Bruce Springsteen to sing about the "robber barons" who "took our homes, They left our bodies on the plains, The vultures picked our bones."[6]

Springsteen wasn't alone. Most of the political spectrum—Democrats and Republicans, critics and defenders of the free market, Nobel laureates in economics and average citizens—were appalled. They agreed that the bailouts and bonuses violated basic notions of fairness and capitalism's risk–reward system, reinforcing perverse incentives to make similar mistakes in the future.[7] Though not necessarily speaking for all these groups, Occupy Wall Street provided the most public, visible expression of protest. As Springsteen noted with gratitude, "Occupy Wall Street changed the national conversation....Previous to Occupy Wall Street, there was no push back at all saying that this was outrageous—a basic theft...."[8]

Ranulfo didn't attend any political rallies, but he had every right to be mad. He had paid off his entire mortgage, he never took out a business loan he couldn't afford, and his store was not integrally tied to the housing bubble. His customers picked blueberries. They didn't flip houses. In 2008 the bottom didn't suddenly fall out on the blueberry market. Although a few landscapers had benefited from the housing boom, they were a small minority of Ranulfo's customers, not the base.

Nonetheless, El Palmar wasn't spared. As unemployment rose, sales at the store started dropping in 2008 and got worse with each passing month.

One day Ranulfo said, *El tiempo no tiene amigos.* "Time doesn't have friends." He said this matter of factly, but it was one of the saddest things I'd ever heard.

The troubles in the economy spread out like a pool of blood. Failures of small businesses all across the country shot up by 40%.[9] Oregon's unemployment rate in 2009 went up to 10.6%, and small businesses lost 114,306 jobs that year *alone*.[10] Sales at El Palmar dropped so much in 2009, 2010, and 2011 that it cost thousands of dollars to keep the store open. By 2011 they were at the breaking point. The big question was: Could Ranulfo and Pablo survive another year?

Notes

1. Jim had no idea he'd made this much of a difference in Ranulfo's life until years later, when I sent him a draft of this chapter and asked if it was all right to use his full name in it.
2. Tett (2009, 238–239).
3. As another illustration of the crucial role of time in finance, note that there was a raging debate over "mark to marketing accounting," that is, whether the financial firms should have to set the values of their assets according to their current market prices on each particular day.
4. The source here is Neil Barofsky, the head of the investigative unit for the Trouble Asset Relief Program and a Washington outsider, a New York prosecutor with experience with money laundering and fraud. Barofsky (2012, 183–184) notes that the New York Federal Reserve did initially make a halfhearted request for the banks to take a loss, but, not surprisingly, they declined.
5. Small businesses employed 49.37% of the private workforce in 2008, whereas Wall Street employed a mere 0.14%. These percentages are calculated according to statistics given by the Small Business Administration and *The New York Times*. The SBA website states, "Of the 120.9 million nonfarm private sector workers in 2008, small firms employed 59.7 million and large firms employed 61.2 million." Small Business Administration, Office of Advocacy, "Frequently Asked Questions," January 2011. www.sba.gov/sites/default/files/sbfaq.pdf. Accessed July 8, 2012. The 178,000 figure for jobs provided by New York investment banks in 2008 comes from Patrick McGeehan, "City and State Brace for Drop in Wall Street Pay," *New York Times*, N.Y./Region, July 26, 2008.
6. Springsteen, "Death to My Hometown," a song with an Irish-rebel sound on his *Wrecking Ball* album, Columbia Records, 2012. Almost the entire album consists of songs protesting and exposing the devastation of the Financial Crisis. Even the title track, "Wrecking Ball," written to commemorate Giants Stadium in New Jersey before it was torn down, ends up sounding emblematic of the Crisis ("So hold tight to your anger....When your best hopes and desires are scattered to the wind, and hard times come and hard times go...").

7. What especially disturbed economists, regulators, and average Americans was the message the bailout sent to the banks: they're too big to fail, so they can keep taking gigantic risks and creating financial crises at the taxpayer's expense, reinforcing a system of perverse incentives. For example, Barofsky, the head of the TARP investigative unit, was appalled at how easily the Treasury caved into the banks (see Barofsky 2012). It's worth noting that Barofsky is a life-long Democrat who voted for Obama, notwithstanding the critics who later assumed that his views could only be motivated by partisan politics. Or to take another example of critiques that transcend political divides, consider what Russ Roberts, a libertarian, free-market economist, said about the bailouts: "It's historically unprecedented—the transfer of public money to people who are already the richest people in human history." Nobel laureate Joseph Stiglitz, who doesn't usually share Roberts' free-market perspective, agreed when he told Roberts in this same podcast interview: "It was totally unnecessary that we rescued the shareholders and the bondholders and the bankers. If we had played by the rules of capitalism, we would have…contributed less to this problem that everybody recognizes of moral hazard. Because the banks realize that when they gamble, especially these too-big-to-fail banks, if they gamble and win, they walk off with the profits; when they lose, the taxpayer picks up the tab. *I think it was unconscionable.*" "Stiglitz on Inequality," Econtalk podcast, July 9, 2012, http://www.econtalk.org/archives/2012/07/stiglitz_on_ ine.html. Accessed July 20, 2012; emphasis added. While I agree that the Treasury Department could and should have forced the banks to make more concessions, I am also sympathetic to the opposing argument that, under these grave circumstances, the government needed to act quickly and decisively. There were no good options, but certainly a better balance could have been found, especially if they had factored in the loss of faith in Washington and Wall Street that would result from the bailouts. The true costs of that loss of faith became apparent in the unusually acrimonious election season of 2016. Even when I was writing my first drafts of these chapters in 2013 and 2014, I still didn't realize until 2016 how widespread and deep-seated the anger was across the country.

8. Fiachra Gibbons, "Bruce Springsteen: 'What was done to my country was un-American'," *The Guardian*, February 17, 2012, http://www.theguardian.com/music/2012/feb/17/bruce-springsteen-wrecking-ball. Accessed on March 20, 2013.
9. Catherine Clifford, "States with Worst Business Failure Rates," *CNN Money*, May 20, 2011. http://money.cnn.com/2011/05/19/smallbusiness/small_business_state_failure_rates/index.htm. Accessed October 15, 2016.
10. This figure is taken from February, 2009, and comes from the United States Department of Labor, Bureau of Labor Statistics, "Local Area Unemployment Statistics," http://data.bls.gov/timeseries/LASST41000003. Accessed June 4, 2013. On the loss of jobs in Oregon small businesses, see Small Business Administration, Office of Advocacy, "Small Business Profile: Oregon," February 2013. www.sba.gov/sites/default/files/or12.pdf. Accessed October 10, 2016.

CHAPTER 20

Wrecking Ball

Fall, 2008–Fall, 2011

As the growing likelihood of Ranulfo's bankruptcy sank in, my sadness turned to anger. All that immense gratitude converted itself into fury. In my entire life, I had never watched boxing, but suddenly I found myself watching it all the time on YouTube, feeling in my own body every blow given and taken on screen. I started working out at the gym again and shed the extra pounds I had inadvertently put on over the past five or ten years of middle-aged happiness. I found depths of anger that I didn't even know existed, and the scary part was I couldn't tell where they were taking me. I had previously accepted Ranulfo's image of me as his boxing trainer, but now the lines started to blur, especially after I read these words by Kate Sekules, a female boxer, about the union between trainer and boxer: "In books, on TV, fighters use the first person plural—he is not an 'I,' he is a 'we': 'We cut off the corners so he had nowhere to run.' The trainer does it, too: 'We fought hard, but it wasn't enough tonight.' Trainer and fighter are the most intimate team."[1] Those words fit Ranulfo and me. Our team had become so intimate that I felt like I had been personally wounded by the Financial Crisis. No longer content to cheer from the sidelines, I wanted to jump over the ropes and get in the ring to defend Ranulfo.

To focus all my mental sparring and diffuse anger, I kept coming back to one question: Who the hell did this to Ranulfo?

This is the point where someone usually quotes *The Godfather* and says to remember that this is "business," and you shouldn't take it personally. But I don't accept that distinction. I think it's just a lie to make people feel better about the unethical, inhumane things they do at work. Viewers (especially men) are eager to repeat the "strictly business" line from that movie in an attempt to assuage their guilty consciences.

I mean, does anyone really believe that Michael Corleone's motives are "strictly business" when he gets revenge on the guys who broke his jaw and tried to kill his father…*twice?* I never did, but plenty of guys say they do, so I'm going to cite the ultimate authority in this case. I don't mean Nietzsche, who exposed Western civilization's schizophrenic attitudes toward objectivity and vengeance, or Keith Hart, the anthropologist who showed that the separation of supposedly objective rules and subjective feelings is a very recent, Western phenomenon, rooted in the way we set up modern political and economic institutions.[2] No, I'm talking about Michael Corleone in Mario Puzo's original *Godfather* novel. In that book, when someone tries to tell Michael he has to separate business from his personal feelings, he retorts, "It's all personal, every bit of business…They call it business. OK. But it's personal as hell."[3] And then Michael goes on to say he learned this crucial lesson from his father, Don Corleone himself. By conveniently omitting Michael's honest view of subjectivity in the movie, the filmmakers created a huge, appealing lie about the necessary separation of "strictly business" and "personal."

The way I saw it, someone had broken Ranulfo's jaw, and if this was business, I had no problem admitting that I took it very personally and needed to find out who did this to Ranulfo. On the other hand, I wasn't going to accept the first answer to come along. I was appalled by the knee-jerk reactions from people who immediately pointed fingers before doing any investigation, relying, instead, on their pre-conceived notions and moral outrage. If they were on the far left, the cause of the Crisis was obviously greed and evil corporations. If they were on the far right, the obvious cause was the government and poor people. Both sides were completely sure they knew who did it because they were simply applying their usual, one-size-fits-all explanation.

I didn't know if I could make any better sense of the Crisis, but I had to try. Surrendering to incomprehension or knee-jerk reactions would have been a second crushing defeat. As a writer said about finance jargon,

"Incomprehension is a form of consent."[4] So I read everything I could about the Crisis. And after reviewing expert studies from a range of political perspectives, I decided Wall Street was the worst culprit for four major reasons (not one of which was that they're "greedy," as if greed hadn't existed before).

First, the banks knowingly lied to investors. The big Wall Street banks, from JPMorgan Chase to Citigroup, sold investors bundles of lousy mortgages that didn't meet their advertised lending standards. This was the key: If the investors had been told the mortgages were shoddy, many already going into default, they could have prevented the crash by slowing down on their purchases. But the banks kept lying to the investors about the default rates, telling them everything was fine. They knowingly committed acts of financial fraud, like a company advertising that their juice boxes contain 20% "real juice" when they actually contain no juice at all, just water and carcinogens.

Unfortunately, *The Big Short*, the most moving and influential movie to come out on the Crisis, blew this key point. Characters lobbed angry accusations of fraud, but nobody explained how it worked. To the contrary, Ryan Gosling's character, the narrator, says that the bankers just didn't see the crash coming, perpetuating the myth of oblivion. Even the final epilogue scenes don't mention the historic government settlements that proved the banks had committed systematic, illegal fraud. What a PR gift to Wall Street. Incomprehension got them off the hook yet again.[5]

Second, the banks saw the crash coming better than anyone. They were at the center of the mortgage business, sensitive to the tiniest twitches and hiccups in the market. They repeatedly referred to themselves as "the brightest people in the world" and "the greatest minds of the century." As one banker said before the Crisis, "[W]hy wouldn't you invest with the smartest people in the world? They must know what they are doing."[6] If only a fraction of this boasting had a basis in reality, if a tiny subset of the bankers had the slightest clue how badly their diminished lending standards were degrading the quality of subprime loans, they must have known that the mortgage business was rotten to the core.[7] Indeed, later investigations confirmed that they did. Reporters McLean and Nocera put it this way: "After the crisis of 2008, a common refrain arose that no one saw it coming. But that was never true. State attorneys general had filed lawsuits [against subprime lenders]. Housing advocates had continually beat the tom-toms." An executive at one bank, Lehman Brothers, wrote a memo in 1995 describing mortgage company Famco as a "sweat shop" specializing in "high-pressure sales for people who are in a weak state." Yet just three years later Lehman Brothers sold millions of mortgage-backed-securities for Famco. McLean and Nocera wrote, "Did Wall Street know what was going on? You bet it did."[8]

Third, Wall Street ran the housing market. By fronting the money to loan "originators" (who didn't have their own capital) and deciding which loans to buy and sell, Wall Street essentially dictated the housing market.[9] It was like a crooked game of cards. It's easy to see the dealer running the game on the street corner and the dupes falling for it, but the one who really runs the show is the unseen mafia boss who hires the dealer, puts up the dealer's starting pool of cash, pays the dealer's commission, and collects most of the profits at the end of the day. That mafia boss was Wall Street. By lowering lending standards to the point where anyone with a pulse could get a loan, this mafia insured that the market would collapse in a bloody paroxysm.

Fourth, by blowing themselves up, the Wall Street banks turned a potential arrhythmia in the economy into a heart attack.[10] If they hadn't suddenly gone broke in September, 2008, setting off a panic in the corporate credit and stock markets that put the entire economy in a tailspin for years to come, we would not have suffered a full-blown crisis in 2008. As Melville said, "If your banker breaks, you snap."

Obviously Wall Street wasn't the only culprit. Homeowners and investors had foolishly gobbled up bad mortgage deals, and the ratings agencies, regulators, and press hadn't sounded the alarm. Other factors included low interest rates, overly complicated risk models, and growing foreign investment. All these factors played a part, but Wall Street was far and away the biggest culprit, with the most devastating impact on the greatest number of people.

So I figured out who the enemy was, but I was still left with a mere abstraction: Wall Street. These weren't real people. Investment banking was simply not part of my daily experience. It's not like the supermarket or hardware store or the local bank where you deposit checks. It's a nebulous, abstract process. And the bankers were smart enough not to show their faces outside their offices, penthouses, limos, and swimming pools, except for a few quick trips by CEOs who had to testify in Washington. Without a public face, they were hard to see as anything other than a mysterious force in a remote place, a cycle of booms and busts. Fighting investment banking was like screaming at the air. Even Occupy's talk about "the 99%" vs. "the 1%," as effective as that was in breaking the sound barrier, the silence about income inequality, still cast the bankers as numbers, more abstractions, not real people.

And it was the impersonal abstractness of the bankers that drove me crazy—all that destructive power hidden behind such blank indifference. This wasn't just any mysterious power; it was a supreme, malignant power that refused to answer or show itself. The banks that survived the Crisis, the ones that laid waste to the economy and put Ranulfo and millions of others in danger of bankruptcy, grew bigger than ever, soon paying their CEOs around $20 million a year, with average compensation for employees set at $750,000.[11] That made me want to puke. I had to know who these people were, to see behind their stony mask. I suddenly felt, in other words, like Captain Ahab chasing Moby Dick: insulted, heaped upon, tasked by a giant, inscrutable power.[12] All along, I had seen Ranulfo as the Captain Ahab who would strike through the mask, but he had no interest in this battle. He had his opinions about what caused the Crisis, but he didn't focus on affixing blame. Like other Americans, he focused on staying alive. I was on my own. To strike through the mask, I had to apply the many lessons I'd learned from Ranulfo about fighting abstractions like time: Make it personal. Use metaphors and symbols. Plead. Communicate. Reevaluate. Strike if you have to.

Metaphors would be perfect for this fight because they make abstractions—money, banking, justice—feel real, concrete, and personal...like a turtle. So I started to look around, to see what metaphors were available for investment bankers. Though far less creative than Ranulfo, the bank CEOs who testified before Congress in 2009 and 2010 certainly understood the power of metaphor, which is why they consistently used metaphors of natural disasters—"hurricanes" and "storms"—to characterize the Financial Crisis, making it sound like an inevitable, natural cycle, and therefore not their fault. The highlight of the Financial Crisis Inquiry Commission hearings came when the Chairman rejected one of these nature metaphors. After the CEO of Goldman Sachs, Lloyd Blankfein, compared the Crisis yet again to a "hurricane," Chairman Angelides pointedly corrected him. He said these weren't acts of God; these were acts of men and women who knew what they were doing.[13]

I couldn't even tell if the bank CEOs were putting on a rhetorical act for the cameras in Congress, deviously using nature metaphors to avoid blame and increased regulation. The bankers actually used these same nature metaphors when they were talking privately among themselves, especially water metaphors for finance markets—pervasive terms like "liquidity," "floating rates," "underwater," and "riding the wave."[14] Just like the natural-disaster metaphors used by CEOs in public, these metaphors removed the sense of volition and personal responsibility. The tides just ebb and flow, the water naturally regenerates itself, and nobody has to take any responsibility for their mistakes or unethical acts.[15] And the metaphors matter. They reinforced the bankers' lack of a sense of personal responsibility, judging by insider accounts like *The Big Short*, in which Michael Lewis chronicles the life of Steve Eisman, an investor who followed the housing market since the 1990s. Eisman witnessed horrible abuses on Wall Street, what he considered a "rape" of the country, yet he never once heard any bankers express remorse. "Not once in all these years," he said, "have I come across a person inside a big Wall Street firm who was having a crisis of conscience. Nobody ever said, 'This is wrong.'"[16] That arrogance, that lack of remorse, just made me more determined to find the right metaphors, so I could get others to understand what the bankers really did.

Unfortunately, the public wasn't helping. In the absence of clearer understanding of investment banking, average Americans and the media reverted to those same nature metaphors—"hurricane," "tsunami," "tidal wave," "volcano," "earthquake"—to depict the Crisis, if not absolving the bankers of blame, at least confusing the matter.[17] The one metaphor that seemed to have a chance of harnessing public outrage came from a 2009 *Rolling Stone* article by Matt Taibbi about Goldman Sachs, which started off by stating, "The world's most powerful investment bank is a great vampire squid wrapped around the face of humanity, relentlessly jamming its blood funnel into anything that smells like money."[18] That "vampire squid" image suddenly took off in the media and blogosphere, to the point where Goldman Sachs officials, in one of the only funny moments of the Crisis, felt compelled to respond by quibbling about what exactly real "vampire squids" do in the ocean.

Many commentators thought "vampire squid" was an unfair term for bankers, but I actually thought it worked in their favor. Vampires are downright cool, at least the kind that were popular in the early 2000s, sexy aristocrats like the Cullen family in the *Twilight* movies. And though squids aren't as cool or good-looking as the Cullens, they act on instinct, so, like other ocean metaphors, they obscure questions of personal responsibility. The term "squid" also had a comical ring to it, as in "Squidward," a harmless character in *Sponge Bob Square Pants*, the popular children's cartoon. If "vampire squid" went too far in one sense, it didn't go far enough in others.

Metaphors had hit the wall. Investment banking was so abstract, and prior knowledge about it so scarce among the general public, that banking metaphors didn't have enough foundation to build on. They just got sucked into a black hole. No common set of metaphors spilled from the lips of late-night comedians, retired old ladies, and taxi drivers, nothing with enough resonance to channel public anger. Occupy and Springsteen couldn't do it all by themselves.

It wasn't for lack of creativity, either. Great metaphors were unleashed through Occupy's placards and Springsteen's 2012 *Wrecking Ball* album, a powerful assault on the bankers and call to arms.[19] The title track, "Wrecking Ball," was originally written as a tribute to the Meadowlands, a football stadium being demolished in New Jersey, but it also served as a perfect metaphor for the Financial Crisis.[20] In the face of all the destruction, Springsteen sang, "Come on, take your best shot, Let me see what you got, Bring on your wrecking ball." I took him to be saying that, even though the bankers are reducing the economy to rubble with a wrecking ball, you can still defeat them by calling them out. And I believed him. At age 62, Springsteen was still jacked. He looked like he could take two or three bankers with one arm tied behind his back.

But the bankers were too smart—and too spineless—to come out of their high-rise offices and face Springsteen, the Occupy protesters, angry furniture movers, or anyone else. They hid behind their security guards, lawyers, and tinted windows, secure in their facelessness. The best metaphors in the world couldn't stick to such a cold void.

That void drove me crazy. If there's anything else Ranulfo taught me—as if his lessons about dreams, metaphors, risk-taking, and humor weren't enough—it's that you've got to fight abstractions with personal communication. You have to get time to tell you its secrets, and see if it wants any friends. So, to pose the more personal questions I was dying to ask the bankers but never could, I'm now going to present an imaginary dialogue with a banker who's an amalgam of everything I've read about Wall Street.[21] This is the only section in this entire book where I fictionalize (not counting a few pseudonyms), but, as the endnotes show, it's a fantasy based in real facts and figures.

For this scene, I have invited a representative banker, a composite figure, to join me at one of those communal readings of *Moby-Dick* in the U.S. Treasury lobby in Washington DC, a fitting location, I believe, given our mutual interests in money, water, and whales.

A Melville Meeting in Washington

After the reading of Chapter 99, the crowd takes a break, to discuss *Moby-Dick* in pairs. Picking up some free chowder, I sit down at a table with a man in his 50s, wearing a black business suit, green tie, and polished wing tips. He says his name is Parker, he came down from New York for the day on some business with the Treasury for his bank, and while waiting for his appointment, he stopped in the lobby.

I'm excited. This is my chance to ask a real investment banker what he thinks about *Moby-Dick* and money, what mysteries light up his imagination.

Fortunately, Parker doesn't ask what I do for a living, so I don't have to explain that I'm a college professor, which might make him mistakenly assume that I think I have the "right" interpretation of *Moby-Dick*, when it's actually too mysterious to be reduced to a single reading. Just to be sure, I start off by saying, "It's kind of hard to take all this Melville language in at one time. It's like Shakespeare: worth it, but not easy, right?"

He laughs and agrees, taking another scoop of chowder while I open my copy of the novel.

"So what were some of your favorite parts?", I ask.

Parker immediately says, "Oh, I love all those descriptions of the water, like when Ishmael talks about how everyone loves to stare at the water, the lakes and ocean, and he's got that great line about how meditation and water are forever wedded."[22]

"Yeah, that's great," I say. "I once read that people who stare at water make the same kind of brain waves that people make when they're meditating. Psychologists hooked up electrodes to the subjects' heads and found this out." Smiling, I add, "So just by looking at water, without even trying, we're all Zen masters."

Parker lets out a quick laugh, and says, "Well, it makes sense since our bodies are mostly water, more than half from what I remember, so it's natural that we connect with water. That's why I like *Moby-Dick*...and being out in my boat on the high seas."

"I know what you mean. That's why I love body surfing with my kids."

Making this sudden connection with a total stranger, I feel the impulse to praise the watery world that unites us all, but, instead, I use the opening to switch tack and say, "But you know what bothers me? Ishmael is always going on about how everything's great at sea, how it's all one happy family, and, sure, sometimes I bet it is, but sometimes he sounds like a nut-job, like that part about just laughing it off when you get smacked by your boss."

The banker laughs and nods as I open to the passage, which is easy to find because it appears in the first chapter, right after Ishmael talks about water and meditation.

"OK, here it is," I say. "Ishmael is talking about being ordered around by the sea captains, and then he says this: 'Well, then, however the old sea-captains may order me about—however they may thump and punch me about, I have the satisfaction of knowing that it is all right; that everybody else is one way or other served in much the same way—either in a physical or metaphysical point of view, that is; and so the universal thump is passed round, and all hands should rub each other's shoulder-blades, and be content.'"

"See, now that's messed up," I say with a smile. "Your boss should not be punching you. Ishmael makes it sound like it's all fine, that everyone just punches and gets punched, but I bet it's always the deckhands getting punched by the sea captains, and never the other way around."[23]

Parker slows down on his chowder and says, "That actually sounds like Wall Street. The senior executives love to scream and swear at the junior analysts, and it can get pretty intense. Not so much at my bank, but I know some people take *serious* abuse."

"Actually," I say, "what scares me the most is how Captain Ahab is so cut off from everyone around him. Like that scene where the carpenter makes Ahab's wooden leg, and instead of being grateful, Ahab curses his dependence on other people." Turning to that page, I read out what Ahab says about the carpenter: "'Here I am, proud as a Greek god, and yet standing debtor to this blockhead for a bone to stand on! Cursed be that mortal inter-indebtedness which will not do away with ledgers.'"[24]

I would love to ask Parker, "So is that how you see me and the rest of the country, as blockheads who you wish you could get rid of? Is that why you call yourselves 'the smartest people in the world' and your clients 'dumb money,' because you see yourselves as Greek gods?"

But that wouldn't be polite, so I just state the obvious conclusion: "That's Ahab's tragic flaw. He can't see that debt ties us all together."

"Right, see, thank you," Parker says appreciatively. "People get mad at bankers, but they don't understand that we provide a valuable service. By taking in investors' money and loaning it out to companies, we move capital to where it's needed for new economic growth, and that helps everyone in the long run."

I want to say, "But housing isn't a productive business, like a start-up company that needs a big loan to develop a great new technology, or micro-credit in Uganda or the inner city that leads to new growth.[25] Houses helped compensate for stagnant wages, but economically they were a dead-end. By shifting billions of investing dollars and savings away from productive new businesses, you *prevented* economic growth." I would love to know how he'd respond, but I can't raise this point because it would cut too close to the bone, potentially undermining his profession's one claim to redeeming social value.

Instead, I say, "You're right. We do need bank credit. Blankfein went too far when he said Goldman Sachs was 'doing God's work,' but he was actually right that investment banks help companies grow by raising capital for them."

Even though I'm bringing up the Blankfein example to support him, Parker shifts uncomfortably in his seat, probably because that "God's work" line set off such a furor with the public, coming right after the banks blew themselves up, took the bonuses, then sent the economy into a tailspin.[26]

Before he can bolt, I simply state, "But Ahab is so self-centered that he doesn't care that he's going to kill his entire crew and abandon his wife and child on shore."[27]

Parker smiles and says, "Yeah, but Ahab was a great man. He knew what he wanted and he went for it."[28] Then he quickly excuses himself, leaving me to clean up his cracker crumbs and empty bowl of chowder.

I considered yelling at him right there in the lobby, but that wouldn't have done any good. Security would probably throw me out for raising my voice, and the other museum-goers would figure I deserved it for not being nice.

Notes

1. Sekules (2000, 45).
2. Although Hart takes *The Godfather* as the inspiration for the central issue and title of his book, *The Hit Man's Dilemma: Or, Business, Personal and Impersonal* (2005), he does not focus on the details of this movie per se. Rather, he draws on Weber's historical sociology to provide large-scale treatments of social changes in the movement to modernity, and his examples from popular narratives—which he believes effectively dramatize the personal vs. impersonal dilemma—include Shakespeare's tragedies, Indian and Japanese movies, and European gangster movies in general. For more discussion of Hart and the issues he raises in relation to *The Godfather*, including gender dimensions, see Sutton and Wogan (2009, 23–46).
3. Puzo (1969, 145).
4. John Lancaster, "Money Talks: Learning the Language of Finance," *The New Yorker*, August 4, 2014, 33.
5. This is a fast-moving movie (*The Big Short*, Director Adam McKay, 2015), and there is a lot at stake here—the movie is so popular and brilliantly made that it may exert a large influence on public understanding of the Financial Crisis—so I feel compelled to spell out my argument at length.

    For roughly the first half of the movie, we are led to believe the bankers only made one rather innocent mistake: They naively believed the mortgage industry would keep going strong, as it had for decades. Bankers at Goldman Sachs and elsewhere laugh at oddball traders like Dr. Burry (Christian Bale) who want to bet against their mortgage securities. In this telling, the bankers just couldn't see what was coming. We only get to know one banker who could see the crash coming (Ryan Gosling's character), but he was an exception that proved the movie's rule of banker naivety. He tells the crew for Mark Baum (Steve Carell) that nobody at the banks is paying attention to the worsening mortgages, that they're all asleep at the wheel. When he tries to sound the alarm at his own bank, they dismiss him with insults like "Chicken Little" and "Bubble Boy."

    This depiction of clueless bankers is wrong, and it exonerates them by failing to show that, in fact, they knowingly lied to investors about the rising default rates and debased loan standards on the mortgages inside the bundles they were selling. Rather than show the managers higher up in the bank who bundled the mortgage securities and knew about their default rates and missing documentation, "The Big Short" only shows oblivious, young bankers at the point of sale who think Burry (Christian Bale) is crazy, which is like showing friendly car salespeople who haven't talked to the automaker's engineers or middle managers, so they don't realize what defects are inside the cars they're selling and how likely they are to blow up on impact. The massive, systematic fraud committed by Wall Street banks has been proven over and over again by historic Justice Department settlements for billions of dollars. The title of the press release for one such settlement sums it up: "Bank of America to Pay $16.65 Billion in Historic Justice Department Settlement for Financial Fraud Leading up to and During the Financial Crisis" (https://www.justice.gov/opa/pr/bank-america-pay-1665-billion-historic-justice-department-settlement-financial-fraud-lending, August 21, 2014. Accessed June 19, 2015). News of these settlements didn't usually make the front pages because they didn't involve jail sentences and, in a plea-bargain type of legal fiction, sometimes lacked a technical admission of guilt, but the number of settlements, the reasons given for them in the legal statements of facts, and their record-breaking monetary penalties clearly demonstrate financial fraud.

The second half of the movie seems different. Main characters throw out many angry accusations about the market prices for bonds being rigged, and together with the long scenes in Vegas, there's an overall feeling that the banks are up to no good. However, even here, the movie is misleading. Our wise guide and host throughout the story, Gosling, repeats what he said in the first half of the film, that the bankers' problem is stupidity, not fraud, and in a memorable line, he flat out rejects the very possibility of ever identifying fraud ("Tell me the difference between stupid and illegal and I'll have my wife's brother arrested"). The movie doesn't ever go on to show that, no, actually, you *can* tell when and how these banks committed fraud, and the Justice Department and civil lawsuits did exactly that.

I'm not asking the film to deviate from its narrative structure, already set in place by Michael Lewis' book (2010). Staying completely within this structure, the film could have easily dramatized the sections in Lewis' book on Wall Street's role in housing scams going back to the 1990s, and it could have hinted at the proof of banker fraud that Lewis didn't have access to when he published his book in 2010. These small but crucial additions would have been perfectly allowable within the creative license the screenwriters had already given themselves in adapting Lewis's book, such as making Jared Vennett a central character and narrator, adding explanations by famous celebrities, giving an epilogue that brings the audience up to 2015—none of which appears in the book. At the very least, adding just one brief explanatory cut-away scene or written epilogue would have gone a long way toward clearing up the movie's confusion about banker fraud. The screenwriters brilliantly created an engaging drama that many Americans watched, so they had a major opportunity to get the public to understand Wall Street's fraud and its crucial role in the crash. The filmmakers stirred up anger, but unfortunately they also perpetuated a fundamental misconception.

6. Ho (2009, 39–49). Ho refers to this as "the culture of smartness," and demonstrates how it pervades the bankers' worldview. Ultimately Ho shows how boom-and-bust cycles result from specific social practices at the banks: "Investment bankers' cultural models of both short-term, relentless deal-making *and* employee liquidity are, in a sense, learned 'on the job,' imbibed through their own experiences and embodiment of their particular organizational culture....In such a context, financial crashes and busts are not natural cycles but constructed out of everyday practices and ideologies..." (2009, 291–292).

7. Obviously not every employee had this knowledge, since the banks were large corporations with thousands of employees. See the distinctions made in an earlier note among different types of "bankers." Smith (2012), for example, makes sharp distinctions between the reckless actions of certain people at Goldman Sachs, which he contrasts with the firm's previous, more long-term, client-oriented traditions, especially among salespeople who advised investors.

8. McLean and Nocera (2010, 86–87, emphasis added). On JPMorgan Chase's timely exit from the mortgage business in the last couple years before the Crisis, see Tett (2009). On the other hand, don't think that JPMorgan (which merged into JPMorgan Chase partway

through Tett's account) avoided the mortgage securities fraud prevalent on Wall Street. To the contrary, JPMorgan Chase, like all the other big New York banks, later had to pay billions of dollars for their fraudulent actions, as indicated by the title of this Justice Department announcement: "Justice Department, Federal and State Partners Secure Record $13 Billion Global Settlement with JPMorgan for Misleading Investors about Securities Containing Toxic Mortgages," November 19, 2013, https://www.justice.gov/opa/pr/justice-department-federal-and-state-partners-secure-record-13-billion-global-settlement. Accessed July 17, 2015.

9. Fannie Mae and Freddie Mac also got in on this business in the early 2000s, but free-market advocates tend to exaggerate their importance. Sure, Fannie and Freddie influenced Wall Street and Washington from the beginning, but they were not the main engine driving the subprime market; the majority of sales of mortgage-backed-securities came out of Wall Street (McLean and Nocera 2010, 7). If the U.S. government had a major influence on the housing market and eventual crisis, it was through their scaling back of regulations on the housing market, and the implied promise of "too big to fail" bank bailouts.

10. I'm not going into detail here on why the banks went bankrupt in 2008 because the basic reason has already been covered: excessive risk-taking, owing to a perverse set of incentives. The main factor was increased leverage, but another major factor pushing the banks over the edge was derivatives, which created hidden interconnections between the banks through collateralized debt obligations and credit default swaps. These derivatives tied the major banks together, insuring that once one or two went down, they'd take others down with them, and set off a panic in credit markets, since it wasn't clear how far these ties extended because they were traded "over the counter" (not on a major stock exchange). The bank executives were, at best, willfully ignorant of the dangers of these derivatives because they were pursuing maximum profits, ignoring warning signs that went back to the crisis in the Asian markets in the late1990s. Drawing the direct link between those 1990s derivatives and the 2008 Crisis, Partnoy writes, "Yes, we saw it coming. How could we not?" (2009, 248). Putting aside the questions of exactly who knew what when, and why they didn't act on that knowledge, the simple point here is that the opacity and extensive-

ness of the derivatives business was another major factor leading to the financial weakness and (near) bankruptcy of investment banks in 2008.
11. By 2009 four mega-banks—JPMorgan Chase, Bank of America, Wells Fargo, and Citigroup—controlled half the market for new mortgages and two-thirds for credit cards, and five banks controlled 95% of the market in derivatives contracts (Johnson and Kwak 2010, 180). The $750,000 average applied to Goldman Sachs in 2009 (ibid.). In 2012 the CEO of Goldman made $21 million, and the JPMorgan Chase CEO made $23.1 million in 2011 (Jessica Silver-Greenberg and Susanne Craig, "Fined Billions, Bank Will Give Dimon a Raise," *New York Times*, Front section, January 24, 2014).
12. After vowing to strike through the mask, Ahab says about Moby Dick, "Sometimes I think there's naught there. But 'tis enough. He tasks me; he heaps me..." (Melville 1851, Chapter 36, "The Quarter-Deck").
13. Quotations from the Financial Crisis Inquiry Commission all appear with full citations in an excellent article by Rohrer and Vignone (2012). My discussion of metaphors used during the Financial Crisis Inquiry Commission hearings is also heavily indebted to this article, but I deviate from Rohrer and Vignone in my discussion below of the "vampire squid" metaphor, where I place more emphasis on the way it removed Wall Street culpability.
14. Most of these water metaphors come from interviews with journalists and traders in the foreign exchange market, as reported in a journal article by Oberlechner et al. (2004). Although the interview subjects for this article were all European, other authors (e.g. Rohrer and Vignone 2012, 16) note that the "money is liquid" metaphorical equation is quite common among American bankers as well. On the prevalence of Captain Ahab allusions in the American business world in general, see Insko (2007). For a whale metaphor closer to the case at hand, note that the term "London whale" was widely used as a nickname for a risky derivatives trader in the London office, Bruno Iksil, who lost roughly $5 billion on trading in 2012, only a couple years after the Crisis had supposedly led to greater oversight on risky trades at JPMorgan Chase. Iksil later said he resented the nickname "London Whale," and claimed

it was devised by rival traders to criticize the size of JPMorgan Chase's bets (Lucy McNulty and Gregory Zuckerman, "'London Whale' Breaks Silence," *Wall Street Journal*, February 22, 2016, http://www.wsj.com/articles/london-whale-breaks-silence-1456189964. Accessed October 5, 2016.) Be that as it may, Iksil's nickname remains an apt example of the long-standing and ongoing use of "whale" as a term for someone who makes large bets, whether in high finance or casino gambling.

15. Oberlechner et al. (2004, 146) point out that ocean metaphors remove the sense of personal responsibility in financial market activity, while adding a sense of cycles ("ebbs and flows") and constant regeneration.
16. This quote comes from Steve Eisman, of Front Point Partners, who put it even more harshly when he said, "The upper classes of this country raped this country....You built a castle to rip people off" (Lewis 2010, 232).
17. Metaphors matter for economists, too. As one economist said, metaphors and stories are essential methods for making sense in all the sciences, including economics: "Metaphors and stories, models and histories, subject to the discipline of fact and logic, are the two ways of answering 'why'" (McCloskey 1990, 10).
18. Matt Taibbi, "The Great American Bubble Machine," *Rolling Stone*, April 5, 2010, http://www.rollingstone.com/politics/news/the-great-american-bubble-machine-20100405. Accessed on March 28, 2013.
19. As for the creative signs in Zuccotti Park, one of the protestors, anthropologist Michael Taussig, wrote, "This is not only a struggle about income disparity and corporate control of democracy. It is about the practice of art, too, including the art of being alive" (Taussig 2013, 17–18).
20. Springsteen stated in a *Rolling Stone* interview that *Wrecking Ball* was "as direct an album as I ever made," but I believe "direct" is a relative term when it comes to a Whitmanesque songwriter like Springsteen. Even though Springsteen was relatively direct with his lyrics on *Wrecking Ball* compared with his other albums, he still put forth plenty of metaphors. For the full interview, see Andy Greene, "Exclusive: Bruce Springsteen Explains His Experimental New Album," *Rolling Stone*, February 17, 2012, http://www.rollingstone.com/music/news/exclusive-bruce-springsteen-

explains-his-experimental-new-album-20120217. Accessed August 2, 2013.

21. For example, Eric Lonergan, an investment banker in London, wrote an interesting book on the social and philosophical meanings of money, and on the first page, he says, "Markets connect a great many, so they are abstract and quantitative. But always human" (2009, 1). It's that combination of abstraction and humanity that I'm addressing.

22. I have no way of knowing whether many Wall Street bankers like this exact *Moby-Dick* passage, but I think it's fair to infer, based on their frequent use of whale and water metaphors, that they would. It's actually hard to know how many bankers have read *Moby-Dick* at all. Probably not many, if the reading habits of James Cayne, the former CEO of investment bank Bear Stearns, are any indication; Cayne said he has only read a few books in his adult life, the main one being a book on Machiavellian business leadership (Cohan 2009, 325). But actual reading of Melville's text doesn't really matter, now that Moby Dick and Captain Ahab (and water metaphors) have become such integral parts of our cultural fabric. I'm just glad *Moby-Dick* is still in there somewhere, and I agree with Insko (2007, 29) that the interesting challenge is to investigate how people use *Moby-Dick* imagery and what that usage reveals about their views of the world.

23. Royster (1986) is particularly good at identifying this "universalizing" impulse in Ishmael, the tendency to gloss over exploitative labor relations with celebrations of humanity in general. Royster says, "Ishmael is never so happy as when he is finding in some dull, arduous, or onerous task an allegory of universal truth" (1986, 313), and he rightly notes not only the way Ishmael turns the blows of sea captains into "an illustration of higher democracy," but also the "noticeably ironic" tone of that *Moby-Dick* passage (1986, 314), which obviously complicates any reading of it.

24. Melville (1851), Chapter 108, "Ahab and the Carpenter." In the Powermobydick online edition, the indefinite article "a" is omitted for some reason between "as" and "Greek god" (and I make another such modification below to the hyphenation in another Melville quotation).

25. For an early, excellent analysis of the importance of bank credit for economic development, see Gershenberg's analysis (1972) of banking in newly independent Uganda.
26. "Blankfein Says He's Just Doing 'God's Work,'" *New York Times*, Dealbook, November 9, 2009. For more examples of uses of religious imagery among employees of Goldman Sachs, usually intended in a positive way to celebrate their company, see Mandis (2013). The investment banks still raised capital for companies in 2008, but that became a smaller part of their business after they went public and got more heavily into trading. For example, McLean and Nocera write, "The IPO was a critical turning point for Goldman Sachs….The trading side of the firm…eventually overwhelmed the investment banking side, in terms of profits, stature, and ethos" (2010, 152). On other changes after Goldman Sachs became a publicly traded company, see also Smith (2012) and Mandis (2013).
27. Ishmael is the only member of the crew who survives at the end.
28. This stance is consistent with Insko's finding that most of the Melville references in the business press portray Captain Ahab as a "model of dogged persistence, a kind of modern-day, goal-oriented careerist whose aims might even be praiseworthy, even if seemingly unattainable" (Insko 2007, 24). It's also consistent with the way even clearer critiques of Wall Street actually had the opposite effect, inspiring young people to become stockbrokers. For example, after Partnoy's book came out with a scathing critique of the derivatives business, he found out some people were upset that they hadn't joined in at the time. Partnoy writes, "During a particularly depressing period, several Irish business school students e-mailed me for job-hunting advice, and one derivatives wannabe wrote that *F.I.A.S.C.O.* was 'actually the best book I have ever read.' I felt I had created a monster" (2009, 250). Michael Lewis reports similar dismay at the response to his scathing indictment of Salomon Brothers and 1980s Wall Street (1989). While working on this book, he gave a talk to students at the London School of Economics, and this was the audience response: "After the talk I was besieged not with abuse, and not with questions about the bond market, but with questions about how to get a job at Salomon Brothers" (1989, 253).

CHAPTER 21

Respect for the Turtle

Summer, 2014

So did Ranulfo and Pablo survive?

It was very rough...but, as of 2014, yes, El Palmar is still open for business.

In your face, naysayers!

Screw you, Wall Street!

Thanks for nothing, Washington!

They're still alive!

And the best part is, they were saved by dirt. Literally—dirt. While sales dropped at the store, the laundromat continued to turn a profit, since everyone still needed to wash their clothes. If it weren't for those dirty clothes, Ranulfo and Pablo wouldn't have made it.

So Ranulfo's dreams were right: dirt *is* good for business. As Ranulfo said in retrospect, still half amazed, "People leave their dirt and their money here, and they go away with clean clothes. Dirt is money. Now I see that dirt is a good thing."[1]

He never could decide whether dirt or cleanliness came first in the universe, but he accepted their deep interconnection. "You can't have cleanliness without dirt," he said, then added in jest, "I'm going to get a crown made out of dirt...The Champion of Dirt!" His dreams made him a firm believer in dirt and the principle that things are not always what they seem. He even now referred to Don Quixote as "the greatest crazy man we've had in history," adding, "He was crazy…but he saw beyond the ordinary. And sometimes you have to be crazy."

Of course, Ranulfo wasn't just a dreamer, either, calling up NASA and saying he was ready to be an astronaut. He got saved because he did what homeowners and bankers hadn't done: he pulled out when he couldn't afford something. The decision not to get the bakery not only kept him out of debt, it left him with about $30,000 in savings, just enough to weather the storm, to survive on dirt.

Not that the scare hasn't left a mark. Ranulfo now tends to refer to the economy as a monster that he's trying to knock down, and he doesn't view time as tenderly as he did before. Recently he said, *El tiempo no necesita aliados. Es egoísta, pero hay que buscarle el lado débil.* "Time doesn't need allies. It's selfish, but we have to find its weak spot."

As for me, I agree with the economists who think the Wall Street banks should be broken up into small-enough-to-fail sizes and restored to private ownership so they'll be motivated to control themselves, like Ranulfo and other business owners who put their own money on the line. Nothing is going to change, though, until the entire political system is cleaned up. The banks make massive campaign contributions, help write the new legislation on finance regulation, and figure out how to game it before the ink dries. Even a Congressman on the Financial Services Committee recently admitted in the press, "It's appalling, it's disgusting, it's wasteful and it opens the possibility of conflicts of interest and corruption. It's unfortunately the world we live in."[2]

When news like this gets me down, I laugh and think of myself as the helpless baby in the E*TRADE commercials, the one in diapers who wails, "I just want to punch the economy in the face!" Other times I dream that the 99%, babies and all, will take back the economy. Slowly, with all those babies, we might even create a "human economy"—meaningful enterprises, such as employee-owned businesses like Ranulfo's and Pablo's.[3]

In the meantime, I've been watching plenty of baseball, though I sometimes couldn't understand why my kids kept playing it. They've broken fingers diving into base, scraped up their legs and arms, and been hit by plenty of hard fastballs. Yet I've also seen my sons make diving catches and slide into base half a heartbeat ahead of the tag, their hands stretched out in front of them as if they were flying face down in the sand. The game has taught them about courage and craftsmanship and rooting for other people and wanting something so badly that your soul aches day and night. As Billy Beane said in *Moneyball*, "How can you not be romantic about baseball?"[4]

These days I don't get particularly moved watching baseball players throwing punches in defense of teammates. I still love that loyalty, but it doesn't bring tears to my eyes the way it did back in 2006 and 2007. Almost nothing does. I'm glad I didn't end up like Kenny, reciting the Serenity prayer to strangers in parking lots, but a part of me misses those days. Ranulfo and I were fighting together for the bakery and new insights. Our kids were open to the world. Andy's death made me confront my own mortality. Everything seemed possible.

Maybe I don't need to watch loyalty on TV anymore because now I have it in real life. For all these years, Ranulfo and I have stuck by each other. I've continued visiting the store every week, and I still love standing behind the counter with Ranulfo, laughing, marveling, theorizing, bagging the customer's groceries. I was touched when he said, "Pete, we're not just friends, we're twins."

Perhaps the biggest lesson Ranulfo taught me was to take more risks. I can't say I opened a small business and put my savings on the line, the ultimate risk, but I did try to be more daring in my own, lower-stakes world. That's why I wrote this book this way, as a narrative full of personal emotions, wild jokes, and embarrassing details, rather than hiding behind the usual impersonal veil of academic analysis. Writing like this might not seem like much of a risk—and compared to putting your family savings on the line, it's not—but in the world of academics, where reputation is the coin of the realm, it makes me vulnerable to criticism and resentment for having crossed the line. Anthropologists can accept everything from cannibalism to witchcraft, just about anything that another culture can come up with, but, as one anthropologist recently said, when it comes to writing style, the field is "incredibly snobbish, resolutely turning its nose up at anything smacking of populism or 'not proper anthropology'...."[5] *Corner-Store Dreams* is definitely not "proper anthropology."

In typical, proper anthropological writing, human beings only appear in brief glimpses, snippets here and there of scattered quotations and descriptions, all marshaled to illustrate the author's generalizations and theories about group patterns ("As this farmer's quotation shows, the Mambino place a high premium on heirloom objects embedded in a concatenation of material culture that..."). Instead of real people, anthropological publications usually provide stick figures—caricatures, not flesh-and-blood individuals. As ironic as it sounds, there's little room for writing about real humans in the discipline that studies humans. Most anthropology reads like a financial audit—comprehensive and intensely detailed, but lifeless to all but a few insiders. By this measure, my book is just a fluffy story, maybe fine for students, but not serious ("theoretical") analysis.[6]

All this might seem hard to believe. If you've met any anthropologists, you'd probably agree that they're sensitive, well-meaning people who genuinely want to help others. And if you know anything about ethnography, you know that narrative writing like mine shares the same goals: concrete details, specific times and places, humanity.[7] So could most anthropological writing really be that wooden? Mary Louise Pratt alluded to this puzzle in the 1980s when she said that anthropological writing "tends to be surprisingly boring. How, one asks constantly, could such interesting people doing such interesting things produce such dull books?"[8] Yet almost 30 years later, "dull books" still dominate the landscape. Surveying the field recently in search of anthropology that might reach a wide public, Norwegian anthropologist Thomas Hylland Eriksen honestly admitted that, for most readers, "Anthropological monographs and articles tend to be dense, technical, and frankly boring...." He laments that, as a result, anthropology is still a self-contained world with virtually no impact on the public: "it is absent from nearly every important public debate in the Anglophone world."[9]

Granted, it's encouraging to see Eriksen and a few others making articulate calls for a public anthropology that breaks out of the ivory tower.[10] These calls have created a hypothetical space for public outreach and a gnawing sense that something is wrong in the discipline. Yet "popularizing" is still a professional risk, and even the few anthropologists who try to reach the public rarely make narrative the centerpiece of their publications. As Eriksen says, "In contemporary anthropology, pleas for narrative have almost become a cliché...but we rarely get on with actually telling stories."[11]

In the face of such critiques, anthropologists like to point to exceptions like Ruth Behar, who has written beautiful anthropological narratives and enjoyed success as a MacArthur Grant recipient and tenured professor at the University of Michigan. But if you listen to Behar herself, you realize that she's actually the exception that proves the rule of anti-narrativism. Behar recently summed up her place in the field this way: "I worry because I do not consider my work to be representative of what most anthropologists consider anthropology...where I reside, still uncertainly, often disloyally, and sometimes, I feel, illegally...I worry because I know that even though anthropology has changed in the last few decades...

it really has not changed all that much, not enough yet."[12] If even Ruth Behar feels this way, I definitely have reason to worry.

And I still wrestle with Pratt's question: Why do such interesting people write such "dull books"?

To put it generously, anthropologists know too much. They get so enthralled that they feel compelled to provide eight examples where one would have sufficed, making their writing impenetrable to anyone other than insiders. In their enthusiasm, anthropologists disregard the quintessential writing rule noted long ago by Voltaire: "If you want to bore the reader, tell him everything." As Eriksen says, "This is where our predicament lies: what anthropology has to offer appears to be irreducible complexity and ambiguity...."[13] And it's not just a matter of "popularizers" needing to write well to appeal to general readers. Better writing would help anthropologists be better thinkers and theorists, since articulating one's points clearly and succinctly requires conceptual mastery.[14] Many anthropologists know this, but empirical overkill and analytical writing have been the dominant modes in the profession for so long that diversity of expression is still discouraged. Once a self-reinforcing system of rewards is in place, whether in a bank or the ivory tower, it's hard to change.[15]

Ten or fifteen years ago, I could still laugh off Pratt's complaint about anthropology's "boring" writing because I loved the puzzles, and I compensated for the flat prose by filling in with my own vivid memories of fieldwork and travel. In my own publications, I stuck to the analysis and resisted extended stories. But the closer I got to Ranulfo, the more such anthropological writing struck me as inhumane. I could see the value of analytical writing and didn't wish it would disappear, but by the time it came to write this book, I knew I couldn't write it in the standard dry-as-ashes style. I wanted to provide "analysis," but only if it came wrapped up in a personal story, not the usual generalizations about large social patterns, what Hart calls the social scientist's "addiction to impersonal abstractions and suppression of individual subjectivity," another legacy of modern society—the academic equivalent of *The Godfather* viewers who pretend that they can take something deeply personal and make it "strictly business."[16] I could no longer accept that artificial separation. I had to mix it up. Whatever happened to me, I had to hope that eventually anthropology would give narrative writing more airtime.

I also couldn't go along with the usual separation between fieldwork and publishing. Ranulfo stayed involved throughout the writing of this book, checking over my drafts multiple times. Together, we recalled and analyzed everything from Kalimán and Don Quixote to the bakery construction costs. More details are provided in an appendix but the short version is this: writing this book has brought us even closer together, rather than putting our friendship in a deep freeze.

Other dreams and projects beckon us, too. A few months ago Ranulfo told me, "I'm going to fire my accountant and have you take over the monthly payroll and taxes." I was in over my head again, but also touched by his trust, just as I had been a few years earlier when he gave me power-of-attorney, in case anything came up while he spent a month in Mexico with his parents. Again, don't tell me business isn't personal.

So if anybody asks what this book is about, I'll say—"turtles." Like the day when Ranulfo told me, "I want to get shoes filled with lead, so I can walk like a turtle." Or when he watched an online video of an alligator trying to eat a turtle. The turtle was stuck inside the alligator's mouth for a couple hours, until finally the alligator gave up trying to bite through his shell, and let him go. With a smile, Ranulfo reported, "The turtle's shell was too hard for the alligator."

That's Ranulfo. Alligators stalking him, fires burning to his left and right, buildings crumbling, dust and debris flying everywhere—and the turtle keeps moving, slowly but surely.

Notes

1. Ranulfo said, *La mugre es dinero.*
2. Eric Lipton and Ben Protess, "Banks' Lobbyists Help in Drafting Financial Bills," *New York Times,* Front section, May 24, 2013.
3. Hart et al. (2010).
4. *Moneyball,* Director Bennett Miller, 2011.
5. Quoted in Eriksen (2006, 27). Eriksen is quoting a British anthropologist here, and he gives other examples of anthropology's "elitism," concluding that "anthropology still cultivates its self-identity as a counter-culture, its members belonging to a kind of secret society whose initiates possess exclusive keys for understanding, indispensable for making sense of the world, but, alas, largely inaccessible to outsiders" (2006, 28). For an earlier exploration of the faulty-yet-self-serving dichotomy between "serious" vs. "popular" anthropological writing, see Campbell (1996). As Campbell says, "Binaries like that are cute; they are slick; and they let us all off the hook" (1996, 58).
6. The experience of Kurt Vonnegut, Jr. makes a good baseline for comparing the changing role of narrative writing in anthropology. In the 1940s, Vonnegut wrote his master's thesis at the University of Chicago about underlying structures in various foundational narratives, showing, among other things, that the story of Cinderella combined the underlying model found in most of the world's creation myths, while adding a positive reversal at the end, when the prince takes Cinderella to the ball, the same penultimate reversal structure found in the Old Testament story of redemption, for example. Vonnegut later referred to his master's thesis as "my prettiest contribution to my culture" (1981, 285). The University of Chicago's Anthropology Department, however, didn't see it as a great contribution: they unanimously rejected his thesis in 1947. So instead of becoming a professional anthropologist, Vonnegut left Chicago and went on to achieve literary fame as a novelist. An apparent reversal in his anthropological status came in 1971, though, when the University of Chicago retroactively awarded him a master's degree in anthropology for one of his novels. However, Vonnegut himself didn't view that degree as the end of the story, a Cinderella-like marriage of anthropology and literature. In his later years, he summarized the whole affair this way: "I was thrilled to

discover that [narrative model of creation myths] years ago, and I am just as thrilled today. The apathy of the University of Chicago is repulsive to me" (Vonnegut 1981, 316). (Sense any lingering bitterness?) Fortunately, since Vonnegut's time at the University of Chicago, discussions of the mutual interconnections between literature and anthropology have become much more accepted. See, for example, Narayan (2012), Segal and Handler (1990), and Wulff (2016). But while these latter books are excellent, respected works about the intersection of anthropology and narrative, showing how far the field has come since Vonnegut's day, it's still relatively rare to find anthropologists publishing their own book-length narratives or having them awarded the same professional standing as analytical accounts, as will be discussed below.

7. That's yet another advantage of narrative writing: by placing the anthropologist and his or her interlocutors in the same dialogical moment, it provides an answer to Fabian's famous critique (1983) of anthropological writing for "denying coevalness," that is, for not placing the anthropologist and his or her interlocutors in the same time frame in their written accounts. Although Fabian's critique is still widely known in anthropology more than 30 years after it came out, I don't believe that it has ever been adequately countered. Adding chapters about a group's history (e.g. the history of manufacturing or post-colonial state control in that area) to one's ethnography doesn't solve the problem, either, if the ethnography still decontextualizes and de-temporalizes the individual moments of fieldwork, leaving those moments as nothing but illustrations of some larger "theoretical" point. The anthropologist and the people in those decontextualized examples are still not shown to be moving through time together, at least not in the fleshed-out way of almost any character-centered narrative where you see the anthropologist interacting with his or her interlocutors and change occurring over time.

8. Pratt (1986, 33).

9. Eriksen (2006, ix). Eriksen's diagnosis in this 2006 book is still perfectly relevant today, and confirmed by other anthropologists with comparable levels of honesty and concern for the field. For example, in 2013 Driessen wrote, "Unfortunately, too much anthropology is boring, unattractive, and unapproachable for wider audiences" (2013, 391).

10. For recent calls for "public anthropology," see Borofsky (2010), Driessen (2013), Eriksen (2006), and the various articles in "Special Issue: Engaged Anthropology: Diversity and Dilemmas," *Current Anthropology* 51: S201–330, 2010. Just to be clear, not all those who advocate for anthropological outreach are calling for or publishing full-fledged narratives.
11. Eriksen (2006, 36). Certainly some changes in anthropological writing have taken place in the last decade or two, but recognizing these changes is actually an impediment when such recognition leads to a false sense of security and inflated sense of progress. I'm reminded of this problem when a colleague will tell me how much better—more personal and narrative-based—anthropology writing is nowadays than it was 30 years ago, but then when I check out one of the anthropology books they recommended, I find that all it has are a few passages with extended anecdotes, while the rest of the 300-page book is written with the usual analytical voice and smattering of quotes from stick figures—hardly what I would call a unified, personal narrative. These experiences give me the feeling that analytical writing is still so dominant in anthropology and our standards are so low that when another anthropologist hears a phrase like "narrative anthropology," oftentimes we're not even talking about the same thing.
12. Behar (2011, 110).
13. Eriksen (2006, 30). Ruth Behar, again, is one of those rare exceptions that proves the rule. Behar's writing is elegant and lean, each word carefully chosen and precisely placed for maximum impact. I admire her as much for what she says as what she doesn't say. She avoids the clogged arteries typically found in anthropological writing. Even with this lean style, I often get the feeling that she could have said more, especially after she's just made a major, potentially explosive point. Rather than spell out all the connections explicitly and at great length, she makes the point in a clear, devastating way, and then moves on. She respects her readers, trusting that they got the point and will make further connections on their own.
14. On the importance of writing for conceptual clarity and theoretical understanding in anthropology, see Campbell (1996), Eriksen (2006, 63), and Sutton (1991).
15. On institutional inertia and reward systems, see Borofsky (2010) and Campbell (1996). Behar also diagnoses anthropology's

ingrained, falsely dichotomous view, according to which stories are fun and fluffy, not serious "theoretical" analysis, and you couldn't possibly combine the two. As Behar put it, "there's a huge fear of good writing in anthropology—the assumption being that good writing has a tendency to be precious, to be too full of itself, to be self-indulgent (always a no-no in our discipline), to be a distraction from the pressing reality at hand that needs to be analyzed rigorously" (2012). Elsewhere, Behar describes how she learned about anthropology's insistence on "academic rigor" during graduate school, where she put aside her more personal, poetic observations about sensory and emotional phenomena during her fieldwork in Spain (2013, 87–91).

16. Hart (2005, 57). I wanted to join the small group of anthropologists trying to write more humanely, like Ruth Behar (1996), who, as noted earlier, has called for and led the way with "vulnerable anthropology."

Acknowledgments

In *Bird by Bird*, my favorite book of writing advice, Anne Lamott talks about the importance of finding good readers for your drafts, people who "will tell you the truth and help you stay on the straight and narrow, or find your way back to it if you are lost" (1994, 164). Fortunately, I have had several such readers for this book.

The novelist Keith Scribner helped me improve my writing at every level, from conceptualizing the book's basic structure to polishing individual sentences. With patience and insight, he encouraged me to rewrite a first draft that lacked a strong narrative thread, and he pinpointed and celebrated what was working well in later drafts. If I had a vexing punctuation, grammar, or wording question, he always had the answer. To the extent that this book is literary enough to belong in a series dedicated to "Literary Anthropology," it's because of Keith, and for that—and our friendship—I'm deeply grateful.

David Sutton helped with the anthropology. He rooted for me when I got the story up and running, but he also gently steered me back to relevant anthropological scholarship whenever I started getting lost in the narrative. Throughout multiple readings and long phone calls, he gave me astute suggestions and helped me think through my interpretations. I wouldn't have even walked into Ranulfo and Pablo's video store in 2005 if David and I hadn't been working on our own book about movies at that time. As always, David has been there every step of the way, and I can't imagine anthropology without him. Thank you, Dave, for another great road trip of the mind.

At Willamette University, two colleagues gave me insightful comments on early drafts based on their knowledge of Latino cultures and writing. When Patricia Varas, from the Latin American Studies program, offered an extremely close reading of a draft, it was reassuring to see that she understood exactly what I was shooting for, right down to the humor, and I benefited greatly from her Kalimán-like ability to spot things that I hadn't noticed. I feel very lucky and grateful to have had Patricia not only as a reader, but also as an interlocutor, confidante, and advocate throughout this entire process. Ivan Welty, a philosophy professor at Willamette, also gave me crucial comments at an important juncture. Ivan let me know that I was on the right track, but he encouraged me to keep going, to fill out the story, especially the parts about my role as an anthropologist. Largely because of his comments, I jumped back into the writing and increased the manuscript length by at least 30%. I appreciate Ivan's open-minded, probing way of seeing the world and what he has done for this book.

As amazing as these readers have been, there's one person who got even more deeply involved in this book: my wife, Maria McIvor. She didn't just read multiple versions of every chapter, she discussed them with me at length at all times of the day and night: over breakfast, driving in the car, standing together on the sidelines at baseball games, after dinner. She was generous with exclamation points and encouraging comments in the margins, but she also told me when something needed more work—and she was always right. Like everything else, we lived this book together. The word "gratitude" doesn't adequately express what I feel for Maria.

I also want to thank the people who read separate chapters and sections. The first time I ever got the sense that there might be a book in here was after writing up a couple fieldwork vignettes for a workshop with Joanne Mulcahy and Kim Stafford at the Northwest Writing Institute. Years later, Joni Roberts, Suzanne Scheld, and Eileen Kane also read early drafts of the first one or two chapters. All these readers encouraged me at crucial, early stages by letting me know that Ranulfo's humor and energy were coming through on the page, and they also gave useful suggestions that influenced my future writing.

I would also like to thank the people who read over individual passages and confirmed that I had accurately represented the events described there: namely, Jim Schiess (second construction estimate on the bakery), Pablo Juárez (bakery plans, buying the store building), Mauricio Juárez

(ESL class), Shanel Parette (Ranulfo's visit to class), Scott McCauley (Sick Bastard), Rich and Billy Knipe (Andy Knipe's funeral), Zach, Liam, and Peter Wogan (Oaxaca, baseball). I also appreciate the feedback and suggestions I've received at social science conferences on aspects related to this research.

Finally, I would like to thank the people associated with Palgrave Macmillan who made this book a reality: the "Literary Anthropology" series editors Deborah Reed-Danahay and Helena Wulff, Palgrave editors Alexis Nelson and Kyra Saniewski, the anonymous reviewers, and the copy editor. Heartfelt thanks also go to Ilan Stavans and Ruth Behar for agreeing to read and comment on this book, even though we'd never met before, and to Jaime Arredondo, for everything he's done for farmworkers in the Willamette Valley.

To all, my sincere thanks.

Appendix A: Ranulfo's Reactions to This Book

Ranulfo and I worked out plans for this book off and on for years, but our discussions got more grounded and specific in the spring of 2013, once Ranulfo started reviewing my drafts of individual chapters. I told him, as I had from the start, that I'd change anything he objected to because I didn't want to write a book that would hurt his reputation, feelings, or our friendship. Being the one to put the words on the page and define events, I worried about taking more of a lead than I ever had before in our relationship, but that didn't turn out to be a problem. As Ranulfo said, "It's an exchange. Sometimes I drive and sometimes you drive, but we're trying to get to the same place." As he read the chapters, he quickly saw we had the same vision. We didn't always share the same interpretations, but he felt that we were getting at the same reality. And, overall, he liked what he saw. He said, *Lo bueno es que compartimos la misma visión.* "The good thing is we share the same vision." And he added, *Pienso que la gente se puede identificar.* "I think people will be able to relate."

Feeling good about our shared vision, we focused on Ranulfo's comments on individual chapters. Throughout the spring and summer of 2013, he read every new chapter carefully (in English) at home, putting highlighter marks next to anything he wanted changed. When we met, usually the next week at the store, he gave me his requests for changes, most of which were quite minor. For example, he corrected the dates for a couple events that happened before I met him. He also asked to have a few details omitted, to protect the privacy of certain people. I made every change he asked for, as he saw when he reviewed the complete, revised version of the manuscript in 2014.

One thing we initially disagreed on was the representation of his childhood poverty. Ranulfo was more interested in a story that stressed that he came from nothing, *la gran nada*. I knew this point was important to him, but I had to tell him that readers would lose interest if all the book did was state over and over that he came from extreme poverty. I believed poverty could be mentioned, but not too often. Once Ranulfo got past the halfway point in the draft, he agreed that it worked fine; the poverty was still in there, but not over-emphasized.

Anticipating possible criticisms, I also asked, "What if people say that I'm robbing your voice by writing about your culture?" Ranulfo flatly responded, "But you're not brainwashing me. We share the same vision. We're forming a connection, like a chain, and the book is training people to do the same thing."

"But what if they say it's not OK for a white guy to talk about Latino culture?"

"Oh, then your answer is: 'I worked very hard to understand this culture. I didn't learn about it overnight.' Anyway, we're splitting the profits, if there are any, 50/50, so they can't criticize you."

Discussing the drafts led to discussions like this, reminiscences about earlier events, and fresh analyses of culture, economics, philosophy, Cantinflas, Moby Dick, accounting, mortgage rates, and everything else. The whole process—writing, reading, discussing, planning—deepened our relationship.

What follows are some of Ranulfo's reactions to specific chapters and sections.

True Story

"This is my favorite part," Ranulfo said while pointing to the first page, where it says "A True Story." "People need to know this is all true. These things all happened."

My Visit to La Palma

Ranulfo especially liked the section on my visit with his parents. He said, "They're the source of everything. They're great people."

APPENDIX A: RANULFO'S REACTIONS TO THIS BOOK   213

His Kids

After his kids, Mauricio and Laura, read the chapter about buying the store from Mr. Hanning, Ranulfo was glad to see they were learning more about their father's business.

Car Conflict

At first he wasn't sure we should include Roberto's car argument. He said, *Pete, te has convertido en criticón.* "Pete, you've become a huge complainer." But later he agreed it was OK to show how we don't always agree, how naturally his first-generation immigrant perspective is different from mine.

Cousin Dying of ALS

In reference to this section, he said, *Muy triste, la historia de Andy.* "Very sad, the story of Andy." He added, "And very honest. If it were me, maybe I wouldn't have put that part in about how you ignored him when you were kids. But his story makes you value life more."

Baseball Card Store

"I liked what Zach said about Larry Doby."

God's Dream

He agreed with my interpretation of the God dream being about his fear of asking for too much, especially in regards to purchasing the Albany restaurant. "Yes, exactly, that was it. I had this fear that I wasn't *la persona indicada,* the right person, to question God. *Como no tengo el derecho de cuestionar, bajo mis costumbres.* Like I don't have the right to question, within my customs."

He still believed it was possible that was truly God in the dream. "God can be anybody. He could be a child, or a homeless person, a customer at the store. That's what that dream made me think. He just showed up as an old man in that dream." At the same time, he couldn't be sure, and he maintained his sense of the ultimate mystery of the dream. "You can't ever be 100% sure. It was a dream."

Overall Dream Interpretations

For the most part, though, he didn't make specific comments on my dream interpretations. When I finally asked directly, he said, *Tal vez sí, tal vez no.* "Maybe yes, maybe no." As just noted for God's dream, he didn't believe anyone could ever know a dream's meaning for sure, even the dreamer. He maintained some of his original interpretations, revised others, and said it was fine for readers to think about mine, like philosophers or scientists who speculate on the meaning of occult phenomena. He said, "Maybe this will open up a hurricane, a chaos, of dream revelations. People will learn it's OK to dream."

Turtles

He was especially happy to see that I included so many of his turtle references. It was after reading one of these passages that he told me about watching the video of the alligator trying to eat the turtle. Another time he said, *Quiero ser el Hombre-Tortuga.* "I want to be Turtle-Man."

Appendix B: Names in This Book

For the sake of privacy, the following pseudonyms were used in this book: Manuel, Antonio, Kate, Kenny, Mr. Hanning, Roberto, and Dave Hedding. A couple minor details in the main text were also changed to protect the anonymity of "Kenny" and "Antonio." Otherwise, all names and details are accurately represented.

Bibliography

Adamson, Joseph. 1997. *Melville, Shame, and the Evil Eye: A Psychoanalytic Reading.* Albany: State University of New York Press.

Appadurai, Arjun. 2016. *Banking on Words: The Failure of Language in the Age of Derivative Finance.* Chicago: University of Chicago Press.

Barofsky, Neil. 2012. *Bailout: How Washington Abandoned Main Street While Rescuing Wall Street.* New York: Free Press.

Barrett, Deirdre. 2001. *The Committee of Sleep: How Artists, Scientists, and Athletes Use Dreams for Creative Problem-Solving—and How You Can, Too.* New York: Crown.

Basso, Ellen. 1987/1992. "The Implications of a Progressive Theory of Dreaming." In *Dreaming: Anthropological and Psychological Interpretations*, Barbara Tedlock, editor, 86–104. Santa Fe: School of American Research Press.

Basu, Sammy. 1999. "Dialogic Ethics and the Virtue of Humor." *Journal of Political Philosophy* 7: 378–403.

Blinder, Alan. 2013. *After the Music Stopped: The Financial Crisis, the Response, and the Work Ahead.* New York: Penguin Press

Behar, Ruth. 1993. *Translated Woman: Crossing the Border with Esperanza's Story.* Boston: Beacon Press.

Behar, Ruth. 1996. *The Vulnerable Observer: Anthropology that Breaks Your Heart.* Boston: Beacon Press.

Behar, Ruth. 2011. "Believing in Anthropology as Literature." In *Anthropology Off the Shelf: Anthropologists on Writing*, Alisse Waterston and Maria D. Vesperi, editors, 106–116. Malden, MA: Wiley-Blackwell.

Behar, Ruth. 2012. "Literature, Writing & Anthropology: Interview with the Author." *Cultural Anthropology: Journal of the Society for Cultural Anthropology*, July 9, 2012, http://www.culanth.org/?q=node/590. Accessed on October 18, 2013.

Behar, Ruth. 2013. *Traveling Heavy: A Memoir in Between Journeys*. Durham: Duke University Press.

Bellamy Foster, John, and Fred Magdoff. 2009. *The Great Financial Crisis: Causes and Consequences*. New York: Monthly Review Press.

Borofsky, Rob. 2010. *Why a Public Anthropology?* Kaneohe, Hawaii: Center for a Public Anthropology, Hawaii Pacific University.

Brettell, Caroline B., and Deborah Reed-Danahay. 2012. *Civic Engagements: The Citizenship Practices of Indian and Vietnamese Immigrants*. Stanford: Stanford University Press.

Burns, Peter, and James G. Gimpel. 2000. "Economic Insecurity, Prejudicial Stereotypes, and Public Opinion on Immigration Policy." *Political Science Quarterly* 115: 201–25.

Butler Flora, Cornelia. 1984. "Roasting Donald Duck: Alternative Comics and Photonovels in Latin America." *Journal of Popular Culture* 18: 163–83.

Caillois, Roger. 1961. *Man, Play, and Games*, Meyer Barash, translator. New York: Free Press.

Campbell, Alan. 1996. "Tricky Tropes: Styles of the Popular and the Pompous." In *Popularizing Anthropology*, Jeremy MacClancy and Chris McDonaugh, editors, 58–82. London: Routledge.

Campbell, Bruce. 2009. *¡Viva la Historieta! Mexican Comics, NAFTA, and the Politics of Globalization*. Jackson: University of Mississippi Press.

Canfield, Jack. 2001. *Chicken Soup for the Baseball Fan's Soul: Inspirational Stories of Baseball, Big-League Dreams, and the Game of Life*. Deerfield Beach, Florida: Health Communications.

Cavalluzzo, Ken, and John Wolken. 2005. "Small Business Loan Turndowns, Personal Wealth, and Discrimination." *Journal of Business* 78: 2153–77.

Chavez, Denise. 2002. *Por el Amor de Pedro Infante*. New York: Vintage Español.

Cohan, William D. 2009. *House of Cards: A Tale of Hubris and Wretched Excess on Wall Street*. New York: Doubleday.

Conover, Ted. 1987/2012. *Coyotes: A Journey Through the Secret World of America's Mexican Migrants*. Los Gatos: Smashword Editions.

Collins, Randall. 2004. *Interaction Ritual Chains*. Princeton: Princeton University Press.

Coser, Lewis A. 1971/1977. *Masters of Sociological Thought: Ideas in Historical and Social Context*, 2nd edition. New York: Harcourt Brace Jovanovich, Inc.

Crapanzano, Vincent. 1980. *Tuhami: Portrait of a Moroccan*. Chicago: University of Chicago Press.

Domínguez Barajas, Elías. 2005. "Sociocognitive Aspects of Proverb Use in a Mexican Transnational Social Network." *In Latino Language and Literacy in Ethnolinguistic Chicago*, Marcia Farr, editor, 67–95. Mahwah, New Jersey: Lawrence Erlbaum Associates.

Donaldson, Scott. 1973. "Damned Dollars and a Blessed Company: Financial Imagery in *Moby-Dick*." *New England Quarterly* 46: 279–83.
Douglas, Mary. 1966/2002. *Purity and Danger: An Analysis of the Concept of Pollution and Taboo*. London: Routledge.
Driessen, Henk. 2013. "Going Public: Some Thoughts on Anthropology in and of the World." *Journal of the Royal Anthropological Institute* 19: 390–93.
Drummond, Lee. 1996. *American Dreamtime: A Cultural Analysis of Popular Movies and Their Implications for a Science of Humanity*. Lanham: Rowman & Littlefield Publishers.
Eriksen, Thomas Hylland. 2006. *Engaging Anthropology: The Case for a Public Presence*. London: Berg Press.
Fabian, Johannes. 1983. *Time and the Other: How Anthropology Makes Its Object*. New York: Columbia University Press.
Farr, Marcia. 2006. *Rancheros in Chicagoacán: Language and Identity in a Transnational Community*. Austin: University of Texas Press.
Fernández L'Hoeste, Héctor. 2009. "Race and Gender in the Adventures of Kalimán, El Hombre Increíble." In *Redrawing the Nation: National Identity in Latin/o American Comics*, Héctor Fernández L'Hoeste and Juan Poblete, editors, 55–80. New York: Palgrave Macmillan.
Flores, William V., and Rina Benmayor, editors. 1997. *Latino Cultural Citizenship: Claiming Identity, Space and Politics*. Boston: Beacon Press.
Foster, George M. 1970. "Character and Personal Relationships Seen Through Proverbs in Tzintzuntzan, Mexico." *Journal of American Folklore* 83: 304–17.
Foster, George M. 1973. "Dreams, Character, and Cognitive Orientation in Tzintzuntzan." *Ethos* 1: 106–21.
Foster, George M. 1979. *Tzintzuntzan: Mexican Peasants in a Changing World*. New York: Elsevier.
Fraga, Luis Ricardo, John A. Garcia, Rodney Hero, Michael Jones-Correa, Valerie Martinez-Ebers, and Gary M. Segura. 2010. *Latino Lives in America: Making It Home*. Philadelphia: Temple University Press.
Gershenberg, Irving. 1972. "Banking in Uganda Since Independence." *Economic Development and Cultural Change* 20: 504–23.
Giamatti, A. Bartlett. 1998. "The Green Fields of the Mind." In *A Great and Glorious Game: Baseball Writings of A. Bartlett Giamatti*, Kenneth S. Robson, editor, 7–14. Chapel Hill: Algonquin Books.
Glazer, Mark. 1987. *A Dictionary of Mexican American Proverbs*. Westport, Connecticut: Greenwood Press.
Graeber, David. 2001. *Toward an Anthropological Theory of Value: The False Coin of Our Own Dreams*. New York: Palgrave.
Graeber, David. 2005. "The Auto-Ethnography That Can Never Be and the Activist's Ethnography That Might Be." In *Auto-Ethnographies: The Anthropology of Academic Practices*, Anne Menely and Donna J. Young, editors, 189–202. Toronto: Broadview Press.
Graeber, David. 2011. *Debt: The First 5,000 Years*. Brooklyn: Melville House.

Hart, Keith. 2005. *The Hit Man's Dilemma: Or, Business, Personal and Impersonal.* Chicago: Prickly Paradigm Press.
Hart, Keith, Jean-Louis Laville, and Antonio David Cattani, editors. 2010. *The Human Economy: A Citizen's Guide.* London: Polity.
Hartmann, Ernest.1998. *Dreams and Nightmares: The New Theory on the Origin and Meaning of Dreams.* New York: Plenum Trade.
Hinds, Harold E., Jr., and Charles M. Tatum. 1992. *Not Just for Children: The Mexican Comic Book in the Late 1960s and 1970s.* Westport: Greenwood Press.
Ho, Karen. 2009. *Liquidated: An Ethnography of Wall Street.* Durham: Duke University Press.
Hollan, Douglas. 2003. "The Cultural and Intersubjective Context of Dream Remembrance and Reporting: Dreams, Aging, and the Anthropological Encounter in Toraja, Indonesia." In *Dream Travelers: Sleep Experiences and Culture in the Western Pacific*, Roger Ivar Lohmann, editor, 168–187. New York: Palgrave Macmillan.
Hollan, Douglas. 2004. "The Anthropology of Dreaming: Selfscape Dreams." *Dreaming* 14:170–182.
Holmes, Seth. 2013. *Fresh Fruit, Broken Bodies: Migrant Farmworkers in the United States.* Berkeley: University of California Press.
Insko, Jeffrey. 2007. "'All of Us Are Ahabs': *Moby-Dick* in Contemporary Public Discourse." *Journal of the Midwest Modern Language Association* 40: 19–37.
Jacobson, C. Jeffrey, Jr. 2009. "The Nightmares of Puerto Ricans: An Embodied 'Altered States of Consciousness' Perspective." *Culture, Medicine and Psychiatry* 33: 266–89.
Johnson, Simon, and James Kwak. 2010. *13 Bankers: The Wall Street Takeover and the Next Financial Meltdown.* New York: Pantheon Books.
Kane, Eileen. 2010. *Trickster: An Anthropological Memoir.* Toronto: University of Toronto Press.
Kerouac, Jack. 1951/1999. *On the Road.* New York: Penguin Books.
Kessler, Alan. 2001. "Immigration, Economic Insecurity, and the 'Ambivalent' American Public." Center for Comparative Immigration Studies, University of California-San Diego, Working Paper 41. http://escholarship.org/uc/item/6k5531rt#page-1. Accessed September 20, 2016.
Kierkegaard, Søren. 1843/1992. *Either/Or: A Fragment of Life*, Alastair Hannay, translator. New York: Penguin Classics.
Kirtsoglou, Elisabeth. 2010. "Dreaming the Self: A Unified Approach Toward Dreams, Subjectivity and the Radical Imagination." *History and Anthropology* 21: 321–35.
Kottak, Conrad P. 1978. "Rituals at McDonald's." *Journal of American Culture* 1: 370–86.
Krohn-Hansen, Christian. 2012. *Making New York Dominican: Small Businesses, Politics, and Everyday Life.* Philadelphia: University of Pennsylvania Press.

Lamott, Anne. 1994. *Bird by Bird: Some Instructions on Writing and Life.* New York: Anchor Books.
Lears, Jackson. 2003. *Something for Nothing: Luck in America.* New York: Viking Press.
Lewis, Michael. 1989/2010. *Liar's Poker: Rising Through the Wreckage on Wall Street.* New York: W.W. Norton & Company.
Lewis, Michael. 2010. *The Big Short: Inside the Doomsday Machine.* New York: W.W. Norton & Company.
Light, Ivan Hubert, and Steven J. Gold. 2000. *Ethnic Economies.* San Diego: Academic Press.
Lohmann, Roger Ivar. 2007. "Dreams and Ethnography." In *The New Science of Dreaming*, volume 3, Deirdre Barrett and Patrick McNamara, editors, 35–69. Westport: Praeger.
Lohmann, Roger Ivar. 2010a. "How Evaluating Dreams Makes History: Asabano Examples." *History and Anthropology* 21: 227–49.
Lohmann, Roger Ivar. 2010b. "Introduction: The Anthropology of Creations." *Anthropological Forum* 20:215–234.
Lonergan, Eric. 2009. *Money.* Acumen: Durham.
Mageo, Jeannette Marie, editor. 2003. *Dreaming and the Self: New Perspectives on Subjectivity, Identity, and Emotion.* Albany: State University of New York Press.
Mageo, Jeannette Marie, editor. 2011. *Dreaming Culture: Meanings, Models, and Power in U.S. American Dreams.* New York: Palgrave Macmillan.
Mandis, Steven G. 2013. *What Happened to Goldman Sachs? An Insider's Story of Organizational Drift and Its Unintended Consequences.* Boston: Harvard Business Review Press.
McCloskey, Donald N. 1990. *If You're So Smart: The Narrative of Economic Expertise.* Chicago: University of Chicago Press.
McClure, Heather H., J. Josh Snodgrass, Charles R. Martinez Jr., Erica C. Squires, Roberto A. Jiménez, Laura E. Isiordia, J. Mark Eddy, Thomas W. McDade, and Jeon Small. 2015. "Stress, Place, and Allostatic Load Among Mexican Immigrant Farmworkers in Oregon." *Journal of Immigrant Minority Health* 17: 1518–25.
McLean, Bethany, and Joe Nocera. 2010. *All the Devils Are Here: The Hidden History of the Financial Crisis.* New York: Penguin.
McWilliams, Susan. 2012. "Ahab, American." *Review of Politics* 74: 233–60.
Melville, Herman. 1851. *Moby-Dick; or, the Whale.* New York: Harper and Brothers.
Morewedge, Carey K., and Michael I. Norton. 2009. "When Dreaming Is Believing: The (Motivated) Interpretation of Dreams." *Journal of Personality and Social Psychology* 96: 249–64.

Narayan, Kirin. 2012. *Alive in the Writing: Crafting Ethnography in the Company of Chekov*. Chicago: University of Chicago Press.

Nietzsche, Friedrich. 1886/2002. *Beyond Good and Evil: Prelude to a Philosophy of the Future*, Rolf-Peter Horstmann and Judith Norman, editors, and Judith Norman, translator. Cambridge: Cambridge University Press.

Oberlechner, Thomas, Thomas Slunecko, and Nicole Kronberger. 2004. "Surfing the Money Tides: Understanding the Foreign Exchange Market Through Metaphor." *British Journal of Social Psychology* 43: 133–56.

Ordóñez, Juan Thomas. 2015. *Jornalero: Being a Day-Laborer in the USA*. Berkeley: University of California Press.

Partnoy, Frank. 1999/2009. *F.I.A.S.C.O.: Blood in the Water on Wall Street*. New York: Penguin.

Pratt, Mary Louise. 1986. "Fieldwork in Common Places." In *Writing Culture: The Poetics and Politics of Ethnography*, James Clifford and George Marcus, editors, 27–50. Berkeley: University of California Press.

Puzo, Mario. 1969/1983. *The Godfather*. New York: Signet.

Rapport, Nigel. 1997. *Transcendent Individual: Essays Toward a Literary and Liberal Anthropology*. London: Routledge.

Reed-Danahay, Deborah, editor. 1997. *Auto/Ethnography: Rewriting the Self and the Social*. Oxford: Berg.

Reed-Danahay, Deborah, and Caroline B. Brettell, editors. 2008. *Citizenship, Political Engagement, and Belonging: Immigrants in Europe and the United States*. New Brunswick: Rutgers University Press.

Reith, Gerda. 1999. *The Age of Chance: Gambling in Western Culture*. London: Routledge.

Roberts, Russell. 2010. "Gambling with Other People's Money: How Perverted Incentives Caused the Financial Crisis." Mercatus Center, George Mason University. https://www.mercatus.org/publication/gambling-other-peoples-money. Accessed August 20, 2010.

Rock, Andrea. 2004. *The Mind at Night: The New Science of How and Why We Dream*. New York: Basic Books.

Rohrer, Tim, and Mary Jean Vignone. 2012. "The Bankers Go to Washington: Theory and Method in Conceptual Metaphor Analysis." *Nouveaux Cahiers de Linguistique Francaise* 30: 5–38.

Rosaldo, Renato. 1989/1993. *Culture and Truth: The Remaking of Social Analysis*, 2nd edition. Boston: Beacon Press.

Royster, Paul. 1986. "Melville's Economy of Language." In *Ideology and Classic American Literature*, Sacvan Bercovitch and Myra Jehlen, editors, 313–336. Cambridge: Cambridge University Press.

Rubenstein, Anne. 1998. *Bad Language, Naked Ladies, and Other Threats to the Nation: A Political History of Comic Books in Mexico*. Durham: Duke University Press.

Sánchez, Claudia, and Richard L. Parker. 2007. "Cultural Values in Latin American and U.S. Superhero Comics." *International Journal of Comic Art* 7: 198–224.

Segal, Daniel, and Richard Handler. 1990. *Jane Austen and the Fiction of Culture: An Essay on the Narration of Social Realities*. Tucson: University of Arizona Press.

Sekules, Kate. 2000. *The Boxer's Heart: Lessons from the Ring*. New York: Seal Press.

Senders, Stefan, and Allison Truitt, editors. 2007. *Money: Ethnographic Encounters*. Oxford: Berg Press.

Simmel, Georg. 1907/2004. *The Philosophy of Money*, David Frisby, editor, Tom Bottomore and David Frisby, translators. London: Routledge.

Simmel, Georg. 1912/1950. *The Sociology of Georg Simmel*, Kurt H. Wolff, translator and editor. Glencoe, Illinois: The Free Press.

Shostak, Marjorie. 2000. *Return to Nisa*. Cambridge: Harvard University Press.

Smith, Greg. 2012. *Why I Left Goldman Sachs: A Wall Street Story*. New York: Grand Central Publishing.

Sotres Mora, Bertha Eugenia. 1973. "La cultura de los comics." *Revista Mexicana de Ciencia Política* 29: 13–17.

Stavans, Ilan. 2000. *The Essential Ilan Stavans*. New York: Routledge.

Stavans, Ilan. 2004. *¡Lotería!* Teresa Villegas, artist. Tucson: University of Arizona Press.

Stavans, Ilan, and Frederick Luis Aldama. 2013. *¡Muy Pop! Conversations on Latino Popular Culture*. Ann Arbor: University of Michigan Press.

Steinberg, Theodore. 2006. *American Green: The Obsessive Quest for the Perfect Lawn*. New York: W.W. Norton.

Stephen, Lynn. 2007. *Transborder Lives: Indigenous Oaxacans in Mexico, California, and Oregon*. Durham: Duke University Press.

Stewart, Charles. 1997. "Fields in Dreams: Anxiety, Experience, and the Limits of Social Constructionism in Modern Greek Dream Narratives." *American Ethnologist* 24: 877–94.

Stewart, Charles. 2003 "Dreams of Treasure: Temporality, Historicization and the Unconscious." *Anthropological Theory* 3: 481–500.

Stewart, Charles. 2012. *Dreaming and Historical Consciousness in Island Greece*. Cambridge: Harvard University Press.

Sunderland, Patricia L., and Rita M. Denny. 2007. *Doing Anthropology in Consumer Research*. London: Routledge.

Sutton, David. 1991. "Is Anybody Out There? Anthropology and the Question of Audience." *Critique of Anthropology* 11: 91–104.

Sutton, David. 1998. "He's Too Cold! Children and the Limits of Culture on a Greek Island." *Anthropology and Humanism* 23: 127–38.

Sutton, David, and Peter Wogan. 2009. *Hollywood Blockbusters: The Anthropology of Popular Movies*. Oxford: Berg Press.

Taussig, Michael. 2013. "I'm So Angry I Made a Sign." In *Occupy: Three Inquiries in Disobedience*, W.J.T. Mitchell, Bernard Harcourt, and Michael Taussig, authors, 3–44. Chicago: University of Chicago Press.

Tedlock, Barbara. 1991. "The New Anthropology of Dreaming." *Dreaming* 1: 161–78.

Tett, Gillian. 2009. *Fool's Gold: How the Bold Dream of a Small Tribe at J.P. Morgan Was Corrupted by Wall Street Greed and Unleashed a Catastrophe*. New York: Free Press.

Thompson, Michael. 1979. *Rubbish Theory: The Creation and Destruction of Value*. Oxford: Oxford University Press.

Thorn, John. 2011. *Baseball in the Garden of Eden: The Secret History of the Early Game*. New York: Simon and Schuster.

Treviño Hart, Elva. 1999. *Barefoot Heart: Stories of a Migrant Child*. Tempe, Arizona: Bilingual Press/Editorial Bilingüe.

Urrea, Luis Alberto. 1996. *By the Lake of Sleeping Children*. New York: Anchor Books.

Valdez, Zulema. 2011. *The New Entrepreneurs: How Race, Class, and Gender Shape American Enterprise*. Stanford: Stanford University Press.

Vonnegut, Kurt. 1981. *Palm Sunday: An Autobiographical Collage*. New York: Delacorte Press.

Walley, Christine J. 2013. *Exit Zero: Family and Class in Postindustrial Chicago*. Chicago: University of Chicago Press.

Watson, James L., editor. 1997. *Golden Arches East: McDonald's in East Asia*. Stanford: Stanford University Press.

Weems, Scott. 2014. *Ha! The Science of When We Laugh and Why*. New York: Basic Books.

Wilker, Josh. 2010. *Cardboard Gods: An All-American Tale Told Through Baseball Cards*. New York: Seven Footer Press.

Wogan, Peter. 2004a. *Magical Writing in Salasaca: Literacy and Power in Highland Ecuador*. Boulder: Westview Press.

Wogan, Peter. 2004b. "Deep Hanging Out: Reflections on Fieldwork and Multisited Andean Ethnography." *Identities: Global Studies in Culture and Power* 11: 129–39.

Wogan, Peter. 2006. "Audience Reception and Ethnographic Film: Laughing at First Contact." *Visual Anthropology Review* 22: 14–33.

Wulff, Helena, editor. 2016. *The Anthropologist as Writer: Genres and Contexts in the Twenty-First Century*. Oxford: Berghahn.

Index

A
Adamson, Joseph, 102n12
Aldama, Frederick Luis, 85n3
anthropology, 15, 34, 38n2, 50, 56, 59n2, 59n3, 59–60n4, 61n9, 82, 83, 85n6, 96n8, 100, 132n7, 199–201, 203n5, 203n6, 204n9, 205n10, 205n11, 205–6n15, 206n16
  anthropologist, 15, 34, 38n2, 40, 50, 55, 57, 80, 85n6, 91, 134n13, 151, 161, 180, 194n19, 199, 200, 203n5, 204n7, 205n11
Appadurai, Arjun, 106n10, 122n11

B
bank loan, 21, 54, 62n14, 66, 102, 121n7, 126, 130, 132n11, 174, 182, 188, 190n5
Barofsky, Neil, 175n4, 176n7
baseball, 1, 2, 16, 32, 44, 72, 93, 146, 147, 149–54, 156n10–11, 198, 199
Basso, Ellen, 60n6
Basu, Sammy, 83, 86n10
Beatles, The, 76, 145
Behar, Ruth, 50, 61n9–11, 96n7, 96–7n8, 120n1, 120n5, 156n9, 200, 201, 205n12, 205n13, 205–6n15, 206n16, 209
Bellamy Foster, John, 97n9
Benmayor, Rina, 120n5
Blinder, Alan, 133n10
Borofsky, Rob, 205n10, 205n15
Brettell, Caroline B., 86n7, 120–1n5
Burns, Peter, 96n3
Butler Flora, Cornelia, 48n7

C
Caillois, Roger, 22n3, 64n23
Campbell, Alan, 203n5, 205n14, 205n15

Note: Page numbers followed by 'n' refer to end notes.

Campbell, Bruce, 48n7
Canfield, Jack, 156n6
Cantinflas, 43, 79, 85n3, 85n4, 101, 112, 120n2, 160, 212
Captain Ahab, 3, 4n3, 20, 21, 103, 183, 187, 193n14, 196n28. *See also* Melville, Herman; *Moby-Dick*
Casino, 16–21, 25, 26, 28, 42, 55, 57, 102, 149
Castaneda, Carlos, 34
Cavalluzzo, Ken, 62n14
Chavez, Denise, 100, 105n5
Cohan, William D., 132n3, 132n5, 133n9, 168n2, 195n22
Collins, Randall, 47n1
Conover, Ted, 90, 92, 96n5
Coser, Lewis, 22n2
Coyotes, 33, 35, 49
Crapanzano, Vincent, 59n4, 61n9, 97n8, 122n8

D
Dairy Queen, 1, 88, 162
Denny, Rita M., 85n6
Domínguez Barajas, Elías, 62n16
Donaldson, Scott, 106n13
Don Quixote, 43, 58, 79, 113, 197, 202
Douglas, Mary, 47n2, 117, 119, 122n10–11, 123n15
dreams, 42–6, 49, 50, 52–5, 57, 58, 59n2, 59–60n4, 60n5, 60n6, 61n12, 63n20, 66, 80, 84, 109–19, 120–1n5, 121–2n7, 122–3n11, 126, 131, 137–41, 151, 152, 163, 165, 171, 172, 198, 213, 214
Driessen, Hank, 204n9, 205n10
Drummond, Lee, 156n8

E
Eriksen, Thomas Hylland, 200, 201, 203n5, 204n9–11, 205n13, 205n14

F
Fabian, Johannes, 204n7
Farr, Marcia, 38n3
Fernández L'Hoeste, Héctor, 48n7
Financial Crisis, 134n10, 148, 171, 173, 175n6, 179–81, 183–5, 189n5, 191n5, 191n8, 193n13, 193n14
Flores, William V., 120n5
Foster, George M., 47n3, 48n6, 60n5, 61n12, 62n16, 62n17
Fraga, Luis Ricardo, 105n1

G
Gershenberg, Irving, 196n25
Giamatti, A. Bartlett, 156n3
Gimpel, James G., 96n3
Glazer, Mark, 62n16
Gold, Steven J., 62n15
Graeber, David, 57, 61n8, 63n22, 91, 96n6, 121–2n7, 135n15, 169n5

H
Handler, Richard, 204n6
Hart, Keith, 105n2, 180, 189n2, 203n3
Hartmann, Ernest, 121n6
Hinds, Harold E., Jr., 48n7
Ho, Karen, 134n13, 135n14
Hollan, Douglas, 59n4, 123n14
Holmes, Seth, 105n4

I

immigration, 10, 71, 87, 94, 109, 111, 112, 114–16, 125
  immigrant, 8n1, 13, 18, 29n1, 32, 56, 67, 78, 91, 93, 99, 102, 106n8, 111, 121n5, 156n9, 213
Incredible Hulk, 5, 113
Insko, Jeffrey, 193n14, 195n22, 196n28

J

Jacobson, C. Jeffrey, Jr., 60n6
Johnson, Simon, 134n12, 135n15, 135n16, 193n11

K

Kalimán, 45, 48n7, 48n8, 113, 137, 138, 167, 202
Kane, Eileen, 34, 38n2, 96n8
Kerouac, Jack, 20, 22n6
Kessler, Alan, 96n3
Kierkegaard, Søren, 148, 156n2
Kirtsoglou, Elisabeth, 123n14
Knipe, Andy, 146–50, 153, 154, 156n1, 199, 213
Knipe, Billy, 147, 156n1
Knipe, Rich, 150, 156n1
Kottak, Conrad P., 80, 85n6
Krohn-Hansen, Christian, 62n15, 106n8
Kwak, James, 134n12, 135n15, 135n16, 193n11

L

Lears, Jackson, 22n3
Lewis, Michael, 22n2, 133n10, 135n17, 168n1, 184, 190–1n5, 194n16, 196n28

Light, Ivan Hubert, 62n15
Lohmann, Roger Ivar, 47n3, 60n6, 62n13, 63n20, 120n4

M

Magdoff, Fred, 97n9
Mageo, Jeanette Marie, 59n2, 59n4, 121n6, 123n14
Mandis, Steven G., 133n10, 196n26
McCloskey, Donald N., 194n17
McClure, Heather H., 105n4
McDonald's, 78–81, 85n5, 118, 121n5
McLean, Bethany, 127, 132n1, 133n8, 133n9, 181, 182, 191n8, 196n26
McWilliams, Susan, 107n15
Melville, Herman, 4n3, 23n7–9, 103, 106–7n13, 107n15, 168n3, 168n4, 169n5, 182, 186, 193n12, 195n22, 195n24, 196n28. *See also* Captain Ahab; *Moby-Dick*
metaphors, 54, 69, 103, 122n10, 173–5, 193n14
Michoacán, 35, 38n3, 39, 70, 76
Moby-Dick, 3, 20, 183, 212. *See also* Captain Ahab; Melville, Herman
Morewedge, Carey K., 60n7
Morrison, Van, 76, 152
movies, 1–3, 5, 26, 32, 33, 43, 67, 70, 79, 111, 160, 180, 181, 189n2, 189–91n5
  The Big Short, 181, 184, 189n5
  El barrendero, 101, 106n8
  El hombre del puente, 112, 120n3
  El mil usos, 100, 101, 106n6
  El Padre Trampitas, 89, 96n4
  The Godfather, 67, 73n1, 180, 189n2
  Moneyball, 199, 203n4
  Ni de aquí, ni de allá, 111, 120n1
  The Pink Panther, 33, 38n1
  Por mis pistolas, 112, 120n2, 160

N

Narayan, Kirin, 204n6
NASA, 10, 27, 66, 198
Nietzsche, Friedrich, 56, 63n18, 63n19, 152, 180
Nocera, Joe, 127, 132n1, 133n8, 133n9, 181, 182, 191n8, 192n9, 196n26
Norton, Michael I., 60n7

O

Oaxaca, 7, 28, 31–5, 39, 105n4, 139
Oberlechner, Thomas, 193n14, 194n15
Ordóñez, Juan Thomas, 29n1, 63n17, 105n4

P

Paredes, Américo, 82, 86n9
Parker, Richard L., 48n7
Partnoy, Frank, 132n3, 134n12, 192n10, 196n28
Pratt, Mary Louise, 200, 201, 204n8
Proverbs, 3, 42, 43, 52, 76, 83, 115, 117, 138, 139
Puzo, Mario, 180, 189n3

R

Rapport, Nigel, 59n3
Reed-Danahay, Deborah, 61n9, 86n7, 120–1n5
Reith, Gerda, 22n5, 64n23
Roberts, Russell, 132n4, 134n11, 134n12, 176n7
Rock, Andrea, 63n20, 121n5, 156n7
Rohrer, Trim, 193n13, 193n14
Rosaldo, Renato, 61n9, 86n9
Royster, Paul, 195n23
Rubenstein, Anne, 48n6

S

Saints, 2, 16, 17, 19, 20
Sánchez, Claudia, 48n7
Sancho Panza, 58, 89, 159
Schiess, Jim, 161, 171, 175n1, 208
Segal, Daniel, 204n6
Seger, Bob, 93
Sekules, Kate, 179, 189n1
Senders, Stefan, 96n7
Shostak, Marjorie, 96n7
Sick Bastard, 147, 148, 156n1
Simmel, Georg, 22n2, 57, 59n1, 61n8, 63–4n22, 99, 105n2, 106n11, 167, 169n5
Smith, Greg, 132n6, 133n10, 191n7, 196n26
Soccer, 12, 32, 33, 44, 46, 67, 76, 77, 81, 90, 151, 166
Sotres Mora, Bertha Eugenia, 48n7
Springsteen, Bruce, 92, 173, 175n6, 177n8, 185, 194n20
Stavans, Ilan, 18, 22n4, 48n7, 79, 85n3, 85n4, 86n9
Steinberg, Theodore, 22n3
Stephen, Lynn, 105n4
Stewart, Charles, 48n6, 59n2, 60n6, 63n17, 63n20, 63n21, 118, 119, 121n7, 123n13, 123n14
Sunderland, Patricia, 85n6
Sutton, David, 48n5, 59n2, 164n2, 189n2, 205n14

T

Tatum, Charles M., 48n7
Taussig, Michael, 194n19
Tedlock, Barbara, 59–60n4, 60n6
Tett, Gillian, 132n1, 132n2, 132n7, 133n9, 168n1, 172, 191–2n8
Thompson, Michael, 122n10
Thorn, John, 156n5
Treviño Hart, Elva, 86n12

Truitt, Allison, 96n7
Turtles, 51, 52, 57, 58, 99, 114, 142, 183, 202, 214

U
Urrea, Luis Alberto, 85n2

V
Valdez, Zulema, 105n1
Vignone, Mary Jean, 193n13, 193n14
Vonnegut, Kurt, 203–4n6

W
Walley, Christine, 96n8, 97n9
Wall Street, 66, 94, 106n10, 122n11, 125–30, 132n1, 133n9, 165, 172, 173, 175n5, 176n7, 181, 182, 184, 185, 187, 190n5, 192n9, 193n13, 195n22, 196n28, 197, 198
Watson, James L., 57, 85n6
Weems, Scott, 86n11
Wilker, Josh, 156n10
Wolken, John, 62n14
Wulff, Helena, 204n6

The manufacturer's authorised representative in the EU is Springer Nature Customer Service Centre GmbH, Europaplatz 3, 69115 Heidelberg, Germany. If you have any concerns regarding our products, please contact ProductSafety@springernature.com

Printed and bound by CPI Group (UK) Ltd, Croydon, CR0 4YY
23/03/2026
02076672-0007